Seeking Life Whole

The Fairleigh Dickinson University Press Series on Willa Cather
In Memory of Merrill M. Skaggs

This series is dedicated to publishing outstanding scholarship on the life, writings, influence, and legacy of this acclaimed American writer, whether single-author volumes or essay collections.

Titles in This Series

1. Achsah, Harwood, and Earl Brewster, ca. 1920. Courtesy of Drew University Special Collections.

Seeking Life Whole

Willa Cather and the Brewsters

Lucy Marks and David Porter

Madison • Teaneck
Fairleigh Dickinson University Press

Associated University Presses
2010 Eastpark Boulevard
Cranbury, NJ 08512

The paper used in this publication meets the requirements of the American National Standard for Permanence of Paper for Printed Library Materials Z39.48-1984.

Library of Congress Cataloging-in-Publication Data

Marks, Lucy, 1951–
    Seeking life whole : Willa Cather and the Brewsters / Lucy Marks and David Porter.
        p.   cm.
    Includes bibliographical references and index.
    ISBN 978-0-8386-4199-6 (alk. paper)
1. Cather, Willa, 1873–1947.   2. Novelists, American—20th century—Biography.   3. Cather, Willa, 1873–1947—Friends and Associates.   4. Brewster, Earl.   5. Brewster, Achsah.   I. Porter, David H., 1935-   II. Title.
PS3505.A87Z734   2009
813′.52—dc22
[B]   2008053245

For Scott, Alexander, and Leo Sprinzen
—L.M.

For Helen, Hugh, Everett, Helen, and David Porter, and
Cathrin Lawton
—D.P.

And for Frances Picard Holt
—L.M. and D.P.

Contents

Illustrations

Color illustrations appear between pages 64 and 65.

Color Plate 1. Earl Brewster. *Positano,* ca. 1916.

Color Plate 2. Earl Brewster. *The Buddha Meditating,*
ca. 1918.

Color Plate 3. Achsah Brewster. *Butterflies,* ca. 1917.

Color Plate 4. Achsah Brewster. *Woman with Violin, Man
Reading & Woman Playing Piano,* 1923.

Acknowledgments

As in any work of this sort, there are many thank-yous to bestow. First and foremost we wish to thank Frances Picard Holt and her family. Without Fran's ongoing generosity, wisdom, and encouragement—and her resolve that her grandparents be more than a footnote in history—this book quite simply would not exist. Earl Brewster displayed customary insight, shortly after Fran's birth, in recognizing her as his "special disciple." Her warm, lively friendship has helped to make this project a pleasure.

From the beginning, Drew University and its collection of Cather materials have provided essential support for this project. Andrew Scrimgeour, dean of the Drew University Library, immediately recognized the potential importance of the Brewster papers when they first came on the market, and moved expeditiously to purchase both that initial selection and other portions of the archives as they became available. The generosity of several donors and Cather enthusiasts was essential to funding these purchases, and we wish to thank Barbara and Finn Caspersen and Marilyn Berg Callander. The late Doug O'Dell of Chapel Hill Books provided the initial entrée to the Brewster materials in a letter written to David Porter, and we express our warm gratitude to both him and his wife Maureen for opening this door to us and hence to Drew University. Among those members of the Drew University Library staff who have graciously contributed their wisdom and their professional expertise to this project, we thank in particular Linda Connors, head of Acquisitions and Collection Development, and Masato Okinaka, library conservator.

The late Merrill Skaggs, one of the world's leading Cather scholars and the motivating force behind the myriad contributions that Drew-educated scholars have made to Cather studies over the years, from the start gave invaluable support to our work on this book, encouraging us to delve into the materials of the Brewster archive when they first arrived at Drew, providing far-ranging advice as our research progressed, and in the final year twice reading the entire manuscript closely and critically. It is no exaggeration to say that this book would not exist without Merrill's wise, warm, and witty counsel, and our highest hope is that it may be worthy of her.

Other Cather scholars and students have also been generous with their knowledge and their time, commenting in detail on early drafts of portions of this book, providing invaluable information on areas of their particular expertise, and in a variety of ways helping us to explore the role the Brewsters played in Willa Cather's life and work. Among the many who have helped us, we give special thanks to Richard C. Harris, John J. Murphy, Ann Romines, Janis P. Stout, Robert Thacker, and Joseph R. Urgo.

Mikaela Sardo Lamarche, curator at the ACA Galleries, representatives of the estate of Earl and Achsah Brewster, has been unfailingly helpful and collegial in answering questions and sharing images of the Brewsters' paintings. The ACA's beautiful exhibition (and accompanying catalog) in late 2007–early 2008, Divine Pursuit: The Spiritual Journey of Achsah and Earl Brewster, reintroduced to the art world and beyond the Brewsters' work and milieu.

John Larry Washburn, who actually knew the Brewsters, generously and humorously shared his memories with us. Clare Needham carefully translated from French to English the essays in *L'oeuvre de E. H. Brewster et Achsah Barlow Brewster*.

Williams College, Skidmore College, and Drew University have provided generous and ongoing support for research, travel, and publishing costs associated with this project. Joshua Allen, our friendly editor at Associated University Presses, was ever helpful, efficient, and fun. As indicated in the detailed listing in our acknowledgments, the libraries of a number of institutions have also been indispensable to our work, with special mention here of the following: the National Art Library and the British Library in London; the Willa Cather Collection at the University of Nebraska; the Drew University Library; the University of Virginia Library; the University of Minnesota Libraries; the Smith College Archives; and the Archives of the Faculty of Asian & Middle Eastern Studies, Cambridge University.

David Porter adds: Special thanks to my late wife, Laudie Dimmette Porter, whose passionate interest in Willa Cather led in the early 1980s to our beginning to collect her books—and to my beginning to read them; to our children, Hugh, Everett, Helen, and David, who graciously endured long hours spent in bookshops during those early collecting days, and even longer hours of hearing about this present project in recent years; to my wife Helen, who has warmly encouraged my interest in Willa Cather for the past twenty years and has for the past five been a perceptive and patient sounding board for my evolving work on Cather and the Brewsters; and to her daughter Cathi, who has not only supported this project with her interest and intelligence but has also lent needed perspective through her ever spicy and ironic good humor.

Lucy Marks adds: Special thanks to my parents, Paulina and Robert Marks, and brothers, Ed and Paul Marks, for their generosity and faith in me. Paul was with Scott and me in Taormina when we found the Brewsters' home with its mosaic "PACE" at the threshold, just as Achsah Brewster described it.

Conversations with Deborah Sagner proved invaluable to my understanding of the Brewsters' personalities and relationships. Yvette Kirby's tactful persistence and flawless French led to our exciting discovery of a previously misattributed triptych by Achsah Brewster. I thank them very much.

I am grateful to Barbara Martin, Ruth Gais, Janet Wolkoff, Edith Sprinzen, Susan Entmacher, Carol Berman, Anne Badger, and my colleagues in the Catalog Department at Drew University Library for their patient and good-natured interest in this project; to Alice Schreyer for her warm support and always helpful advice; and to the late Lola L. Szladits, mentor and friend. *Grazie sincere* to Antonella Bucci in Rome and Carmelina Fiorentino in Capri for their energetic detective work.

Most of all, I thank my husband, Scott Sprinzen, and our sons, Alexander and Leo, who from the beginning accepted—even welcomed—the Brewsters into our lives with enthusiasm, encouragement, and great good humor.

❧

We gratefully acknowledge the help of the following individuals and institutions: Linda Connors and Masato Okinaka for permission to quote extensively from the letters and memoirs in the Brewster Collection, Special Collections, Drew University Library; Frances Picard Holt, for permission to reproduce photographs, and to quote from family letters and from Harwood Brewster Picard's memoir, "Fourteen Years of My Adventures," which are in her possession; Mikaela Sardo Lamarche and ACA Galleries, representatives of the estate of Earl and Achsah

Brewster, for permission to reproduce images of the Brewsters' paintings at the gallery; the Archives of American Art, Smithsonian Institution, for permission to quote from the Macbeth Gallery records, 1838–1968 (bulk 1892–1953), Reels NMc5, NMc28, 2575; Stephanie Cassidy for permission to use information from the Student Registration Records, Art Students League of New York; Roland Bauman for permission to use information from the Student File (Earl Brewster), Alumni & Development Records, Oberlin College Archives; Françoise Simmons for permission to quote from letters in the Rhys Davids family papers, Archives of the Faculty of Asian & Middle Eastern Studies, Cambridge University; Nanci A. Young for permission to quote from the Class Records of 1902, Alumnae Biographical Files, Box 1617, Smith College Archives, and to use information from the Office of the President William Allan Neilson Files, Box 4; Louise Laplante, Smith College Museum of Art, for information about Earl Brewster's painting in that collection; Jennifer S. Morrow, for information about Calvin Brewster and Flora Chapman's attendance at the Western Reserve Eclectic Institute; Alan Lathrop for permission to quote from the Claude Washburn Papers, Upper Midwest Literary Archives, University of Minnesota Libraries; Katherine L. Walter and Carmella Orosco for permission to quote from and reproduce an edited typescript of Earl Brewster in the Robert and Doris Kurth Collection, Archives & Special Collections, University of Nebraska-Lincoln Libraries; Richard Workman for permission to quote from Achsah Brewster's letters to Dorothy Brett, and to use information from Earl Brewster's letters to Frieda Lawrence Ravagli and Angelo Ravagli, Harry Ransom Humanities Research Center, the University of Texas at Austin; the Clifton Waller Barrett Library of American Literature, Special Collections, University of Virginia Library, for permission to quote from the Papers of Vachel Lindsay, MSS 6259, and to refer to inscriptions in two of Lindsay's books in that library; Pollinger Ltd. and the Estate of Frieda Lawrence Ravagli for permission to quote from the letters of D. H. Lawrence; and Grover Smith for permission to quote from his 1969 edition of Aldous Huxley's letters.

Introduction

To the list of Willa Cather's closest friends and confidants—Louise Pound, Isabelle McClung Hambourg, Edith Lewis, Dorothy Canfield Fisher, and Zoë Akins, for instance—we now know that we should add the names of Earl and Achsah Brewster. Cather's friendship with the Brewsters, which has only recently come to light, began when Cather first came to New York in the early 1900s and extended to the end of her life. Not only did the Brewsters become cherished fellow artists and friends, but they also clearly piqued the curiosity of Cather the novelist, for in both character and range of experience they were idiosyncratic, even eccentric, and lived in a world very much of their own making.

The Brewsters had moved from New York to Italy immediately after their marriage in 1910; except for a short visit in 1923, they never again returned to America. With their daughter, Harwood, they spent nearly twenty years in southern Italy, interspersed with travels to Greece, France, Ceylon, and India. Following six years near the Côte d'Azur, they finally settled in northern India, where they remained until their deaths.

Dedicated painters and writers, intellectual and deeply spiritual, the Brewsters were in equal measure a product of their time and truly sui generis. Born in 1878, they were influenced by such turn-of-the-century artistic, religious, and cultural currents as abstractionism, antimodernism, Theosophy, and the newly rediscovered Buddhism. Their love of nature, their pursuit of beauty and simplicity in art and life, and their rejection of a materialistic society place them within a philosophical movement that reaches back to Whitman and the Transcendentalists, and anticipates modern-day interest in Eastern religions. Like the Transcendentalists, the Brewsters sought "elegance rather than luxury, and refinement rather than fashion" (Shi 1985, 128), though managed still to accommodate a flair for silk and brocade, a habit of carting around the family silver, and an uncanny ability to find themselves in some of the loveliest homes in Europe while on the verge of destitution.

17

From the beginning, their art was influenced foremost by the decorative mural paintings of Puvis de Chavannes and the Italian primitives, while the often abstract style of their work, its wide-ranging spirituality, and its use of color and form to express emotion, put them also in the company of Gauguin and the expressionists. Their paintings were reproduced in several major art journals, and were shown regularly at the Paris salons, generally to critical rather than public success; they are still found in Italian and French churches, religious and educational institutions in the United States, and temples and government buildings in northern India.

The Brewsters had a radiant and unshakeable sense of a noble purpose in art and life that had little to do with societal recognition or reward. Never seeking to be anything but their truest selves, they yet exerted a strong, almost magnetic, appeal for some of the most prominent figures of the early twentieth century, as varied as Willa Cather, D. H. Lawrence, and the extended Nehru family, who were inspired and perhaps challenged by their uncompromising values and priorities.

Willa Cather became acquainted with Achsah perhaps as early as 1904 and met Earl shortly before he and Achsah married and sailed for Europe in 1910. In the teens Cather came to know the Brewsters not only through the occasional letter but also through their paintings, several of which she and Edith Lewis acquired during this period for their New York home. The 1920s brought Cather face to face with the Brewsters on two European trips. During these trips Cather gave the Brewsters inscribed copies of her books, she and Lewis acquired more Brewster paintings, and Cather and the Brewsters discovered a close convergence among the principles and ideals that were shaping her writing and their art. Although Cather saw the Brewsters for the last time when she and Lewis visited them in southern France in the summer of 1930, the flow of letters, and the exchange of books and paintings, continued, surviving the Brewsters' permanent move to India in 1935 and even the daunting barriers posed by World War II.

※

This book had its beginnings in 2002 with the arrival at the Drew University Library of a small archive of books and letters that had been in the possession of Frances Holt, daughter of Harwood Brewster Picard and granddaughter of Earl and Achsah Brewster. The materials in this archive had obvious relevance to Drew's Willa Cather collection: several Cather books inscribed to the Brewsters by the author, others inscribed by Edith Lewis or by members of the Brewster family, and five letters from Cather to the Brewsters. What no one expected, however—and what became increasingly clear once the materials arrived—was that the archive would bring to light an important and long-hidden chapter in Cather's life. Further materials acquired in subsequent years, among them nearly 1700 Brewster letters, a copy of a memoir written by Harwood Brewster Picard in 1977, and above all Frances Holt's gift of Achsah Brewster's 436-page unpublished memoir, "The Child," have confirmed the significance of this long relationship between Cather and the Brewster family. For the purposes of this book, Fran Holt has also generously provided access to additional Brewster letters, family photographs, and a substantial memoir that Harwood wrote in 1926, at the age of fourteen, though these documents remain in private hands.

Our primary purpose here is to bring this long and rich relationship, which Willa Cather cherished, and which had a considerable impact on her work, to the attention of Cather readers and scholars. We begin with the Brewsters themselves, since what they meant to Cather derived from who they were and from the distinctive lives they lived as practicing artists. Lucy Marks's opening chapter draws on a wide range of primary sources from American and English collections. The first section briefly reviews the Brewsters' well-known friendship with D. H. Lawrence and introduces them in their own right, focusing on their artistic and intellectual interests and achievements, and the influence they exerted within an illustrious circle of acquaintance. Section two describes family background and formative influences, the remarkable circumstances of their first meeting in 1904, and their courtship and marriage in 1910. The Brewsters' nearly two decades in Italy (1910–29) are documented in section three, including Harwood's birth in 1912, their extensive travels, Earl's Buddhist studies, their friendships with D. H. Lawrence, Willa Cather, and others, and their artistic and scholarly publications. The fourth section covers the Brewsters' six years in southern France (1929–35), the publication of their 1934 volume of Lawrence's letters, Earl's growing interest in Vedanta Hinduism, and the circumstances of their final move to India in 1935. Section five discusses the decades in northern India, including their friendship with the Nehru family, and the quasi-celebrity they achieved in Almora and beyond. Examined throughout are the Brewsters' artistic, intellectual, and spiritual pursuits, their relationships with family, friends, and with each other, and the ideals and incongruities that informed their lives.

David Porter's second chapter endeavors both to establish the facts of Willa Cather's long relationship with the Brewsters and to understand what it meant to all parties involved. The chapter's first section surveys the long course of the friendship from its beginnings in New York in 1904–10 to its lively continuation long after Cather and the Brewsters last saw each other in 1930. The second section focuses on the many ways in which the Brewster archive expands our knowledge of two trips—the one Lewis and Cather made to Europe in 1920, which concluded with a hitherto unknown rendezvous with the Brewsters in Naples, and the one Cather herself made to France in 1923, during which we now know that she saw the Brewsters frequently. It was through Edith Lewis, who had roomed with Achsah at Smith College, that Cather and the Brewsters came to know each other, and the chapter's third section considers the important and sometimes poignant light that the Drew materials cast on both Lewis herself and her long relationship with Willa Cather. The fourth section, which focuses on the abundant archival materials that cluster around the years 1920–24, documents the extraordinary synergy of artistic ideals and principles that developed between Cather and the Brewsters during this period and that as early as 1922 began to leave its clear traces in Cather's writing. The Brewsters' impact if anything becomes more marked in the years that follow, as the chapter's fifth section shows by its discussion of three later Cather works, her novel *Death Comes for the Archbishop* and her stories "Old Mrs. Harris" and "The Old Beauty." The epilogue to chapter 2 focuses on "Recognition," a poem that Cather wrote in 1922 with the Brewsters specifically in mind.

Part 2, which begins with a detailed checklist of materials in the Brewster Archive (chapter 3), offers a selection of resource materials, virtually all of them hitherto unpublished. Chapter 4 surveys the Cather books owned by the Brewsters, many of them inscribed by Cather or Lewis, and paraphrases the five letters from Cather to the Brewsters that are contained in this archive, while chapter 5 contains the draft of a short essay Earl Brewster wrote on Willa Cather in 1949. Chapter 6 is devoted to generous selections from Achsah Barlow Brewster's lengthy 1942 book,

"The Child," chapters 7 and 8 to shorter excerpts from two memoirs that the Brewsters' daughter Harwood wrote in 1926 and 1977 respectively. Chapter 9 offers a representative sampling of letters written by Achsah and Earl, with the first dating from before their marriage in 1910, the last from shortly before Earl's death in 1957.

In selecting what to include in part 2, our first purpose has been to complement the essays of part 1 with relevant supporting materials, including, in many cases, the full text of documents and passages that are but mentioned or excerpted in those first two essays. We have also, however, tried in part 2 to suggest the richness of the archives themselves and the variety of voices represented—Achsah's in contrast to Earl's, for instance, or the piquant ebullience of Harwood at age fourteen as against the more considered tone and manner she adopts some fifty years later. We hope our book itself will offer a solid and wide-ranging introduction to the Brewsters and their friendship with Willa Cather, but we hope also that both the essays in part 1 and the documentary materials in part 2 will suggest further avenues for exploration in the future.

A word about the editorial principles that have governed our treatment of the Brewster materials which we cite in part 1 and from which we publish selections in part 2. Achsah's "The Child" and Earl's 1949 essay on Cather both show signs of their authors' ill health and advancing age: in particular, names, locations, and chronology are sometimes garbled. In the case of these documents, and of Harwood's 1977 memoir, we have corrected obvious typographical mistakes and minor factual slips without comment, and have made note only of those errors that are more serious or of particular interest. In the case of the Brewsters' letters and of Harwood's "Fourteen Years of my Adventures," however, we feel that the occasional slips in spelling and the like contribute to the freshness and immediacy of the documents. We have accordingly preserved them as they appear, without peppering the text with *sic* wherever they occur; when the errors are more significant or confusing, we have added notes for the sake of clarity and accuracy.

Abbreviations

THE FOLLOWING ABBREVIATIONS ARE USED IN THIS BOOK:

ABB   Achsah Barlow Brewster
BG   *Bhagavad Gita*
CRD   Caroline Rhys Davids
CW   Claude Washburn
EHB   Earl Henry Brewster
HBP   Harwood Brewster Picard
LL   Letters of D. H. Lawrence (see References for full entry)
RR   Rudolph Ruzicka
VL   Vachel Lindsay
WM   William Macbeth

Seeking Life Whole

I

1

Earl and Achsah Brewster: A Biographical Sketch

LUCY MARKS

INTRODUCTION

THE STORY OF THEIR MEETING WAS LIKE A FAMILY FAIRY TALE, TOLD and retold through the years by husband, wife, and daughter. Its charmed inevitability seemed both harbinger and proof of charmed lives. In 1904 Earl Brewster, an art student in New York, painted the head of an imagined young woman for a magazine cover. His friend, Vachel Lindsay, saw the picture and complimented Earl on its excellent likeness of Achsah Barlow, herself a painter. But Earl looked blank—he had never heard of Achsah Barlow. Lindsay arranged a meeting, a lively dinner at Achsah's apartment. The three spoke of predestination, each struck by what seemed the profound significance of Earl's portrait of a woman he had never met. Then Achsah left New York to study art in France and Italy, and shortly after she came back, Earl himself went to Europe to paint. Upon his return in late 1909, their acquaintance was renewed, and predestination played out its role. Within a year Achsah Barlow, the flesh and blood embodiment of Earl Brewster's imagination, became his wife.

❧

American painters Earl and Achsah Brewster are remembered today for their decade-long association with D. H. Lawrence and his wife, Frieda. Fellow writers, painters, intellectuals, and, not least, fellow wanderers, the couples developed a sympathetic bond that prevailed despite their conspicuous, almost comical, mismatch of temperaments. The friendship has been well documented in Lawrence's many letters to and about the Brewsters and their daughter, Harwood; in the Brewsters' 1934 memoir of Lawrence; and in numerous Lawrence studies. A parallel chronicle of the relationship survives as well in at least six of Lawrence's writings that reflect their intimacy and shared experiences. Two poems, two short stories, a novella, and a book of travel essays[1] all testify to the dynamic interaction between the families throughout the 1920s.

Who were the Brewsters? The published record as summarized above reveals at best an oblique view of their lives from 1921 to 1930, seen largely from Lawrence's perspective, as though their existence were confined to his orbit. In fact, they were serious artists and formidable intellects in their own right. By the time they met Lawrence on Capri in 1921, they had lived in Europe for more than a decade, exhibited regularly in Paris and Rome, and would shortly publish a kind of manifesto on their philosophy of art. Their work appeared in reviews such as *Colours* and *Art et Décoration*. Achsah, who had spent three summers at the MacDowell Colony,[2] was invited to participate in Maurice Denis' Atelier d'Art Sacré. Her *Sermon on the Mount* triptych was admired by the archbishop of Paris, who had it placed in a church in Crécy-en-Brie. An accomplished pianist, she also wrote essays, novels, and short stories, published several articles, and despite ill health, produced a massive memoir, "The Child," shortly before her death. Earl became a scholar of Buddhism and Vedanta Hinduism, mastered Pāli and Sanskrit, and contributed regularly to such publications as *Asia,* the *Buddhist Annual of Ceylon,* the *Aryan Path,* and *Prabuddha Bharata*. His compilation of the life of the Buddha from the original Pāli has gone through more than four editions, including one in French.

Together they read widely, deeply, constantly, with Sundays set aside for Plato, whom Achsah referred to as if he were a weekly dinner guest. Their sophisticated familiarity with Western and Eastern thought and culture was juxtaposed with a childlike ingenuousness that at times provoked in others impatience or derision; more often, it inspired generosity, loyalty, and protectiveness. Achsah dubbed their tight-knit family unit of father, mother, and daughter "our 'blessed trinity'" (ABB to HBP 2/26/36), but in the many years abroad, their gift for friendship, their bonhomie, and peripatetic existence led to an ever-widening company of friends. Among their circle, besides D. H. Lawrence, were such prominent literary, artistic, and political figures of the day as Willa Cather, Vachel Lindsay, Aldous Huxley, Llewelyn Powys, Bernard Berenson, Elihu Vedder, Nora Joyce, Geoffrey Scott, and three generations of the Nehru family.

Indeed, Lawrence was only one of several writers for whom the Brewsters provided inspiration and material. Poems by Willa Cather and Vachel Lindsay, as well as three memoirs, a novel, an essay, and a BBC broadcast, all attest to the affection, respect, and even fascination they aroused in others. Several years before Earl's death in northern India, *Life* magazine sent a photographer to take pictures for an article, never published, entitled, "Happy Himalayan Hermit."[3]

Unconventional and unworldly, steadfastly devoted to their art, and passionately engaged in the life of the mind, the Brewsters spent decades wandering through Europe and Asia in search of a permanent home and livelihood—a journey that mirrored both their artistic quest to realize in color and line the essence of human emotions, and their spiritual pursuit of connection or Oneness with the universe. Still, uncompromising in their ideals and sense of self, they exhibited many contradictions. Although they clung to their identity as Americans and to their heritage of New England pilgrim aristocracy, they moved ever further into geographic exile, until a reunion with family and country was no longer possible. The freedom they sought in Europe came increasingly at the cost of financial dependence on others, diminishing options, and finally indigence. Modest, self-effacing, never sycophantic, they still took pride in their association with well-known figures, who conferred a certain validity on their unorthodox lives and choices. Although deeply spiritual, they were by no means ascetic, delighting in spacious homes, fine antiques, stylish clothes. Art for art's sake might mean going without lights and plumbing, but not without a grand piano.

Their quest ended in northern India, where they remained until their deaths, painting, writing, and studying. The serenity they found in Almora proved magnetic to those neighbors and visitors of many different cultures, each seeking his own truths, for whom the Brewsters gradually evolved into spiritual parents. Indeed, Achsah was at times addressed as "Mother," and more than one visitor asked if Earl might not adopt him. Aspiring always to "rise to something nobler" (EHB to ABB 10/5/13), they seemed to find in the shadow of the Himalayas a footpath leading to their ideal, and welcomed others along the journey.

YOUTH AND COURTSHIP

Earl Henry Brewster was born in the mill town of Chagrin Falls, Ohio, near Cleveland, on September 21, 1878, the second son of Calvin H. Brewster and Flora Elizabeth Chapman, and younger brother by nearly ten years of Ara Calvin Brewster. The Brewsters were descended from Elder William Brewster, one of the Mayflower Pilgrims, a heritage in which they took great pride. Calvin and Flora attended the Western Reserve Eclectic Institute (later to become Hiram College); afterward Calvin ran a dry goods store, Brewster and Church, in Chagrin Falls. He died in 1885, when Earl was just seven. Ara became head of the household, took over at Brewster and Church, and supported the family. Earl would later recall a happy, comfortable childhood, with summer vacations in Maine and New Hampshire, and the security of a quasi-paternal brother and doting, protective mother, who allowed her younger son to neither swim, skate, nor dance (EHB to HBP 10/8/30). Sensitive and artistic, he was aware even as a child of his strong emotional response to color and form, and to the murals of Pierre Puvis de Chavannes, whose dreamlike allegories of the human experience remained his ideal and inspiration (Brewster 1923, 5–6). Earl's childhood absorption in the tranquil, premodern realm created by Puvis later fed his need to escape the pressures of an "overcivilized" American bourgeois society (Lears 1994, xv), and seek a spiritual reality within himself and through his art. His antimodernist vision of a quiet retreat, serene and remote, "as simple as true and as beautiful as in a canvas by Puvis de Chavannes" (8/14/10), would lead him to the other side of the world.

During a brief stint at Oberlin Academy in the fall of 1897,[4] Earl became absorbed in the study of Eastern religions, which had been explored earlier by the Transcendentalists, and popularized by Edwin Arnold's immensely successful 1879 poem, *The Light of Asia*. The World's Parliament of Religions, held in conjunction with the 1893 Columbian Exposition, fueled widespread interest in Buddhism and Vedanta Hinduism, while the Theosophical Society, founded in 1875 by Helena Blavatsky, also looked to Buddhism for spiritual guidance, though it incorporated elements of the occult. Earl had become interested in Theosophy when Annie Besant, one of Blavatsky's followers, lectured on the subject in Cleveland in the 1890s. Already as a child he had had intimations of reincarnation (EHB to Ara Brewster 6/10/47); now he felt powerfully drawn to the East as a symbol of everything the materialistic, scientific West was not: mythical, ritualistic, spiritual (Knott 1998, 77–78).[5] Although he and Besant never met, Earl was convinced that she advised him telepathically. Besant became the first of several forceful, authoritative women who influenced the development of Earl's spiritual beliefs and guided his study of religious texts and languages.[6] Coincidentally, he would soon meet a Hindu man, Jagedesh Chatterji, who invited the nineteen-year-old student to accompany him to Kashmir as his secretary. At this point, Flora Brewster put her foot down, and it would be nearly three decades before Earl realized his dream of seeing India.

Oberlin Academy was followed by a year at the Cleveland School of Art. At a class in outdoor painting Earl met Frederick Shaler, and the two moved together to New York at the end of 1899. Earl enrolled at the Art Students League and later the New York School of Art, working with such prominent teachers and artists as William Merritt Chase and Frank Vincent DuMond, whom he recalled with particular gratitude (Brewster 1923, 6–7). During much of the next decade, he and Shaler shared a studio at 42 Washington Square South. Commercial art jobs, the occasional sale of a painting, and a frequently pawned gold watch kept him afloat. He continued to study Eastern religions and cultures, read Paul Carus and Lafcadio Hearn[7] as well as the *Bhagavad Gita* and Chinese philosophy, and became president of the local Theosophical Society. A fellow art student, Vachel Lindsay, introduced him to Miss Achsah Leona Barlow, whose portrait he had unaccountably conjured up for a magazine cover, but she left for Europe before Earl, diffident and unsure of himself, could muster the courage to pursue her acquaintance.

His work received increasing exposure and recognition. From 1906 to 1910, he was represented in group shows at the Society of American Artists, the Pennsylvania Academy of Fine Arts, the Corcoran Art Gallery, the Boston Art Club, and the National Academy of Design, where William Merritt Chase bought *The Gray Harbor* for his personal collection. Earl's part in an April 1908 show at the New York School of Art attracted favorable attention from the *New York Times,* as well as the watchful interest of art dealer William Macbeth.[8] Earl characterized his paintings from this period as "pure impressionism," but already he felt drawn to an abstract style "as free from the servitude of forms and all objective elements as an Oriental rug" (Brewster

1923, 7). Buoyed by his critical success and eager to test himself on a wider stage, he sailed for Europe in the spring of 1908.

The next year and a half were spent in France and Italy, first in Paris, then with Flora in Taormina, on the eastern coast of Sicily. Oddly, just as one of Earl's paintings had led to his introduction to Achsah Barlow, another prompted his decision to go to Sicily: the chance remark by an acquaintance that one of his pictures resembled the landscape there (Picard 1984, 201). He delighted in its "Theocritan" setting, where he painted in the company of shepherds and goats. To Rudolph Ruzicka, a close friend from art school days,[9] he raved about its "vast phenominal veiws," its landscape "beautiful and rare in composition" (12/28/08); with more restraint, he assured William Macbeth of there being "very much indeed that is quite within the painters range, and that composes in a manner that seems to me very beautiful" (12/7/08).

Back again in France by April 1909, he was already sounding blasé. "Perhaps," he confided to Ruzicka, "the second visit to Paris no one finds quite so thrilling as the first." He compared the "harmonies of color" in the Mediterranean coastal landscape to New York and New England, and found Europe wanting. The exception was Sicily, where he discovered "a touch of that primitive nature which I love equally well from an artistic standpoint (and more from other standpoints)." Europe had challenged and inspired him, but enthusiasm was flagging, and he no longer wished, as he once thought, to remain permanently (5/16/09). After Flora went home in June, he took a last look at Italy before sailing to New York in the autumn of 1909.

While Earl returns to America with a roll of canvases for William Macbeth, it is time to bring Achsah Leona Barlow into the story. She was born in New Haven, Connecticut, on November 12, 1878, the youngest daughter of John Harwood Barlow and Ida Elena Hubbard, and sister of Alpha and Lola. John Barlow had emigrated from northern England as a child. A contractor at the Winchester gun factory and later head of the Ideal Manufacturing Company in New Haven,[10] he was successful enough to leave each of his daughters a good inheritance. Achsah was named for her maternal grandmother, Achsah Ann Dickinson, through whom she claimed kinship with Emily Dickinson. Like her famous forebear, she almost always wore white. Connected on Ida's side as well to the New England Mathers, Achsah retained a strong sense of an illustrious heritage as an integral part of her self-image.

In early 1887 Ida Barlow died of tuberculosis. Her sisters moved in with the family and devoted themselves to helping John Barlow raise his daughters. Like Earl, Achsah was the much-indulged youngest child, still their "dear baby girl" at age twenty-eight (John Barlow to ABB 11/26/06; Picard 1977, 3), "little baby girl" at twenty-nine (A. Brewster 1942, 322), and "little baby niece" at forty-five (324).

In 1898 she followed Alpha and Lola to Smith College.[11] Among her closest friends there was her sophomore roommate, Edith Lewis, who joined in playing hooky from compulsory Bible class (ABB to HBP 9/27/30), and would later become Willa Cather's companion. Only toward the end of her college years did Achsah make up her mind to study painting, led instinctively by the need to express emotion through the use of color, and by her vision of the "essential" role of the artist in society (Brewster 1923, 17). After graduating from Smith in 1902, she moved to New York to study at the Art Students League with Frank Vincent DuMond, and with Robert Henri at the New York School of Art. One night a fellow student, Vachel Lindsay, brought his friend Earl Brewster to dine at her apartment. By an astonishing, perhaps momentous, coincidence, Earl had painted Achsah, sight unseen, for a magazine cover. As it happened, Lindsay himself had long admired the quick, confident woman, both serious and vivacious, always dressed in white, the "puritan-bacchante" (4/27/19) who would inspire several of his poems.[12] Whatever the men may have had in mind, however, Achsah was making her own plans. In the fall of 1906 she left to continue her studies in Paris, "to do or die,"[13] and to test herself in the proving ground of the international art world (Adler 2006, [11]).

Her first months in Europe were spent working from live models at the Institut des Beaux Arts and the studios of Lucien Simon and Castelluchio. From Paris she moved on to England, Belgium, Holland, France, and Italy, visiting galleries and sending home "delicious" details of cities explored and families befriended (A. Barlow, 4). John Barlow provided steady encouragement and regular funds, exhorting her to "work work work and no such word as cant,"[14] while Lindsay expected she would win "so many laurels you can hardly peep through them" (12/22/06). By November 1907 Achsah was back in New Haven, where Lindsay wrote, hoping to see her paintings from "Yurrup" (11/18/07). The following spring, 1908, Earl Brewster left New York for his own European art tour, returning in the fall of 1909. Shortly afterward, he finally made his move.

During their nine-month courtship, conducted largely through letters, Achsah Barlow and Earl Brewster vividly evolved the artistic and philosophic principles to which they dedicated themselves, using themes and images that would recur for the next fifty years. Their distinctive personalities emerged as well in their approach to matters practical and abstract. By the time they were married on December 1, 1910, they had said enough to know that the essence of their future together would consist in the ceaseless endeavor to live up to those principles, to "keep the ideal alive" (EHB to ABB 8/14/10), and to remain true to themselves, whatever the cost might be.

They had already met again in New York when Earl first wrote on February 23, 1910, inviting Miss Barlow to view the canvases in his studio at 42 Washington Square South. She was impressed with his paintings, "so big and true," and intrigued by the earnest, idealistic Mr. Brewster, who seemed "to be able to live in the world and not of it" (3/26/10). Within weeks the letters posted between New York and New Haven vibrated with the thrill of discovery. Buddhism, Lao-Tze, Tolstoy, Thomas Carlyle, Hiroshige, Ibsen, Symbolism, St. Francis of Assisi, Mallarmé, Paul to the Corinthians, Puvis de Chavannes—there seemed hardly enough paper to contain all they had to say. They exchanged books and art reproductions, compared literary and philosophical interests, and traded impressions of their European experiences, clearly delighted by both the scope of their intellectual engagement and the recognition of a sympathetic understanding. "There are a thousand things I could write," Achsah marveled. "You seem to set the ink streaming from my pen" (7/3/10).

A deeply spiritual and strikingly cross-cultural sensibility informed their lives. Earl segued easily from Buddhism to Lao-Tze, whom he found "as intimate as the psalms or Walt Whitman," and reminiscent of Ibsen (4/3/10); he compared Achsah's favorite text, 1 Corinthians 13, to the doctrine of the unity of life in the *Bhagavad Gita* (*BG* 2001, 6:29). Charity, honesty, and the unity of life, he declared, formed his creed (4/16/10). Understanding him perfectly, Achsah sent off a Buddhist proverb about man's trials and aspirations (4/13/10), and compared the teachings of the Buddha to the Golden Rule (4/29/10). From moral principles to artistic motifs, they moved instinctively and seamlessly between Eastern and Western images and concepts, propelled by an Emersonian "eclectic and synthetic" interest in the quintessential wisdom of all faiths (Buell 2003, 179).[15] In later years, Achsah's Christmas crèche typically included the Christ Child protected by a seven-headed brass cobra, and surrounded by angels and Indian deities (ABB to HBP 12/29/37).

That spring Earl was struggling to regain confidence in his painting, and a firmer resolve to continue on his chosen path. To William Macbeth he had confessed financially "embarrassing" circumstances, and offered a 50 percent commission on sales for Macbeth to give his work a better showing (2/2/10). Unsure of either his talent or commitment, he turned again to the *Bhagavad Gita,* this time to its precept of taking action for its own sake, "working for the sake of work," without thought of outcome or reward: "We ought to be happy and peaceful if we would renounce the fruit of our actions—for we act I believe the best that we know how to act—how can one do more?" (5/15/10; *BG* 2001, 3:19). He would return to this passage all his life, inspired by its explicit negation of ego, and perhaps cheered by its indifference to pressures imposed from without.

During the summer of 1910—the Barlows in New Hampshire, Earl and Flora Brewster in Maine—Achsah and Earl pondered the meaning of artistic success. Her energetic optimism and calm self-assurance were a foil for his self-doubt, frustration, and "nervous temperament" (11/3/10).[16] Where Earl saw a future governed by forces largely beyond his control, whether the current art market or the whims of creative enthusiasm, Achsah was inspired by a sense of self-determination and renewed possibilities in each new day. They shared a romantic idealism, but his gave full rein to the dreamer and escapist, while hers was based on an optimistic certainty of every human's potential to grow into his best self, and of goodness and beauty in a world that had produced saints and philosophers. In the often difficult years ahead, Achsah's vision rarely failed her, even as she confronted illness, poverty, and the irrevocable separation from those held dearest. Her wide-reaching embrace of mankind drew to her people of all stripes.

By mid-August, they were edging toward the question of their future. Achsah's memories of Venice prompted Earl to wonder if Italy were "a fatal and direful enchantment that will never wear away." Ever since returning to America he had felt out of step with his surroundings: "I feel so strongly the charm of certain other lands that I find it difficult even in thought to associate myself with my own environment. And alas those lands are sometimes quite of my own imaginings. . . . Where one's work aside from painting would be the care of trees, toil amid plants and the earth, & tending a spring or fountain. . . . What is there in modern life to compensate for these joys?" (8/14/10).

For Achsah, Italy was no direful enchantment, but a "living satisfaction," indeed where she hoped to spend much of her life. Plucking him from his Puvis-like reverie, she crystallized the philosophy they were working out together, and envisioned its application: "I believe with Tolstoi that the only happiness of life lies in its simplicity and genuineness—enough work to make sleep a luxury, frugality enough to make food a boon and time enough to chat with and love everyone you meet. I don't suppose Italy is necessary to these elements but I know it is easy to do so in Italy" (9/2/10). "Simplicity and genuineness," realized through steady work, thrift, and contemplative leisure, provided the framework for all they sought to achieve in the years ahead: to strip away all nonessentials and arrive at a purity of expression in life and art.

They arranged to meet again in New Haven when she returned that fall. Meanwhile, back in New York with Flora, Earl felt affirmed and invigorated by Achsah's vision of an ideal future, seizing on it as their common cause. He severed his connection with the commercial art world, "even if I must remain poor the rest of my life," contemplated a trip to Sicily that winter, and wished to discuss the project when they met again: "I want my next move to be of permanent significance" (10/10/10). Achsah's reply was all he could have hoped for. She applauded his decision to renounce commercial artwork, though begged to differ with his concept of poverty: "Our wealth is in proportion to what we are, not what we have" (10/18/10).

Earl's buoyancy, however, changed swiftly to panic ("all is confusion—like my mind") when Flora left New York shortly before his trip to New Haven. Face to face now with his prospective rite of passage from the safely dependent role of youngest son to responsible head of a household, Earl floundered as he tried to have it both ways: "[My mother] is very very dear to me and it was hard to have her go. I tried to persuade her to go with me to Europe—but she felt it was not right to do so at present. Oh Achsah I think if one could only <u>know</u> the right it would not be hard to follow. And in perfect obediance there is so much of freedom—in many ways" (10/18/10). Marrying Achsah was the single most decisive action Earl would take throughout their life together, one that he himself set in motion and saw through to its conclusion. Yet during the next half century, where they went, and when and why, was often in "obedient" response to the suggestions or decisions of others. Spiritually and intellectually, Earl's "basic principles were unshaken by heaven or earth" (A. Brewster 1942, 21). It was the practical aspects of day-to-day adult life—that is, engagement with the world as an autonomous individual—that proved so troublesome. "Knowing the right" meant having to decide between alternatives, to make a commitment, accept responsibility, even to compromise, all singularly difficult hurdles for him to surmount.

Whatever Achsah herself may have felt upon learning that her thirty-two-year-old lover had just invited his mother along on their proposed Sicilian tryst, Earl's visit to New Haven a few days later, on the weekend of October 21, unequivocally banished all thought of anyone but themselves. "Beloved," she wrote afterward, "Was it all some beautiful vision!"(10/24/10). She compared her blissful state to Olive Schreiner's tale, "A Dream of Wild Bees," in which a woman dreams that her unborn child will be denied fame and wealth for something far greater than worldly success: "This shall be thy reward—that the ideal shall be real to thee" (Schreiner 1987, 147).[17] If Schreiner's story defined their highest aspirations, Achsah now included among these the man who had lately kissed her: "I think I must be the child to whom the 'ideal seems real,' not only seems but is real" (10/24/10). She had already achieved her reward: Earl would remain her ideal-made-real for as long as she lived.

He, too, was thinking of Schreiner's story, particularly its inherent sacrifice. "I crave almost with a priest's desire—simplicity." "Asceticism," too, he had added, but tellingly crossed out the word. Apparently there were limits. Acknowledging the risks, he nonetheless longed "to shake off every compromise, to say—either the ideal or nothing; to fling the little ideals of little souls away and to move thro the world with you—following only the laws of our own being" (10/25/10). The exigencies of outward circumstances could be left to others, as long as he and Achsah remained faithful to their inner reality.

By late October they were discussing wedding dates, ships to Europe, and, delicately, finances. Earl's concerns here were well-founded, as he had sold no paintings that year, despite the efforts of William Macbeth, and his prospects seemed bleak. Unperturbed by her future husband's precarious position, wishing only that she were an heiress, Achsah hunted up her bankbook and urged Earl to seek advice from John Barlow, who had promised her a gift of $1000 to add to her savings of $2500. On the Brewster side, to Earl's relief, Flora directed Ara to send him

$200. Now the father of three daughters, Ara remarked dryly to his younger brother, "Well you are ten years older than I was when I was married, and perhaps you will be able to get boys instead of girls. Here is hoping so anyway" (11/4/10).

The wedding date was fixed for December 1, 1910; "at home" cards in "Taormina, Sicily," were printed up. Achsah repeatedly reassured her family "that we may not stay in Sicily for-ever" (10/31/10), while Flora feared that in all the excitement her son would forget to eat. "Sicily and the sunshine for me," Earl exulted (11/17/10), confident that Achsah would make him a stronger man and a better artist. "It seems to me we face a marvelously glorious future. O God grant that from it we may create productions of great beauty. How can we help but do so?" (11/6/10).

They were married in the living room of the Barlow residence, 89 Bristol Street, New Haven, with Achsah's father, sisters, aunts, and a few friends in attendance, Flora with Ara and his family from Chagrin Falls, Fred Shaler, and Rudolph Ruzicka. Not present at the ceremony was Vachel Lindsay, who nevertheless had almost the last word, requesting Achsah to "tell Earl H. Brewster to send me a letter of at least perfunctory apology for removing about half the Youth and Beauty from the United States, and all of the real art Talent" (11/25/10). Two days later, aboard the *Carpathia* of the Cunard line, they sailed for Europe.

ITALY

Achsah had placated her family with assurances that they "may not" stay forever in Sicily, and indeed they did not, but except for a three-month visit in the summer of 1923, they never again returned to America. Far from home, they could evade the pressures of a society that appeared increasingly materialistic and spiritually vacuous; with no formal ties or obligations to their adopted land, there was time to paint and to reflect. And one could live cheaply in Italy. Work, leisure, thrift: the keys to simplicity. Still, philosophy always trumped geography in their lifelong pursuit of a "purer and more abstract realm of thought and feeling than any country can offer" (Brewster 1923, 8). Their travels were along "inward and outward" paths (A. Brewster 1942, 21).

The Brewsters' first home was Fontana Vecchia, a "Theocritan idyll" east of Taormina, with views of Mt. Etna and the Ionian

Sea. Here they worked "almost strenuously" (EHB to RR 7/23/11), Achsah mostly at portraits, Earl at landscapes. From the northern coast, the Lipari Islands appeared to him "like the very land of the hearts desire" (12/6/11). In the summer of 1911 John Barlow and Alpha came to visit, and by early winter Achsah was expecting a child.

They moved on to Paris, where Earl's work would be shown the following fall, John and Alpha stopping first in Venice before joining them. In spring 1912 the Brewsters took a large studio at 16 Quai de Béthune on the Ile St. Louis, with a grand piano, silk furnishings, and view north to the Bastille. It was a time of hopeful anticipation and increasing confidence in their abilities. Earl made some sales in France, and learned that William Macbeth had sold one of his paintings in New York. He proudly told the dealer that the Hillyer Gallery at Smith College had accepted *The Bathers* for their permanent collection, "where I understand it has been well received" (4/24/12).[18]

In mid-March, on his last morning in Venice, John Harwood Barlow died suddenly of heart failure. Never one to hold back when it came to those she loved most, Achsah would later describe him as a "living portrait of Da Vinci as a young man" (A. Brewster 1942, 204). He was buried in Venice; five months later, there was a granddaughter to carry on his name.

Harwood Barlow Brewster was born on the morning of August 22, 1912, at the American hospital at Neuilly-sur-Seine outside Paris. If Achsah's ideal became real in the person of Earl, his daughter approached deification. "The Child arrived to bless us," she wrote, comparing her joy to "the Buddha's bliss upon reaching his goal" (A. Brewster 1942, 2). In her eyes Heaven and Earth participated fully in the event, all elements working in harmony and benediction. Her glassed-in room was like a garden, "all the stars and moon and finally the sun, were there, closer than the doctors and nurses" (1), while "cool shadows and bright shafts of sun, gave strength to mother and child" (4). Achsah would remember always the tall chestnut trees outside, which inspired the choice of their daughter's name, and seemed to designate Harwood as a child of Nature.

That fall Earl exhibited at the Paris Salon d'Automne in the Gran Palais "one of my most recent and beautiful canvases—'The Family by the Sea,'" he notified Macbeth (9/25/12). In November they moved south to Portofino, on the Ligurian coast, and in March 1913 south again to Anticoli Corrado, a picturesque hilltown east of Rome, famous for the beauty of its models.

Their home, San Filippo, had a large fountain in the angle of its L-shaped wings, where Earl bathed and sketched. When Fred Shaler arrived, the friends painted together to the tune of a shepherd's pipe.

With a view to moving his family still further south, Earl spent a week on Sicily, sketching, sightseeing, and house hunting. Turning north again to Paris, he readied their paintings for the 1913 Salon d'Automne, and haunted the galleries and art schools. Picasso's "esoteric" canvases seemed to herald a new acceptance of "free individual expression," encouraging Earl in his own work (EHB to ABB 10/3/13); the paintings of Maurice Denis, who later admired Achsah's religious murals, were "much in line with the kind of thing you and I would like to do" (10/13/13). This was the first of many trips that Earl would make in search of galleries to show their pictures, new landscapes to sketch and explore, and houses to rent cheaply, driven as much by a vague yearning and vagabond indecisiveness, as by artistic ambition and financial necessity. When he and Achsah were apart, their letters ranged over centuries of philosophy, art, religion, and literature, as they pondered how best to balance contemplation with action, to grow into their best selves. "Our quest was beauty, without and within, like Socrates" (A. Brewster 1942, 340).

That fall Achsah exhibited with both the Salon d'Automne and the Société des Artistes Indépendants, and the following year with the Secessione in Rome, venues organized in reaction to the art establishment to showcase innovations in painting and sculpture. On the strength of her Paris work, she was made a member of the Union Internationale des Beaux Arts et Lettres, and invited to exhibit with them in 1914.[19] During the next fifteen years, until the end of the 1920s, the Brewsters participated regularly in these and other shows, where Achsah earned the larger share of artistic recognition. Only after they moved to India did Earl's work find a more appreciative audience.

Their old art school friend, Rudolph Ruzicka, came out from Rome to Anticoli at Christmas 1913 with marzipan fruits for the tree, and Earl dressed up as Santa Claus. Adding to their celebration, the French papers had favorably reviewed their work in the Salon d'Automne (EHB to WM 12/30/13). Several months later, in March 1914, they moved south again to the Amalfi Coast.

Carosiello was a guest house on the grounds of the Palazzo Rufolo in Ravello, that "cloud cuckoo land"[20] overlooking the

Gulf of Salerno (A. Brewster 1942, 15). A terraced garden led down to a private beach, where Achsah and Edith Lewis, visiting from New York, swam that summer in long black stockings and bloomers. Here they "plunged deeply into painting" (23), the pattern and pace of their work reflecting the personality of each. Earl, cautious, patient, and modest, spent months on the same canvas, working at times with several versions, apologizing to William Macbeth for sending home so few pictures. His focus on artistic process rather than product was a kind of empirical quest in itself that paralleled his itinerant life and spiritual search. Achsah, spontaneous, forthright, and decisive, aimed to complete a canvas each day, the bigger the better.[21] As she observed, "Earl's knowledge and skill grew with constant practice, while I burst forth into experiments and exaltations" (409).

They remained at Carosiello for two and a half years, until August 1916. By way of Theosophy, Earl had become an "ardent" disciple (A. Brewster 1942, 21) of Hinayana (Theravada) Buddhism, an austere branch of Buddhism which favors monasticism and rigorous meditative efforts (Ross 1968, 84, 123)—another indication of his estrangement from a world focused on material achievement and rational analysis (Tamney 1992, 42).[22] His Buddhist practice and study, which Achsah joined in part, included daily yoga, meditation, vegetarianism, and memorization of sacred texts. With Caroline Rhys Davids, lecturer at the London University School of Oriental Studies and eventual president of the Pali Text Society, Earl discussed scriptural passages, Pāli terms,[23] and Buddhist art (8/14/16). Although three years would pass before they met, she arranged for him to contribute to several Buddhist publications, and later proposed that he write a life of the Buddha (E. Brewster 1926, [xi]). Another serious student of Oriental philosophy, Lucile Beckett, lived nearby at Villa Cimbrone with her father, Baron Grimthorpe, himself a member of the Buddhist Society in London. Earl would later experience an epiphany which revealed to him a psychic and mystical bond with Lucile.[24] Their esoteric correspondence on the interpretation of Christian, Buddhist, and Hindu scriptures continued until his death.

From Carosiello Earl severed his last formal tie to the contemporary American art scene in a mutual parting of ways with William Macbeth, who had sold none of his work for several years. "I do not find my inspiration in any particular one of the modern schools," he told the dealer. "I am inclined more and more to believe that the simplicity of primitive painting is adequate and more suitable for what the painter has to say, unless his interest is purely external, than the more clever technique of later times." His own art had likewise grown simpler, "not for the sake of mere naiveté but only in simpler ways do I find it possible to convey the spirit of what I have to say" (2/12/16). He asked that Macbeth allow Edith Lewis to select from those canvases still at his gallery, and send the rest to Achsah's sister, Lola Derby, in New Haven (11/27/16).

Italy's entry into World War I in May 1915 impinged very little on the Brewsters' idyll, but the sale of Carosiello the following year forced another move. By the fall of 1916 they were settled with Fred Shaler at Rocca Bella in Taormina, a pink stucco house with a large studio, grand piano, and view of the Greek theater. Several months later, after visiting a local festival, they stopped at a café where Fred asked for water. He contracted typhoid and died on December 27, 1916. Earl, who had nursed his beloved friend, was awakened some time later by a vision of a figure that stooped over his bed to kiss him.

The Brewsters stayed in Taormina until the spring of 1917, when stray shots from German submarines began landing in their garden. Wishing to contribute to the war effort, they moved to Florence to assist at the American hospital, Earl in the infirmary, Achsah in occupational therapy and later a laboratory. There was little time to paint, but they toured I Tatti with Geoffrey Scott and the Berensons, and visited the "ultra modern" painter, Alberto Magnelli, who knew Picasso, Leger, and Max Jacob (A. Brewster 1942, 55). Libero Andreotti, the foremost Italian sculptor at the beginning of the twentieth century, invited the Brewsters to collaborate with him in a three-person show, but this plan was never realized (83). Another acquaintance there, the Englishwoman Nellie Morrison, would later introduce them to D. H. Lawrence. Lucile Beckett, too, had come to Florence with her youngest son, Manfred. It was on the tram from Fiesole that Lucile was suddenly "revealed" to Earl, "dear and shining and beautiful" (83). He recognized "almost clairvoyantly" that he had "found another being related to India" (3/1/51).

By the fall they were house hunting once again, debating the merits of Paris and southern Italy, and deciding finally on Rome for the duration of the war. Their large studio at Via Margutta 54,[25] with velvet couches and brocade chairs, had a piano and picture window looking up to the Pincio and Villa Medici. Here Earl molded the first of his two statues of the Buddha in meditation (later cast in bronze), a frequent subject also for his pictures. He and Achsah painted New Testament scenes as well, including numerous Madonnas and child. In their studio hung her mural, *Gethsemane;* Lucile bought Earl's canvas of the *Last Supper* for the Ravello cathedral.

They would live in Rome for two years, until autumn 1919. Harwood attended a Montessori school on the Pincio, Achsah sketched daily with the "Circolo Artistico," Earl experimented with abstract painting and read widely in modern Western philosophy—Schopenhauer, Hegel, Kant, Bergson[26]—to enrich his study of Buddhism. Their circle of friends, mostly expatriates, included artist Elihu Vedder and his daughter, Anita; set designer Gordon Craig, son of the actress Ellen Terry; and Margaret Mather of the New England Mathers, with whom Achsah claimed kinship through her mother. A great favorite was Mrs. Rhys Davids's cousin, Algar Thorold, head of the British Propaganda in Rome, with whom Earl began his study of Sanskrit. Achsah prided herself on the "brilliant" gatherings at Via Margutta 54, where, it was said, "the British Propaganda had its centre" (A. Brewster 1942, 100).

The Brewsters took part in several exhibitions during 1918, including the Esposizione Internazionale di Belle Arti della Società Amatori e Cultori di Belle Arti, followed by a joint show of their work in the foyer of the Opera House, and another at the Casino on the Pincio, for which a small catalog was printed. Several of Earl's landscapes were displayed, as well as paintings that showed clearly the influence of Puvis de Chavannes and the Italian primitives: decorative murals in a narrow range of color tones; religious images; figures set, friezelike, in a flat landscape; a mood of remoteness and detachment (Cushman 1992, 41, 47; Wattenmaker 1975, 23–24). Although largely representational, their pictures achieved an abstract quality through the simplification, rather than elimination, of form (Randhawa 1944, 31). Apparently no sales were made, as Achsah commented more than once that "the times were out of joint for our art" (A. Brewster 1942, 144, 147).

Throughout the next decade, one or both of them would exhibit each year in Paris; the few pictures sold often went to friends. Occasionally Earl himself became too attached to a favorite canvas to part with it (EHB to RR 7/5/24). Despite constant money worries, however, he "shook off every compromise" when it came to his artistic integrity. Refusing an invitation to contribute woodcuts for a book of views of Rome, he complained to Rudolf

Ruzicka that the woodcuts were treated in "too trivial a fashion and that the publication itself really had no good reason for coming into being" (4/6/18). Similarly, Achsah later declined repeated invitations from Maurice Denis and Georges Desvallières to join their Atelier d'Art Sacré, fearing that affiliation with a specific group might jeopardize her artistic independence. As she loftily declared, "We are more interested in the quality of our wine than the bush advertising it" (9/9/36).

Easter 1918 was spent with Lucile and Manfred at Villa Cimbrone, where they celebrated the Buddha's birthday with costumes and poetic tributes on a rose-strewn terrace. On Capri they met Axel Munthe, and visited Lady Sybil Scott and her daughter, the future Iris Origo, at Elihu Vedder's beautiful villa, Torre dei Quattro Venti. Six months later the war was over. Friends were returning to England and France, and Earl thought this might be the moment finally to go to Ceylon, seat of Hinayana Buddhism, to continue his study of Pāli. But when it came time to buy their tickets for the Orient, he had second thoughts about taking his wife and seven-year-old daughter to a remote country where he knew no one. Where to now? "Our hearts turned towards the wonders that were Greece" (A. Brewster 1942, 148), the new plan being to remain there if they could find a place to live. After celebrating Christmas 1919 in Florence with a party at the Berensons, they sailed from Brindisi.

The Brewsters spent ten days in Athens in January 1920, visiting the Acropolis, reading Plato, eating pastries. There was no house to be found, and when they decided to return to Italy, the many drachmas they had bought were already devalued. They were living chiefly on the income from investments that John Barlow had left Achsah, with the occasional sale of a painting and regular gifts from family.[27] Expenses and exchange rates had to be carefully weighed and calculated. This was their tenth move in as many years. Harwood later insisted that "we were always settling down for the rest of our lives, wherever we went" (Picard 1984, 206), surely an oxymoronic game plan. In the end they settled down permanently only when all options had run out and the decision was effectively made for them. "I am an absolute Fatalist," Earl later told Claude Washburn, "though it is true we have to talk and plan and think as though we were free" (6/30/26). His search for "wherever we went" was an integral part of his identity,[28] in life as in art. They would move roughly twenty times in the next fifteen years.

The first few months of 1920 were spent at hotels in Naples

and Sorrento. At the Albergo Santa Lucia in Naples they met Sridara Nehru, first cousin of Jawaharlal Nehru, and his wife, Raj, with whom they felt an immediate rapport, the seeds of a friendship between the two families that would last nearly four decades. In May the Brewsters took a small house in Sorrento, Villa Daphnis, with a dovecote and turret. Despite cramped studio space, they turned out a number of canvases, many donated to churches and schools in accordance with Achsah's belief that decorative murals were a necessary element in society and essential to life, "at least to life that is such as it should be" (Brewster 1923, 17). That fall, Edith Lewis and Willa Cather saw the Brewsters in Naples before sailing to New York in November. Winter was coming on, Villa Daphnis growing damp, and studio space was still unsatisfactory. Achsah wrote to Anita Vedder asking if they might rent the villa on Capri, Torre dei Quattro Venti. Before the end of the month they had settled in.

Capri was home base for much of the next nine years, and Quattro Venti an "enchanted pleasure-house" (A. Brewster 1942, 170), with its balconies, Moorish dome, and sweeping view of the Gulf of Naples (Soria 1970, 231). Elihu Vedder's large, well-lit studio accommodated even Achsah's outsized murals, and the grand piano provided another artistic outlet when painting proved difficult. A young German, Ernst Hoffmann,[29] joined Earl in his Buddhist pursuits. Even within Capri's large bohemian community the Brewsters stood out for the local inhabitants, not least, apparently, because they were legally married. Achsah's habit of dressing all in white, her veils, scarves, and capes fluttering in the breeze, earned her the nickname "the sailboat" (Cerio 1950, 508); Harwood's white tunics and the ribbon encircling her forehead gave a Grecian effect (Nardi 1947, 440). Quattro Venti, like Via Margutta in Rome, soon became a gathering place for expatriate artists and intellectuals (Winkler 1990, 7), attracted to the music recitals, philosophical conversation, and especially to their charming, erudite, somewhat eccentric hosts. Years later, Edith Lewis recalled Achsah's ability to "bring together light, color, fragrance in a simple room, so that it became unforgettably lovely";[30] Earl himself, a man of "rare sympathy, insight and character" (Washburn 1968, 23), inspired "an admiration . . . amounting to reverence" (CW to Mrs. Washburn 3/3/ 26).

In April 1921 Nellie Morrison brought D. H. Lawrence to Quattro Venti. She had seen Achsah's painting of St. Francis and was struck by its likeness to Lawrence, who was then visit-

ing friends on Capri. For the third time, one of their paintings
played a pivotal role in the Brewsters' lives. The rapport was in-
stantaneous and exhilarating. "We felt at one with him, stimulated to express our deepest emotions. . . . He moved from the
same centre that we did" (A. Brewster 1942, 199). There was,
moreover, the remarkable coincidence that the Lawrences had
lived at San Filippo and were now at Fontana Vecchia. In her
1934 memoir, Achsah characteristically sweeps across centuries
and cultures as she recalls her first impressions of Lawrence,
likening him to Socrates, Pan, Christ on the cross, Whistler's
portrait of Carlyle, and the sculpted head of a Bolshevik (Brewster 1934, 241–42). Even Earl, normally reserved with strang-
ers, was swayed by Lawrence's gift for rousing others to speak
openly, and recognized his spiritual awareness and fundamental
"devotion to *life*—that power so much beyond our mere mental
consciousness" (13). Lawrence "is a man whose society I found it
a joy to have," he told Rudolf Ruzicka, "and who promises to
come my way again" (5/9/21).

Equally intrigued, Lawrence was soon peppering the Brewsters with letters suggesting future meetings, shared travels,
and shared lives, all the while teasingly critical of Earl's strin-
gent Buddhism. His unexpected joie de vivre and love for the
natural world chimed fully with their own. He was also mulling
over Earl's invitation to join them later in the Orient, for the
Brewsters would soon be sailing east on their "Buddhistic pilgrimage" (Brewster 1934, 244). Earl had not given up his dream
of studying in Ceylon. Recalling the "same old disgusting indecision" that led him originally to postpone the trip (EHB to CW
6/23/21), he had booked their passage shortly after the move to
Quattro Venti.

The plan was to leave Italy in October 1921, spend an indefi-
nite period in Ceylon, and eventually reach Burma. Undecided
still about Earl's proposal, the Lawrences returned to Capri in
late September to make their farewells. "Uncle David" gave Harwood "a terrible impression of being very white" (Picard 1926, 79
[1st series]). Four days later, as Earl accompanied Lawrence and
Frieda to their train, he felt "something passed between the
three of us which made us realize our friendship more deeply
than before, and gave us the promise of its endurance" (Brewster
1934, 27).

They sailed aboard the *Osterley* from Naples to Ceylon, with
stops at Port Said and Aden, arriving in Colombo two weeks
later. The Brewsters were mesmerized by this first glimpse of

the East, where "the slow, rhythmic roll of ocean breakers marked off the heart-throb of a primaeval world" (A. Brewster 1942, 216). To Harwood, the orange clay earth, elephants, and exotic curries made Ceylon seem "like a fairy land" (Picard 1926, 85 [1st series]). Earl soon felt "so essentially at home in an eastern atmosphere that I do not like to contemplate any limit to this sojourn" (EHB to CRD 1/17/22).

The unbearable heat of Colombo soon prompted a move northeast to Kandy Lake, across from the Temple of the Tooth. Each morning Earl and Harwood set out together, she to a missionary school, Earl to a Buddhist temple, where he studied Pāli with a monk in exchange for giving English lessons. Achsah sketched the riotous vegetation, the decorative patterns in shrines, Singhalese men and women. Her dark figures, reminiscent of Gauguin's Tahitian natives,[31] inhabit the same silent, remote world of her New Testament scenes. At Kandy they met Judge Ennis of the Supreme Court of Ceylon, whose wife Lawrence named in his teasing poem about Earl, "Apostrophe to a Buddhist Monk" (Brewster 1934, 50). In January 1922 they moved to Ardnaree, an isolated bungalow in a large wooded estate overlooking Kandy Lake, with a wide veranda, plenty of studio room, and four servants. Earl worked on an article for the *Buddhist Monthly of Ceylon,* and planned on Burma for that fall. "Life was exuberant" (A. Brewster 1942, 243), sometimes too much so for Achsah, who feared snakes. When the Lawrences decided after all to investigate Ceylon, Earl met them at Colombo in mid-March 1922 and brought them to Ardnaree, where they would remain for six weeks.

Lawrence began his sojourn with the Brewsters by recounting their faults, glaring and trivial. Among the former was Hinayana Buddhism, with its belief in the central role of "dukkha" (suffering), as "unshakeable" in Earl as it was unacceptable to Lawrence, whose "imperative need to fight" (*LL* 4 #2423) collided with what he judged to be Earl's passivity and escapism (Ellis 1998, 15). Although Achsah joined in Buddhist meditation and yoga, her confident, optimistic nature "never could emphasize sorrow . . . believing as I do, that we are conceived in joy, born to joy, dying to joy" (A. Brewster 1942, 249). A sunny and perhaps mediating presence was Harwood, to whom Lawrence was genuinely attached, and who felt accepted as a companion, rather than child, in her relationship with "Uncle David" (Picard 1984, 212; Brewster 1934, 307). They corresponded regularly for the rest of his life.

Together the families explored the estate and remote temples, watched "workmen in the ways of life not dominated by machinery" (Brewster 1934, 47),[32] argued, sang hymns, told stories, talked philosophy. "[Lawrence] wished us to live and work together in a deep and sincere relationship, from which would spring a reality beyond any one of us" (49). That their friendship not only survived but flourished throughout the decade was due in no small part to Earl's unflappable equanimity, which allowed him to accept "the word hard to hear" from this "furious" reformer (14), and absorb or reject it in accordance with his own sense of self and "the laws of his being." Lawrence "knew that Earl's truthfulness would lead him through any difficulty" (A. Brewster 1942, 249).

When the Prince of Wales visited Ceylon that March, they all attended the midnight perahera, a vast procession of elephants staged in his honor, which Lawrence later described in his poem, "Elephant." The unreality of the scene, with its fireworks, drums, and dancers, made them long for familiar sights, and talk soon turned to "otherwhere." Lawrence, who had suffered from the heat since his arrival, now "looked like death's head," and felt "a sickening repulsion from everything," the rich food, Buddhist temples, and "teeming life of the place." Achsah, too, felt overwhelmed by the suffocating air, jungle wildlife, and "nervous dread lest something awful might happen" (Brewster 1934, 253; A. Brewster 1942, 251–52). The exotic had become threatening. Regretfully, Earl informed Mrs. Rhys Davids of their intention to return to Europe. "My wife finds the climate here so bad for her that we have decided to retrace our steps. It is a great disapointment to me not to go on to Burmah" (4/5/22).

In late April 1922 Lawrence and Frieda left Ceylon for Australia and America. The Brewsters would not see them again for four years. Shortly after, they too sailed from Colombo, again on the *Osterley*, this time for France to meet Alpha in Switzerland. Relieved to be heading west again, Achsah noted that "Mount Sinai looked less commanding on the way home, back to the Promised Land" (A. Brewster 1942, 254).

They put up at the Grand Hotel in Chexbres-sur-Vevey, where Harwood studied daily in Alpha's room, dubbed the "School of Learning" (Picard 1926, 11 [2nd series]). When twenty-year-old John Derby, Lola's son, arrived from New Haven, he and Earl set off on a tour of Italy. It was early August, and Mussolini was threatening to march on Rome. Less than a year before, Lucile had been caught in a gun fight between Fascists and Socialists in Viterbo.[33] Now en route to Florence, Earl and John found their train commandeered by Fascists, who fired out the windows and burned piles of newspapers on the platform. To John they seemed "like a lot of school boys having a lark" (EHB to ABB 8/3/22).

From Switzerland the Brewsters moved on to Paris, settling in at the Hôtel du Quai Voltaire in preparation for a joint exhibition at the Galerie Chéron in the fall of 1922.[34] This latest attempt to promote their art had been Achsah's idea, for Earl was discouraged enough by their lack of prospects to talk of going into "some simple business" (EHB to RR 1/15/23). He had been "pining for the east" (*LL* 4 #2593) almost since their return from Ceylon, and once back on familiar soil, was forced to confront the fact that they had nowhere to live and no reason to suppose that they would ever be able to support themselves as artists. "I am perfectly sick of the artists life," he wrote Ruzicka, "in so far as his relation to selling etc is concerned—so far as making a livlihood of it,—of course I have no experience in doing so!"(1/15/23). Their return to Europe in 1922 marked the beginning of nearly a decade of increasing disappointment and despondency on Earl's part that would amount almost to paralysis. "Life is too bitter without a great deal of indifference," he told Claude Washburn. "Instead of indiference I fall into torpor, which . . . makes matters so much worse" (EHB to CW 10/15/25).

Christian and Buddhist scenes, landscapes, and Achsah's Ceylon paintings, with their simplified Gauguinesque shapes and brightly colored vegetation, were among the works exhibited that December. The Galerie Chéron considered the show a "great success," despite poor sales and mixed reviews.[35] Few pictures were sold, some to friends at much-reduced prices, the profit covering but half their expenses. However, Chéron would continue to represent them through the coming year, and promised a second show in November 1923. In a further effort to publicize their work, the Brewsters arranged for a monograph, made up of two essays and thirty-two reproductions, to be published in Rome by Valori Plastici "in a rather de luxe fashion. It will be written in French and is supposed to be good advertising" (EHB to RR 1/15/23). Their Parisian friend and fellow painter, Pierre Caous (later chief justice of the Supreme Court of France), translated their essays from English into French.

L'oeuvre de E.H. Brewster et Achsah Barlow Brewster appeared in the spring of 1923. Valori Plastici had been a natural choice, for its owner, Mario Broglio, himself advocated a return to the pictorial values of the past, chiefly those of the primitive Italian painters.[36] Earl and Achsah each contributed a semi-autobiographical essay, which discussed the development of their artistic principles and acknowledged their debt to Puvis de Chavannes. The fundamental components of painting, Earl emphatically and repeatedly declared, were color and form: "red, blue, green, and the secondary and other colors, the cube, the sphere, the cone, straight lines, curved lines, horizontal, vertical, oblique" (Brewster 1923, 12). All other elements should remain subordinate to these, whatever the style or period, geometric, cubist, ancient, modern. Here Earl addressed what he viewed as recent debasing accretions in painting, notably realism. The "primordial elements" of color and form alone produced what the showy technique of "scientific reproduction" (13) could not—"abstract psychic emotion" (10), the goal of all "great and pure" art, regardless of age or culture (12).

Nearly a decade before, Earl had written similarly to William Macbeth, "So far as time is concerned in the question this saying of Emil Bernard is a comfort to me—'There is neither ancient art nor modern art. There is art, which is to say the manifestation of the eternal ideal'" (2/12/16). Bernard, too, greatly admired Puvis, particularly his idealism and intellectualism (Nonne 2002, 78), qualities which critics associated with the Brewsters as well.[37] While Achsah maintained the primacy of "powerful emotions" (Brewster 1923, 16) in guiding the artist's hand, her references to Theocritus, Horace, Plato, Euripides, and Schopenhauer underscored the cerebral rather than sensuous element in their work.[38]

By January 1923 they were back on Capri, "our blessed island. It seemed better than ever" to Achsah, after fifteen months on the road (A. Brewster 1942, 276). New neighbors since their departure for Ceylon included the futurist writer Filippo Marinetti, who admired one of Earl's abstract paintings (EHB to Lucile Beckett 5/15/55), and retired schoolmaster Richard Reynolds and his wife, author Dorothea Deakin. Their three daughters, Diana, Hermione ("Mynie"), and Pamela, quickly became like sisters to Harwood, bound by temperament, interests, and the often isolating experience of expatriation. The four girls studied together, wrote skits, played charades; they would remain intimately linked for the rest of their lives. At Easter Caroline Rhys Davids arrived, Earl's mentor in Buddhist studies and "the living archive of Pali scholarship." Unexpectedly fun as well as formidable, she swam and sunned, asked to be called "Erda," and raised eyebrows by communing with voices from Beyond (A. Brewster 1942, 292–93). It was probably during this visit that she proposed that Earl write a life of the Buddha, the first complete English compilation from translations from the Pāli canon (EHB to RR 7/5/24; E. Brewster 1926, [xv]), which he began work on the following winter. In May she accompanied the Brewsters as far as Rome, for they were again setting off on a long trip: Earl had promised Flora they would visit America that summer.

They sailed from Le Havre after a week in Paris (where they saw Willa Cather), arriving in New York in early June 1923. It was their first trip back since 1910, and their last. They remained in America for three months, staying alternately with Edith Lewis in New York, the Barlows in New Haven, and the Brewsters in Ohio. Harwood was enthralled with her newfound relatives, and charmed by "the perfect equipment of a well-appointed American home," electrical appliances being a novelty (A. Brewster 1942, 319). After their quiet rhythm of work and study, her parents fared less well when confronted with a daily onslaught of visiting, entertaining, and moving about, in a world faster and louder than the one they had left more than twelve years before. Trains rushed them "from Gehenna to Gehenna" (341), where streets were lined with a jumble of faux chalets and Venetian palaces, homes so "perfect" that one felt oneself "an intrusive blot" (338). "Perfection" for Achsah signaled the death of improvisation and creativity. Earl complained to Mrs. Rhys Davids that five weeks seemed like six months. "Our life here is so external . . . that I have no time for those interests which are most a real part of myself" (7/16/23). He longed for the quiet of their studio in Capri. In early September 1923 Edith Lewis waved good-bye from the dock in New York. They had seen almost all of their American family and friends for the last time.

Earl's intention was to be back in Paris by early fall to prepare for their second show at the Galerie Chéron, as well as the annual salons in which they continued to participate. Many old friends were around, including Willa Cather, staying with Isabelle and Jan Hambourg at Ville d'Avray. Nora Joyce, whom they had met the previous fall, advised Achsah in selecting a black cape on the Rue de la Paix. Earl hosted a lavish banquet to reciprocate the entertaining they had enjoyed—"a glorious victory," though he had to forgo a much-needed winter coat to pay for it (A. Brewster 1942, 343).

Their Chéron exhibition of landscapes, religious scenes, and Earl's bronze Buddha had its admirers. Dorothy Canfield

Fisher, reduced to tears before Earl's sketch of the Crucifixion, described having come in "from the dark, noisy chaos of the street, and felt myself calmed and strengthened by that calm strong beauty you two are creating, benedictions on you!" (12/8/23).[39] This show, too, was a financial failure; few pictures were sold, though one was to a niece of Oscar Wilde. Achsah donated her large triptych of the Sermon on the Mount and the Joan of Arc altarpiece to a church in Crécy-en-Brie.[40] However, Paris had lifted and inspired them. Back on Capri by Christmas 1923, they looked forward with renewed optimism and palpable relief to a period of uninterrupted work. "For us, just to be in Quattro Venti on Capri was enough" (A. Brewster 1942, 345).

The Brewsters remained at Quattro Venti for nearly two and a half years, until March 1926. Harwood studied French, Greek, and Latin, and with the Reynolds sisters established a newsletter, "Genius Burning," which they typed and distributed weekly until the end of the decade, despite the occasional absence of one or another of its contributors. Achsah produced numerous murals, to be scattered among schools between Naples and Calabria. Musical evenings were resumed (notably during the Hambourgs' visit [EHB to CW 6/7/25]), plays written, and all visitors corralled into elaborate charades. Earl's work on the life of the Buddha occupied the first half of 1924.[41] Characteristically, he never asked whether he would receive royalties: "It is not done with that in view" (EHB to CW 3/18/24). He had declined Ruzicka's offer of a loan, but while he was off sketching in Calabria in the fall of 1924, Achsah drummed up business by collecting commissions for his work from their friends.[42]

Since his student days at Oberlin, and throughout the years of dedicated study, Earl had dreamed of seeing India. On Capri now he read an excerpt from *My Brother's Face*, by the Indian writer Dhan Gopal Mukerji,[43] and after learning that Mukerji was then traveling in Europe, invited him to visit. Mukerji spent several days with the Brewsters, paying calls and reciting scripture, in a mutually enjoyable mix of high spirits and spirituality. It was enough to seal their friendship and fate. Upon returning to America, Mukerji spoke with his friend Josephine Macleod, who had ties to a monastery near Calcutta. Macleod (known to many as "Tantine") was an influential disciple of the late prominent Hindu Vedantist Swami Vivekananda,[44] at whose monastery, Belur Math, she spent part of each year (Prugh 1999, xxvi, 25). During a stopover in Naples on her next trip east, she stayed for ten days with the Brewsters, who were awed by her regal presence and intimate link to a renowned spiritual leader. By the end of her visit, she had invited them to come as her guests to the Belur Math mission. At first they refused, then hesitated, wavered, and then it was settled. They would leave for India in March 1926.

Once again D. H. Lawrence came for the packing-up and good-byes, joining his friend painter Dorothy Brett, who was visiting the Brewsters on Capri. He had hoped to hire a "little lugger" (*LL* 5 #3589) for an extended Mediterranean trip together, and now sympathized with Achsah's dread of India, perhaps recalling the menacing exoticism of Ceylon (Brewster 1934, 266–67). Earl meanwhile was hurriedly correcting galley sheets for his life of the Buddha, to be published in London by Kegan Paul, Trench, Trubner and Company in October 1926, with an introduction by Mrs. Rhys Davids. Entitled *The Life of Gotama the Buddha (Compiled Exclusively from the Pali Canon)*, it "piece[d] together scraps of biography and autobiography embedded" in the rules and sayings of the earliest Buddhist scriptures (E. Brewster 1926, [xi]).[45] The sheets were posted to London on their way to the ship. Lawrence and Brett closed the gate to Quattro Venti after them. "They waved courage to us as we rolled away" (A. Brewster 1942, 356).[46]

Again the long-range plan was to "settl[e] down for the rest of our lives," as Earl described in a story about the voyage east. Aboard their ship was a man who spoke so compellingly of the Greek island of Syra in the Cyclades that they "decided to spend the rest of our days there if not in India" (Brewster 1934, 99)—a characteristic statement, reminiscent of his earlier proposal to move to Greece if they could find a house. Contingency plans—those omnipresent "if's"—provided a loophole against having to commit to a particular course of action. They docked in Bombay on April 1, 1926, and proceeded immediately to Calcutta and Belur Math, where Tantine settled them into the guest house at the Vivekananda Mission. With her was Boshi Sen, a scientist and disciple of Vivekananda, who became a close friend during their stay in India, and their neighbor when they moved permanently to Almora ten years later. Shortly after their arrival, the Indian Society of Oriental Art in Calcutta hosted an exhibition of the Brewsters' work, arranged by nephews of Rabindranath Tagore (EHB to CW 6/30/26).

By mid-May Calcutta was stifling. With Boshi Sen, the Brewsters made the long trip to Almora, a hill station in the United Provinces facing the Nanda Devi range of the Himalayas. Here they remained into the monsoon season, working, meditating, and exploring the estate surrounding their home. Earl rose early to paint the first rays of sun on the mountains. Boshi set up a make-shift laboratory, with Harwood as his assistant, and taught her to chant Vedantic scriptures; she in turn introduced him to charades. She studied Pāli and Sanskrit with Earl, practiced rags on the esraj, sent weekly contributions to "Genius Burning," and began a memoir, "Fourteen Years of My Adventures." When Tantine arrived, the group climbed higher into the hills to visit Snow View Estate, which a decade later would become the Brewsters' final home.

But things were not going well. Even before they left Belur Math, Earl was finding India "more interesting than simpatico" (*LL* 5 #3716), despite Tantine's prior warnings about dirt, disease, and poverty. By early May, plan B, namely Syra, was already taking shape. Lawrence reported to Brett that Earl sounded "lamentable—he's awfully interested in India, but doesn't really like it: says they can't leave before *October* . . . perhaps winter on one of the Isles of Greece" (5 #3729). Worse than Calcutta was Almora, where both Earl and Achsah became ill, possibly with malaria (5 #3802). Between stories of man-eating tigers, the sight of an enormous baboon in the pantry, and her fear of snakes, Achsah lay awake at night in terror.

Lawrence regretted their distress, but he plainly felt that India had given Earl a much-needed dose of reality, yanking him out of the passive "easy ether" and escapist "lotus-pool" of his brand of Buddhism. As a result of his disillusion with India, Earl would now be "truer to [his] own inner man," Lawrence assured him, less quiescent, more critical, primed to grasp his "own single destiny." He hadn't reckoned on Earl's own inner man preferring an alternate lotus pool to "battle and repudiation" (*LL* 5 #3802). In late November, three months after delivering his lecture on taking charge of one's destiny, Lawrence wrote impatiently to Brett, "Earl says the Grecian isle, Syra, is now the Paradise of his imagination" (5 #3897). But Earl was nothing if not consistent. He had confessed years before to the lure of "certain other lands . . . sometimes quite of my own imaginings." Furthermore, ceding the question of their future to the chance utterance of a stranger on a ship—like floating away, unresisting, in the "easy ether"—absolved him from having to decide for himself what next step to take. Only his obedient presence was required.

In a last burst of sightseeing as the trip wound down, they

took in Agra and Benares, Sarnath, where the Buddha had preached, and Bodhgaya, where he received enlightenment. At Hamirpur they were lavishly entertained by Sridara Nehru, a cousin of Jawaharlal Nehru and commissioner of Hamirpur, whom they had met in Naples six years before. There was just enough time in Bombay to see the Elephanta Caves and shop for sandals and incense. On December 7, 1926, they sailed for Piraeus, and thence Syra.

No paradise, it turned out to be "a rather treeless island devoted to market-gardening" (Brewster 1934, 99), crowded with Armenian refugees and teeming with bedbugs. They stayed just four days before returning to Italy. As a token of their stopover, Achsah later sent to a school they had visited an altar painting of Christ with the shepherds.

The Brewsters arrived back in Naples in January 1927 with neither a home nor a reliable source of income. During the next two and a half years they would move roughly fifteen times, drifting between hotels and villas on Capri or Villa Cimbrone, dependent on the occasional absence of a friend for the loan of a house, and on periodic funds from home. "I am getting so very tired of this kind of existence," Earl lamented (1/20/27). His distress and disappointment in India must have been a crushing blow, after three decades of anticipation. The Lawrences, whom he visited outside Florence in mid-January, found him "improved, really, by India" (*LL* 5 #3949), for "the very disillusion is valuable, and then the glimpse of a new reality" (5 #3946), but the reality at hand left Earl nearly incapacitated. When in the fall of 1929 the Brewsters finally did settle into their own home for an extended period, it was through Lawrence's intervention.

Stepping back into their familiar Capri routine, Harwood resumed lessons with the Reynolds sisters, and they "all fell to painting" (A. Brewster 1942, 391). Lucile and Manfred came from Ravello; charades reached giddy heights. The writers Llewelyn Powys and Alyse Gregory, new to the island, would become the Brewsters' close friends. In April 1927 Earl set out with Lawrence on a five-day walking tour of Etruscan sites, which resulted in Lawrence's book *Sketches of Etruscan Places,* and the novella *The Escaped Cock.*

Despite the constant shifting between homes and hotels— Pensione Bella Vista, Villa Giulia, Villa Cimbrone, Hotel Capri, twice more to Cimbrone, once more each to the Bella Vista and Villa Giulia, and finally Villa Torricella, all in 1927 alone— Capri "seemed like heaven" to Achsah (A. Brewster 1942, 391), after months of feeling unwell and "scared stiff" (*LL* 5 #3949). Her stout optimism and trusting loyalty truly made her "a perfect traveller" for Earl, who admired "the calm ease with [which] you journey—without fretting and stewing. . . . But not only for such little journies are you so perfect a companion—but for the longer journey of life itself you take it in the same way" (1/9/27). Even her "calm ease," however, was tested during this time of uprootedness and worse than usual financial uncertainty. "Our plans are as vague as ever," Earl told Mrs. Rhys Davids (7/31/27). Their families grew increasingly anxious. Now eighty years old and infirm, Flora Brewster weighed in severely, admonishing Earl, "If you gave your mind to finding a market [for your work] as much as you have given to Indian literature, and Bodhism—you would have succeeded" (9/21/29).[47]

Lawrence's letters to and about the Brewsters during the late 1920s resembled the running commentary of a Greek chorus. Alternately teasing and advising, hectoring and sympathizing, he beseeched them, Earl in particular, to make a decision, put up a fight, set a firm course of action: "Heavens, what waifs and strays!" (*LL* 6 #4020); "This indecision for you is like a sickness. You've drifted now long enough to realise that you aren't moving anywhere, you're only becoming water-logged and really derelict" (6 #4053); "*Don't have* ideas about places, just because you're not in them" (6 #4054); "And so you're once more flotsam! For goodness sake, cari miei, take a direction and swim for it. I do think this being washed about by wayward currents is too enervating" (6 #4139); "So the Israelites are turned out of their little Canaan" (6 #4407); "Achsah, my dear, you must come to a few decisions *all on your own,* Earl is out of the running . . . and I seriously think Buddha and deep breathing are rather a bane, both of them. . . . Earl has more or less destroyed his adaptation and dislocated himself from the western environment" (7 #5122). When Lawrence sent Harwood some Christmas money in December 1927, he slyly suggested that she use part of it to buy her father a wigwam (6 #4232).

Lawrence blamed Earl's inertia on his absorption in Buddhism, but Buddhism clearly was another manifestation of Earl's long-time reluctance—for Lawrence "a form of side-tracking" (5 #3802)—to engage actively and autonomously in the exigencies of day-to-day adult life. Barely a month into their courtship, Achsah had noted that he seemed "able to live in the world not of it" (3/26/10). Earl himself acknowledged difficulty "even in thought to associate myself with my own environment":

everyone has dreams and ideals, "but they seem more willing than I to live in this world as they find it" (8/14/10). Recognizing in her a kindred spirit, he wondered if together they could "help people in the ordinary world without descending from ours" (10/25/10). Their shared romantic vision of an ideal life in Italy crowded out all practical concerns. Only weeks before proposing to Achsah, and despite "embarrassing" financial circumstances, Earl renounced commercial artwork, his sole reliable source of income—a decision she applauded, though (or rather, because) she surely realized by then that their futures would be linked.

These were hardly the daydreams or rash idealism of youth. Earl and Achsah were thirty-two years old when they married, had traveled abroad and lived apart from their families. Yet each was still very much under the protection of parents and siblings, both financially and emotionally; each was the classic indulged youngest child, creative, largely freed from conventional responsibilities, accustomed to being taken care of, and ultimately interested more in inquiry than achievement (McGoldrick 1995, 216), in the "joy of the process" (ABB to HBP 3/18/42) rather than product or gain.[48] They wished to be set free, not cut loose. Their financial dependence on family and friends would continue to the end of their lives.

John Barlow supported and encouraged Achsah during the eight years she studied painting in New York and Europe—a vocation that apparently assumed confidence in someone else's monetary assistance, as she never mentioned employment. (In contrast, Alpha worked from the time of her Smith graduation, and would eventually assist with Harwood's school tuition.) Earl managed to support himself in New York, though it seems doubtful that he and Flora could have spent a year and a half abroad without Ara's help.[49] When Earl planned his Sicilian rendezvous with Achsah, he begged Flora to come along, seemingly unwilling or unable to choose between mother and future wife. Harwood associated her parents' late marriage in part with Earl being "very much his mother's son" (Picard 1984, 200). He was similarly reliant on several authoritative women—Annie Besant, Mrs. Rhys Davids, Tantine, and Lucile Beckett—for spiritual guidance and discussion. All of them were old enough to be his mother, except Lucile, who was more a spiritual sister.

There was a childlike unworldliness and naïveté about Earl and Achsah, a sense of their "sitting upon rosy clouds," as Lawrence put it (Brewster 1934, 245), above the fray, concerned with matters spiritual and cerebral, rather than corporeal.[50] The reading recommendations in their courtship letters alone could fill several college syllabi. Nearly a year after their marriage, Vachel Lindsay wrote, "I can't yet quite realize you folk are married yet. It sounds like a fairy-tale to me. It sounds delightfully improper. I don't know just why" (9/9/11). Fairy-tale weddings are fantasies of innocence that conclude with "happily ever after." What surely struck Lindsay as "improper"—a curious comment to make about a married couple in their thirties—was the juxtaposing of his unworldly friends with the earthly reality—the intimacy and physicality—of married life.

Neither Earl nor Achsah had grown up in a family with a husband and wife at the helm. Each had lost a same-sex parent (and role model) before the age of nine, and was raised partly by relatives who stepped into the breach. Ara Brewster, ten years Earl's senior, became a quasi-paternal figure to his brother when Calvin Brewster died; he married young, ran the family business, provided for Earl and Flora, and was soon a father himself. After Ida Barlow's death, her sisters were "like three mothers" to the Barlow daughters. When Achsah (John Barlow's "dear baby girl" into her late twenties) paid homage to the aunts who had raised her, she singled out those characteristics with which she also clearly identified: "crystalline purity, a flavour of goodness," and "white, immaculate soul, unsmirched with any worldliness" (A. Brewster 1942, 321–22). She habitually dressed in white, the color of childhood innocence. Earl himself recalled his boyhood sadness when he grew too old to wear white (Brewster 1923, 6). Vachel Lindsay enjoyed a flirtation with Achsah, but he also called her "a holy woman, not many are as good" (12/22/06). In his 1912 poem, "My Lady in Her White Silk Shawl,"[51] he described her as a "lily," "prim," "with thoughts that find no place / In our harsh village of the West," "distant as far-hidden stars, / And cold," a "Puritan Bacchante" who wakens "wild and innocent love in every worshipper" (Lindsay 1914b, 139). Like the "merry gentle moon," she belonged to another sphere.

What their marital expectations were cannot be known. A month before the wedding, it seemed to Earl that "already a mystical marriage has been made—that our life is now one" (10/31/10). Three weeks later he wrote of the "white flame" that burned for her in his heart, that perhaps not even the "night of Brahm" (when cosmic activity ceases) would extinguish. After death, "shall we not be there in potentiality in the unity. Our love is the very seeking I suppose for that unity." Here he retreats, concerned about that repeated word: "Dear love forgive me if I speak of that ["things" is crossed out] I should not" (11/20/10). Achsah had characterized her role in their relationship as "the child to whom the 'ideal seems real,' not only seems but is real" (10/24/10). She was identifying specifically with the child in Olive Schreiner's story, but the word "child" itself was for her an exalted concept, signifying a Rousseauian state of innocence and "psychic wholeness" (Lears 1994, 146), a closeness to nature and God with undertones of the Christ Child, as she articulated in their 1923 book: "To be an artist one must be a child. The work of one who has purity of heart—*integer vitae*—is a new vision of God" (Brewster 1923, 16). Years later in India, they were drawn to an aphorism of their guru, Sri Aurobindo Ghose, that was couched peculiarly in language the Brewsters themselves might have used: "What is God after all? An eternal child playing an eternal game in an eternal garden" (1/10/37; A. Brewster 1942, 312).

Her image of Earl as the ideal incarnate gave luster even to the hard times. He was "like the sea, wide, deep, open, clear and pure" (A. Brewster 1942, 21); when they were apart, "We . . . rejoice in you and we do magnify your name" (1/13/27). Regarding the newly elected Pope Pius XII, she asserted first that Earl resembled the "beautiful, sensitive, spiritual" pontiff (3/9/39), and then decided that the pope instead resembled Earl (5/17/42); crowned with passion vines on one birthday, "Father looked to me like Aeschylus, Sophocles and Euripides rolled into one, not to mention Dante and Petrarch et al" (9/22/36); his paintings resembled those of Mantegna and Piero della Francesca (5/4/41; 12/1/36).

A child is not prepared for the rituals of adulthood; idealization, whether of people or places, real or imagined, puts the object at an emotional remove from actual experience, indeed functions as an obstruction to direct experience. Passionately devoted throughout their lives together, Earl and Achsah yet never overcame the developmental challenges they faced to sustain a fully adult relationship as husband and wife. Little more than a year after their wedding, and sometime after the start of Achsah's pregnancy, their marriage became celibate.[52] Their avoidance of a full relationship in an adult marriage paralleled their childlike resistance or inability to engage the world on adult terms—to make their own decisions, to determine their own future, even to compromise occasionally for the greater good. "Detachment," from each other and from the world, was the "necessary" price for attaining "a purer and more abstract realm of thought and feeling than any country can offer" (Brewster 1923, 8). By the late 1920s, Earl had pretty well answered for himself the question he had posed nearly two decades before, "whether its better to adapt yourself to your environment—or let it adapt you to its uses" (8/14/10). Eventually their outward journey mirrored the inward, and the Brewsters were carried, unresisting, about as far as they could go.[53]

Lawrence had offered them his villa outside Florence for the spring of 1928, when he and Frieda would move north to Switzerland, but when the Brewsters arrived they were so alarmed by his deteriorating health that they promptly decided to accompany their friends to the Alps. "There was no definite notion of where we were going, only the pleasure of exploring" (Brewster 1934, 282). From June to October they made their way through Switzerland and Germany to southern France. Lawrence was preparing for an exhibition of his pictures at a London gallery, and half-heartedly attempted to have the Brewsters' work included (*LL* 6 #4488, 6 #4508). Although painting was a common bond between them, he cared far less for their art than for their friendship (Cushman 1992, 39, 46), which inspired two short stories from the late 1920s. "Nobody Loves Me" was based on an exchange with Achsah in the mountains near Gsteig.[54] In late August 1928, when the families were briefly apart, "Things" appeared in *Bookman,* a "most amusing story . . . you'll think it's you, but it isn't," Lawrence assured them (*LL* 6 #4656). Earl and Achsah clearly played some role in his satirical portrait of expatriate painters Valerie and Erasmus Melville, but they either laughed it off or hid their hurt (Cushman 1991, 91). The sympathetic affection and loyalty between them and Lawrence ran deep. They parted in France in early October, the Lawrences heading to Var, the Brewsters back to Capri via Nice, where they were delayed for several days, unable to continue their journey until money wired from America had arrived. This was the last trip that Earl, Achsah, and Harwood made together. The following summer Harwood left to attend school in England, Capri friends scattered, and the years in Italy came to an end.

Dartington Hall was a small progressive school in Devonshire, modeled on the one founded by Rabindranath Tagore near Calcutta, and aimed at "children of parents with moderate means" (Young 1982, 9). It was a logical choice, for its philosophical approach to education accorded perfectly with the Brewsters' own. Indeed, it stood for everything that Achsah meant by "child": classrooms were essentially in the garden, workshop, and play-

grounds; its founders recognized a "common ground between religious and artistic experience" (198); and the "most vital
service" it sought to render was "to release the imagination, to
give it wings, to open wide the doors of the mind" (61). Harwood
would enter in September 1929. That summer Lola arrived with
Rachel, and the two sisters and cousins sailed in late July from
Naples to Venice on the first leg of a journey en route to taking
Harwood to school. Influenced by Boshi and her work in his laboratory in Almora, she was planning to become a doctor. "Hurry
up and cure my asthma," Lawrence wrote, "for you've only got
half an Uncle David instead of a whole one" (*LL* 7 #5266).

They worked their way across the continent to England,
where Tantine provided tickets to the full cycle of plays at Stratford-on-Avon. After two and a half trying years in hotels and borrowed villas, with little money and no prospects, Achsah must
have felt as if she were breaking loose and kicking up her heels.
Constantly busy, stimulated, and full of fun, she managed one
breathless letter home to every three or four of Earl's. Meanwhile he was alone on Capri, trying to paint but clearly dis-
tracted, eager for news of their travels, worried first at her
irregular post, then frustrated and fuming, as evident from the
blizzard of exclamation points, question marks, and underlin-
ings that swirl across his pages. It was hard to be separated from
Achsah: "Life is 'dukkha' without you," he had once written.[55] In
the midst of his annoyance now he paused to observe, "I feel that
the stream of our being is nearer in quality, in harmony and
more significant in our relationship with each other and in our
combined relation to the world, than ever before" (9/10/29).

Anxious that Harwood cram in as many academic subjects as
possible, Earl decided she should study Greek, German, mathe-
matics, and science. His own scanty post-secondary school education—several months at Oberlin Academy—was a source of
lifelong regret that no amount of subsequent scholarship and er-
udition could alleviate, and he was determined that his daughter be exposed to as broad a curriculum as possible. Achsah must
have seemed to him an academic blue blood, with her Smith degree and Yale-oriented family. She herself was immediately delighted with Dartington Hall, where "everyone is working away
heart and soul and hand." Her Emersonian approach to Harwood's formal education sidestepped Earl's focus on the acquisition of subject knowledge—for Achsah simply a given and a
starting point—and emphasized instead personal inner growth,
for oneself and as an example and inspiration to others. Among

the "good, simple, true spirit of the people" at Dartington Hall, she felt sure that Harwood would "find a place where she can express herself in helping and in being helped" (9/16/29). It would be a splendid experience, "whatever she does or does not learn" (9/18/29). Several years later, when Harwood was struggling to pass her entrance exams for medical school, Achsah reminded her, "Nothing really matters, certainly not lessons, except goodness and beauty and truth and the shine of bliss that is the proof you are finding them" (1/11/31).

Achsah must have suffered when they parted in Devonshire. If she adored Earl, she worshipped Harwood, with an idealization bordering on apotheosis. Harwood carried the full freight of her "child" appellation: she was the "'holy spirit' of our 'blessed trinity'"(2/26/36), "the fulfillment of the law and the prophets" (A. Brewster 1942, 310), "close to nature. . . . the Stoic of whom I had dreamed as I read Marcus Aurelius before her birth" (173), whom "everyone loved and honoured," along with her father, "as elect souls" (100). Joan of Arc always reminded Achsah of Harwood (11/10/32); Wanda Landowska's recording of Bach sounded just like Harwood's own playing (4/22/42). The frequent motif of mother and child in Achsah's paintings further underscored her romanticized view of their respective roles, and occasioned Lawrence's sarcastic comment, "Achsah's acres of Jesus and the blue Virgin—always herself" (*LL* 6 #4211).

Hyperbole aside, Harwood clearly was an unusual child and young woman, affectionately admired by diverse and discerning friends, from Cather to Lawrence to Mrs. Rhys Davids.[56] She flourished in the rarefied atmosphere of the Brewster household, where her parents' steady habits of work and study made literature and art, religion and music, a focus of daily life, though never at the cost of childhood dolls and storybooks. Sociable, articulate, and self-possessed, she was equally at ease with adults and peers, ready to play games or recite Achsah's favorite passage from Euripides. Achsah closed her memoir on an elegiac note with "the Child's" departure for Dartington Hall and the coming family divide: "School days were ahead. The baby girl was a memory now" (A. Brewster 1942, 416). They would meet again at Christmas.

FRANCE

Where the Brewsters themselves would be by that holiday was still under discussion, for they were very nearly out of funds and

Plate 1. Earl Brewster. *Positano*, ca. 1916. Formerly owned by Willa Cather and Edith Lewis. Courtesy of Frances Picard Holt.

Plate 2. Earl Brewster. *The Buddha Meditating*, ca. 1918. Courtesy of ACA Galleries.

Plate 3. Achsah Brewster. *Butterflies,* **ca. 1917. Courtesy of ACA Galleries.**

Plate 4. Achsah Brewster. *Woman with Violin, Man Reading & Woman Playing Piano,* 1923. Courtesy of ACA Galleries.

ideas. Earl had to ask Ara for a large loan, to be repaid from his inheritance from Flora. At Lawrence's urging, the Brewsters joined him and Frieda that fall in Bandol, between Marseilles and Toulon, with a view to being that much closer to Harwood as well. Château Brun, near St. Cyr-sur-Mer, was a square, three-story stone house set amid vineyards. It had no plumbing, electricity, or oven, but the rent was low, and the two "B's" carved over the doorway augured well.[57] Achsah immediately hired a grand piano, though they were unable to move in until after Christmas, when money arrived from America to make possible the purchase of furniture (Ellis 1998, 520–21). Harwood joined them for the holiday at Hôtel Beau Rivage; before returning to Dartington Hall, she typed Lawrence's *Apocalypse* manuscript. This would be the last time she saw him.

In early February 1930 Earl and Frieda brought Lawrence to a sanatorium in Vence. Earl was leaving shortly for India, having accepted an impromptu invitation to accompany Dhan Gopal Mukerji as his guest on a short trip there. He said good-bye to Lawrence in mid-February, and left France at the end of the month, intending to return to Vence in May. Two weeks later he arrived in Port Said, en route to Bombay, to find Achsah's telegram with the shocking news of Lawrence's death on March 2. "Dazed and sorrowed," he resolved to "honour [Lawrence] most, and keep his presence and friendship best, by trying to live in the realizations of those truths he had realized." His March 15 response to Achsah also included a postscript, written four days later, by which time, far from "dazed," his thoughts were leaping ahead: "Don't let anyone have access to my letters from David, until I return."[58] He had finally hit upon a promising moneymaking scheme.

During their several weeks in India, Earl and Mukerji saw Tantine at Belur Math and, most memorably, were guests of the Nehru family in Allahabad. Their extensive political discussions with Motilal Nehru and his son, Jawaharlal, then president of the Indian National Congress, are recorded in Mukerji's 1930 book, *Disillusioned India*.[59] "The father and son are splendid," Earl wrote to Achsah, "but I like the son best of all—and feel very close to him" (3/25/30).

The Brewsters had intended to spend the winter of 1929–30 at Château Brun and return to Capri in the spring. In fact, they never saw Italy again, and rarely strayed from southern France until their final departure for India in December 1935. There simply was no money. Alpha paid for Harwood's studies in Lon-

don after Dartington Hall; Margaret Mather, their "chief patron-
ess" (EHB to Ara Brewster 5/11/35), covered the rent on Château
Brun; local friends occasionally stepped in with a loan or purchased a painting. Still, the Brewsters often looked to Harwood
to meet their bills out of the money Alpha sent her, and to supply
such necessities as shirts, socks, and books. Achsah breezily dis-
missed their predicament as a question of mind over matter, an
opportunity to assert her priorities: "Remember you inherit the
earth and that the kingdom of heaven is within, and there are
no price marks on either" (10/11/31). Earl by now sounded more
resigned even than depressed: "Our bread is mostly bread of
charity—but it seems to agree with us quite well," he told Rudolph Ruzicka (12/20/32). To Harwood he acknowledged that
there was little chance he could repay her occasional loans.
Everyone must go on faith, "but we more than most" (6/27/31).

Outwardly, their life at St. Cyr was "like the Victorian novel—
quiet, rural, dignified" (ABB to HBP 9/27/30). Earl noted that
"the world seems as little aware of us as always—which I do not
mind" (12/20/32). Their letters to Harwood catalog a daily schedule of reading and study that is staggering in its sweep, from
Plato, Plotinus, and Boccaccio, to Peter Abelard and Gibbon,
modern literature (Tolstoy, Cather, Conrad, Dos Passos), lives of
Joan of Arc and Beethoven, Hindu scriptures, and a four-volume
biography of Vivekananda. As always, Sundays were set aside
for "the divine Plato" (EHB to HBP 4/30/33); indeed, their letters
could almost be dated according to weekly discussions of the dialogues and "the dear, whimsical Socrates" (ABB to HBP 12/13/
37). "Jowett's translation [was] our 'vade mecum,'" Achsah recalled. "Those Dialogues were as real as the sunshine, as divert-
ing as a drama, as breathlessly exciting as a new novel" (A.
Brewster 1942, 126–27).

Earl's spiritual affinities were gradually shifting from Buddhism to Vedanta Hinduism, to which he was reintroduced during the Brewsters' 1926 stay at Belur Math; he had been
acquainted with its teachings from the time of Vivekananda's
well-publicized lectures at the 1893 World's Parliament of Religions (Ross 1968, 68). During their visit to India, Earl spoke at
length with Vivekananda's disciples, and was drawn to this "accepted philosophy of intellectual Hinduism" (51), as were a number of scholars and artists, Western as well as Eastern. Like
Hinayana Buddhism, Vedanta stresses the individual's personal
search for enlightenment, but in accordance first with specific
training exercises, such as the study of religious texts, sessions

with a guru, and analytical discussion, followed later by deepening meditation (52–53). The many months Earl devoted to reading and typing the letters of Vivekananda's influential Irish disciple Sister Nivedita gave him a thorough grounding in Vedantist thought and aspiration.[60] The writings and counsel of his own gurus, Shivananda (Vivekananda's successor at Belur Math), and particularly Sri Aurobindo Ghose, inspired and comforted him for the rest of his life: "Where from any Westerner have I found such understanding?" (12/27/51). Achsah joined in daily meditation, finishing her evening breathing and chanting "while Father is still thus occupied up in his sanctum" (12/27/31).

Harwood came regularly during school vacations. She had finished at Dartington Hall in 1931, and rather than continue for a liberal arts degree at Cambridge, decided instead to attend the London Royal Free Hospital School of Medicine for Women, part of the University of London. This was a most distressing moment for her parents, hardly able to grasp her apparent rejection of the humanities-based curriculum they valued so highly (EHB to HBP 6/27/31).[61] Achsah implied that such a trajectory could contribute to the ills of society: "The trouble with life today is that there are too many efficient specialists who do not know how to relate their little knowledge to the wisdom of the universe" (6/27/31). "Efficiency," like "perfection," functioned as a pejorative in her vocabulary. Their letters are peppered with "I would like you to," "how much I wish you could," "you must," and "you can't," but Harwood stood her ground. After repeated attempts, she eventually passed all five entrance exams in late 1932, and matriculated the following year.

If the Brewsters were unable to stir from St. Cyr, the world found a way to come to them. Willa Cather and Edith Lewis visited from Paris; the Reynolds girls and their father stopped to and from Capri and England. Sridara and Raj Nehru had hoped to visit St. Cyr, but Earl reluctantly declined: his "affairs [were] at too low an ebb" to permit guests at Château Brun (6/26/33). Harwood's London meeting with Gandhi in October 1931 caused a vicarious frisson of excitement to ripple through their correspondence.[62] Newspapers from England and America kept them abreast of the struggle for Indian independence, the economic crisis in the United States, and the rise of Nazism and Fascism in Europe. An oppressive "sense of suspended fear" made Achsah surer than ever of "the futility of politics. Through the ages the enduring things are art, architecture, literature, music and the memories of holy lives" (3/10/33).

The Brewsters' circumscribed existence was itself a kind of freedom, for the years in France were intensely productive. "It is so enthralling to try to create beauty. There is nothing like it" (ABB to HBP 11/23/30). Achsah's mural painting would reach "that stage when it is difficult to stop for eating sleeping or night and the days are so short" (11/29/30). (A decade later she wondered to Brett "how people can live who are not painters" [9/25/41].) Writing rather than painting became her chief creative outlet during this period, however, and she filled her pages at much the same rate as she did her canvases. "Indeed she has written one novel and twenty seven short stories in the last seven or eight months," Earl told Rudolf Ruzicka (11/30/31). Some of these were hopeful magazine submissions. An article about Ceylon, published in *Asia* magazine, brought in fifty dollars (ABB to HBP 1/22/33). By early 1933 she was aiming for the *Atlantic Monthly*'s five-thousand-dollar prize for nonfiction, writing seventy-five thousand words on the joy of life (a subject she was singularly well-equipped to address), and had set her sights on a *New York Herald* award for a book about Italy calculated to spur immediate travel.[63]

For himself, Earl reported qualified artistic progress to Ruzicka ("of course improvement is accompanied with slumps"), though his ongoing experimentation with "pure abstracts" helped his representational work (EHB to RR 2/24/31, 12/20/32). He, too, was writing prolifically—articles for *Prabuddha Bharata;* a short story, "My Lady Poverty," for the *Atlantic Monthly;*[64] a translation of the sayings of the Buddha, as a sequel to his life of the Buddha, published in *Asia* in 1936. His essay, "Dukkha and Sukha," on sorrow and joy—the opposing Buddhist concepts that he and Achsah seemed to embody—appeared in 1931 in a collection of essays on Buddhism.[65]

The Brewsters' most ambitious project during these years was the compilation of Lawrence's letters and their memories of him that appeared in early 1934 as *D. H. Lawrence: Reminiscences and Correspondence*. Between October 1930 and February 1931, they worked with an urgency ("like beavers," "like furious hurricanes" [ABB to HBP 1/18/31, 7/4/31]) born of their deep affection for Lawrence and their pressing need for money. Harwood, too, played an active role, copying out her letters from Lawrence and suggesting revisions. The manuscript was sent to Random House in February 1931. Earl joined the Society of Authors, Playwrights and Composers to obtain legal advice (Harwood kept his dues current), and consulted the more experienced Ruzicka, asserting his primacy of place among Lawrence's circle to justify the rush to publish, before coming around to financial need: "I was Lawrence's most intimate friend during the last years of his life. . . . I am convinced that many of the letters would be of much value to the student of Lawrence, and should therefore easily find a publisher—and bring us quite a bit of money!—which we certainly need, and which would have amused and pleased Lawrence, I am sure, to provide for us, even in such a fashion" (2/24/31).

In the midst of negotiations with Random House, Earl was frustrated to learn that William Heinemann had bought the copyright to Lawrence's letters and was planning its own publication of his correspondence. This appeared in 1932, edited and introduced by Aldous Huxley, another of Lawrence's close friends, whom the Brewsters knew as well. Not surprisingly, Achsah judged that "the very best side of [Lawrence] is not there" (ABB to HBP 10/5/32). In mid-1933 Heinemann finally gave them permission to publish their own volume of letters. Earl wrote to Ara in late January 1934 that the book would come out the next month, "and then we should be having some money" (1/27/34).

Their self-effacing and sympathetic portrait of Lawrence earned critical praise,[66] but little else. Earl was truly at an impasse, worried and depressed at living "on the verge of nothing" (EHB to Ara Brewster 6/3/35). Margaret Mather had fallen ill in Rome at the time that their rent on Château Brun was due; Alpha lost her job and could no longer pay Harwood's school tuition. An exhibition of the Brewsters' work at Mount Holyoke College, organized by Alpha in the spring of 1934, brought appreciative reviews but no revenue.[67] A welcome respite came in early 1935, when they spent several months with Harwood in England. Earl left a number of paintings with London dealers, and told Ara he had made important connections (5/11/35).[68]

At this point a dramatic series of events—sudden tragedies, unexpected possibilities—began to unfold, and by the end of the year their lives would be forever changed. In March 1934 Diana Reynolds had married a Frenchman, Georges Picard, a teacher in Paris and former Rhodes scholar. Their daughter, Claire, was born in February 1935, but Diana soon became ill, and died a month later. Then in May 1935, as Mynie and Pamela Reynolds were walking in Capri, Pamela slipped, hit her head, and fell into the sea. She died just two months after Diana.

This was all a tremendous shock to the Brewsters, for Diana,

Mynie, and Pamela had been like sisters to Harwood for more
than a decade. That summer Harwood visited the Reynolds family on Capri; there, she and Georges Picard fell in love. When she
told her parents she planned to marry the following spring, they
were terribly upset. "He does not seem to us to be strong physi-
cally, he has a baby daughter and he is a Roman Catholic," Earl
confided to Ara, underscoring their chief objection by stating it
twice more: "I can but feel sorry to have Harwood marry into an
environment which will be distinctly Roman Catholic, for
Georges is almost fanatically Roman Catholic. It is the hardest
blow Achsah and I have ever had" (10/17/35). In contrast to their
own all-embracing spirituality, Catholicism seemed narrow-
minded, "not really sufficiently Catholic in failing to recognize
the divinity of other teachers as well as Jesus" (EHB to HBP 4/
22/33). Earl persuaded Harwood to return to London for at least
one more school term.

Meanwhile, circumstances were changing rapidly for Earl and
Achsah as well. In spring 1935 Geoffrey de Sélincourt, a fellow
painter and student of Vedanta,[69] came to live with them at Château Brun and share expenses. His wealthy father, who disap-
proved of art, gave him a meager allowance, Earl told Ara (6/3/
35), but the sum was enough for Geoffrey to devise a plan that
Earl found irresistible: he "offers to meet the financial side of a
journey to India, for himself and Achsah and me, and the taking
of a house there where all three of us would continue our studies
of painting and Hindu thought. We are inclined to accept the
offer" (10/17/35). The Brewsters were utterly out of money and
alternatives. In addition, they hoped that such a move might en-
tice Harwood to join them, perhaps continue her studies there,
or in any event put some distance between her and Georges. By
late fall they had sold their furniture, stored a box of paintings,
given away some books; Achsah donated six murals to local
churches.[70] On December 1, 1935, their twenty-fifth wedding anniversary, Earl wrote to Harwood, "We finally sailed away from
Marseilles at about 3 o'clock yesterday." They would never see
her again.

INDIA

The Brewsters landed in Bombay in mid-December; Christmas was celebrated with Tantine at Belur Math. Between February and April, with "no plans except to move by inspiration"

(ABB to HBP 2/3/36), they traveled through southern India to Pondicherry, home of Sri Aurobindo's ashram, where "the atmosphere mentally is simply heavenly" (EHB to HBP 2/25/36). By mid-April 1936 they had settled with Geoffrey at Snow View Estate in the Kumaon Hills near Almora, first glimpsed ten years before. Here at Bhawani House, in sight of the Himalayas, Earl and Achsah would spend the rest of their lives.

These first months in India were an exhausting mix of intoxicating new experiences and profound sadness. They missed Harwood desperately, urged her to visit, and worried about her coming marriage. In addition, they felt forcibly the contrast between their "deep and active" interior life in India, and the depressing external reality of "dust and disorder."[71] From Bangalore Earl wrote that in the early mornings he often lay in bed "longing for my demise (!), but afterward I feel full of deep deep happiness and clearer visions than ever before" (3/12/36). Now in their late fifties, they suffered the physical discomforts of travel in India. Never in robust health, Achsah was ill nearly from the time of their arrival in Bombay. (Both she and Earl were eventually diagnosed with pernicious anemia, the inability to absorb vitamin B12.) Hardest of all was coming to terms with the fact that they had no alternatives for the present or foreseeable future. Earl protested to Harwood, "Some who criticize us have no conception of what it means not to be able to go where they like, when they like and how they like. Geoffrey is paying our expenses; the last money I have had of my own was the £10 which you sent me from Aunt Edith's purchase of one of my paintings. . . . No one else can realize how difficult such situations are for us" (4/18/36).

Even so, the Brewsters' enforced stability proved immensely energizing and productive, as Achsah's muscular prose conveyed: "We have all taken violently to portraiture"; "We have painted full blast and to great purpose"; "We are indefatigable and draw upon inexhaustible forces."[72] In addition to painting, they were turning out articles and reviews for *Asia* and the *Aryan Path,* and collaborating on short stories. Earl's study of the Rig Vedas inspired a book project, "The Ancient Wisdom in Hindu Thought" (EHB to HBP 3/29/38).[73] In lieu of a piano, Achsah practiced on a tabletop. Geoffrey rented a neighbor's gramophone, so mornings began with Beethoven quartets. There were brief trips to nearby Binsar and Mirtola, and "happy, long evenings together reading about the ineffable" (4/10/37). Earl, now in shawl and turban, was "fulfilling his heart's desire in being here, for which all his life he has been pining" (ABB to HBP 5/31/36).

By the time Geoffrey left for England in mid-November 1936, the Brewsters were a fixture in Almora's distinguished spiritual, intellectual, artistic, and political community. Lest anyone back home think they had washed up at the outpost of civilization, Achsah assured her fellow Smith alumnae that "one of the Emersons, Gertrude, an editor of *Asia,* is a neighbor and dear friend. We have an interesting group of Cambridge scholars near enough to visit back and forth."[74] Among new and old acquaintances during this first year were Earl's fellow student in Buddhism from Capri days, Ernst Hoffmann, now called Anagarika Govinda; the Danish mystic and friend of Rabindranath Tagore, Alfred Sörensen, known as Sunyata; Boshi and Gertrude Sen; anthropologist W. Y. Evans-Wentz; dancer and choreographer Uday Shankar; and the Nehru family, among whom the Brewsters became particularly close to Vijaya Lakshmi Pandit, sister of Jawaharlal Nehru and the first woman minister of India. Achsah got around the problem of too many distracting visitors by simply painting them (9/16/36).

Following a special dispensation from the pope, Harwood and Georges were married in Paris on May 7, 1936, at which point Earl and Achsah ceased their opposition and enthusiastically embraced the young family. Heretofore they had taken care to offer moral support rather than advice. Now the floodgates opened, both parents seeking to ensure that their daughter appreciate her duties to husband and child, so as to "mould the home into beauty-goodness-truth" (ABB to HBP 4/26/36). Missing from Achsah's list of Harwood's responsibilities is housekeeping, or, as she saw it, "frittering your energies in small, evanescent things." She had a horror of her daughter becoming a conventional housewife. Georges needed "understanding & discrimination & shining leisure," not cooking, knitting, and sewing (12/6/36). Best to follow her own rather startling modus vivendi, which was "not to do anything yourself that you can get someone else to do, not to do anything today that can be put off until tomorrow" (8/2/36). This, of course, from someone who nearly always had servants, and who frequently provided others with, as she put it, the "happy privilege to give to those one loves" (12/29/37).

In early 1937, concerned about a coming war, Georges moved his family from Paris to the United States, first to New Haven, and then Winona, Minnesota, where he taught at a Catholic women's college. The Brewsters' regret at uncultured, "raw Minnesota" (ABB to HBP 9/10/38) soon turned to alarm as it dawned on them that Harwood was leading an American middle-class existence in a "tiny second floor flat squeezed into a new American town" (6/12/38). She had married a salaried academic, acquired a refrigerator but no piano, and sent her parents snapshots instead of paintings. Servants were not an option. Earl counseled resistance to American materialism, as if Harwood were bent on hedonism (1/12/38).

There is an almost comical role reversal here, with Earl and Achsah the counterculture bohemians who went off to their Indian mountain top and guru, while their daughter rebelled by marrying a conservative man and leading a conventional life. Indeed, from the time she left Dartington Hall in 1931, Harwood had functioned to a degree in the role of responsible parent in their relationship, paying the Brewsters' bills, sending them clothes. Her own daughter, Frances Diana, was born on October 1, 1938. To Earl's delight, this was also the birthday of Annie Besant, a coincidence that seemed to "signify an unusually deep sympathy" between himself and his new granddaughter (ABB to HBP 11/7/38). He carried her picture on a cushion from room to room, "addressing her as his special disciple" (7/10/39).

Geoffrey's departure meant that they now had to assume all household expenses. Modesty and lack of business skills prevented Earl from asking more than small sums for their work. In addition, the news that Margaret Mather had been a passenger on the Hindenburg (word of her survival reached them many months later) cast doubt on further help from that direction. Earl anxiously asked friends in England and America to sell at any price the paintings he had stored with them. More worrisome still than their finances was the state of Achsah's health, which deteriorated during 1938. She became increasingly weak and unsteady, hardly able to walk, and developed heart problems, all signs of pernicious anemia. Liver supplements, regular injections, and a change in diet were prescribed.[75] For several years Earl functioned alternately as nurse, maid, and amanuensis. Sad and exhausted, hardly daring to leave her side, he wondered at Achsah, "so gay and full of interest in our readings and studies and work" (7/15/40). By late 1940 they spoke of returning to the United States, but she felt unable to manage the trip. "No one knows the pain and suffering she endures. Always she says that she is much better" (11/30/40).

"Not only for such little journeys are you so perfect a companion," Earl had once written, "but for the longer journey of life itself you take it in the same way" (1/9/27). Achsah had a remarkable gift for greeting each day, in good times and bad, with high expectations and an open heart, her glass not half full, but perpetually overflowing: "It is the joyous aspect of looking upon God himself as a playmate in the game of living" (5/6/42). Worry and complaint were alien to her nature: "Our roof leaked but the lilies more than repay one"; rats scampering overhead "sound as if they were playing tag and having fun," while those indoors "specialize on the Pāli-canon!" Rats devoured as well the Brewster family crests that Alpha had sent to Almora, and "digested [the] significance" of their motto, "Verité soyet ma garde." Achsah asked Harwood for replacements.[76]

When she eventually regained enough strength to work, Achsah began jotting down for Frances and Claire some recollections of Harwood's childhood, "spinning memories . . . like an old spider drawing forth his web from himself" (8/3/41). The exercise quickly took on a life of its own; in just over a year she produced a family history, "The Child," which ran to nearly 450 pages, encompassing the period from Harwood's birth to her departure for Dartington Hall.[77] In recreating the "splendor" of past times and places, she soothed her yearning for her daughter, sisters, and friends after years away, the time and distance between them now compounded by an unreliable wartime post. Sending home the manuscript in late 1942, she cautioned Harwood to "take in homeopathic doses, small doses at a time" (10/4/42).

In India the Brewsters finally achieved the sustained artistic recognition that had eluded them in the West. Copies of Earl's statue of the Buddha went to temples in Mirtola, Lucknow, and Sarnath; galleries in Allahabad and Lucknow featured their art; prominent local residents began to acquire their pictures. The deputy commissioner of Almora, M. S. Randhawa, was particularly instrumental in publicizing their work. He owned several of Earl's canvases, hoped to establish a Brewster gallery in Allahabad, published a monograph, *The Art of E. H. Brewster & Achsah Brewster* (1944), and purchased sixteen paintings for public buildings in Delhi. The All India Fine Arts and Crafts Society unanimously elected Earl vice president.[78] Letters throughout the 1940s and 1950s describe numerous sales to political dignitaries, missionaries, spiritual leaders, and tourists. "Your father is a 'vogue' here!" Achsah marveled (10/11/43).

Artistic celebrity proved a mixed blessing. By the early 1940s the Brewsters' studio attracted a daily stream of visitors. With no interest in the limelight, and his accustomed work schedule constantly frustrated, Earl confessed to "a kind of sick feeling" at the approach of callers (EHB to HBP 3/30/42). He "detested" M. S. Randhawa's monograph, which "everyone in India has read," as "too sentimental, that is unintentionally untruthful in spirit," and urged Harwood to evade Randhawa's request for help in establishing a Brewster gallery. Individual appreciation was welcome, "but I hate publicity . . . the write-ups and critics cackle" (6/1/45).

There was a mystique about the Brewsters that went far beyond their art, and drew to Bhawani House people of many nationalities and social strata. Their openhanded simplicity and quiet pursuit of truth and beauty inspired reverence and a protective devotion. The Pandits came regularly with their daughters, whom "Aunt Achsah" introduced to charades; Jawaharlal Nehru sent frequent gifts of flowers, cakes, and magazines. The commissioner of Bareilly named his new daughter for Achsah; the postmaster general of India wished to be thought of as her son. A wandering mystic, dressed in white, twice appeared at their door. Always a seeker, Earl himself became something of a guru to many young men, who found in his humanity and rigorous studies the inspiration for their own search. They wrote music to him, sent presents, and sought out "the peace and quiet of [his] face and [his] home." Perhaps, he told Harwood, "such ones are clairvoyant, but see my ideal only instead of this suffering old man which I see myself to be" (7/31/49).

He, too, was showing symptoms of pernicious anemia, "stagger[ing] around like a drunken sailor, but I managed to keep on painting, house keeping and nursing" (1/7/44). Achsah endured a gruesome course of "hypodermics," which "shiver my timbers at the moment but inspire fresh hope" (6/1/43). Harwood sent information about the disease and its treatment. She was now assisting at a hospital in New York, where the Picards had moved after Georges finished a PhD in French at Harvard. Earl wrote frankly about their deteriorating condition; Achsah said simply that "faith, hope and love are the way of health and delight" (4/18/44). No longer able to paint, Achsah passed the last months of her life reading, listening to music, enjoying the company of friends and the natural world around them. "The days float by like bright butterflies, full of colour," she told Harwood (10/8/44).

She died on February 16, 1945. One morning before dawn Earl heard her exclaim, "Oh now let me go," before she slipped into a coma, waking briefly to say "good night" to him. Dressed in

white silk and covered with narcissus and mimosa, she was cremated in an isolated spot near a river, her ashes scattered on the
water.[79] The cables Earl sent immediately to Harwood and
Alpha were delayed, and they learned of Achsah's death from
the newspaper. She had "not a particle of vice in her," Frieda
Lawrence recalled (3/8/45).[80] Edith Lewis summed up for their
Smith class: "She had a wonderful life. It was an artist's life
throughout. . . . She had a generosity of mind and nature that
could tolerate almost any human frailty except cheapness and
vulgarity. And what courage she had!"[81]

Earl stayed on at Bhawani House until his death in 1957. Although he mulled over the possibilities of returning to America
or joining Harwood in Paris (Georges worked for the United
States Information Service there during the 1940s), poor health
and lack of funds precluded such options. Much of his earnings,
as well as Achsah's inheritance, had gone toward medical treatment. As always, friends and family stepped in. Ara sent regular
checks; Gertrude Sen and Vijaya Lakshmi Pandit attempted to
expand the market for his work; others assisted with clothing,
art supplies, and medication. A constant preoccupation was to
ensure that Harwood receive their possessions after his death.
He continued to mourn their long separation, but his hope that
they would one day meet in Almora was never realized. In the
early 1950s Harwood and Georges were divorced, and she returned to the United States with Claire and Frances. India was
out of the question.

He missed Achsah terribly, writing in equal measure of his
frequent depression and his attempts to overcome it. Friends in
Almora made his home a regular gathering place, even inviting
him to live with them, but Earl loved Bhawani House and its
associations. India, too, never lost its allure. "I myself feel that
it gives me what I essentially need and desire. . . . Externally,
outwardly I live like a visitor in India—more or less—but in-
wardly I feel that I am and always have been Indian. The very
space and atmosphere about me gives what I seem to need"
(EHB to Lucile Beckett 3/27/56).

Keeping to a fixed schedule helped lift his mood. He painted
steadily during these years, at times hardly able to keep up with
the demand for his work. "Never have I been as much in love
with painting as at present. It is a mystery, the joy, the bliss it
brings to me" (EBB to HBP 11/12/47). Equipped on cold days
with two overcoats and a hot water bottle, he worked outside for
ten hours at a stretch, unable to resist the ever-changing views

of the Nanda Devi range outside his door. Postcards and magazines kept him abreast of movements in contemporary art,
though his tastes were rooted in an earlier period. Always he returned to Puvis de Chavannes, "whose work I believe to be
among the greatest known, and which have inspired me to this
very day" (EHB to Ara Brewster 9/15/51).

Despite his isolation and ill health, he followed American and
European politics avidly, from the Japanese surrender six
months after Achsah's death (a "victory of the higher spiritual
forces" [EHB to HBP 8/11/45]), to the Sinai War and Soviet put-
down in Hungary less than a year before his own. In August
1947 Earl became an active participant in Indian politics, when
local dignitaries in Almora invited him to raise the country's
new flag during their celebration of independence. "As the flag I
hoisted unfurled, roses fell from it upon me!" (EHB to HBP 8/
22/47). A prominent lawyer addressed the gathering in Hindi on
Earl's behalf. Later, he shared the country's shock at the news
of Gandhi's assassination (2/4/48).

By the early 1950s many of his close circle—Dhan Gopal Mukerji, Llewelyn Powys, Willa Cather, Mrs. Rhys Davids, Richard
Reynolds, Tantine, Flora, and Alpha—were dead. Increasingly
nostalgic for Italy and lonely for the company of old friends, Earl
now unexpectedly found himself in the literary public eye. Several new biographies of D. H. Lawrence, including those by
Harry Moore, Pietro Nardi, Richard Aldington, and Edward
Nehls, documented the intimacy between the two families.[82] The
Illustrated Weekly of India invited Earl to contribute an article
with his recollections of Lawrence.[83] In 1955, facing destitution
and rapidly deteriorating health, he reluctantly sold Lawrence's
letters, after prolonged negotiation, to the University of Texas.
His efforts to publish a second edition of *Reminiscences and Correspondence* were unsuccessful.[84]

The Brewsters also now figured in several publications and
projects independent of their relationship with Lawrence. Edwin
Cerio's lighthearted memoir, *L'ora di Capri* (1950), was admiring of their intellectual accomplishments, though Cerio appreciated them more as pleasant eccentrics than as artists. A
philosophy professor from Syracuse, Raymond Frank Piper,
wished to include the Brewsters' work in his book, *The Hungry
Eye: An Introduction to Cosmic Art* (1956), but Earl was unable
to supply photographs in time for publication, much to his disappointment (EHB to HBP 7/31/49, 5/27/50). In late 1952 *Life* magazine sent a photographer to Almora in preparation for an

article entitled "Happy Himalayan Hermit." Although Earl dreaded being "dished up by Life," which he "detested," he enjoyed his days with its cosmopolitan photographer, James Burke.[85] John Stanwell-Fletcher's travel book, *Pattern of the Tiger* (1954), included a chapter about Earl that compelled one reader to seek his counsel on Buddhism. (Earl himself found Stanwell-Fletcher's work "overflowing with misstatements, exaggerations and untruths" [EHB to Ara Brewster 2/6/55].) In June 1956 Francis Watson, whom the Brewsters had known since their early years in India, paid tribute to Earl in a broadcast for the BBC's General Overseas Service entitled "Portrait of a Buddhist."[86] Earlier that year, in response to a petition from the Buddhist Society in Australia, Routledge and Kegan Paul brought out a new edition of *The Life of Gotama the Buddha.*

Earl continued to paint and study almost to the end of his life. He drew up a detailed list of his possessions for Harwood—books and paintings; Achsah's jewelry and silver; rugs and brass items. Six months before his death, he sensed indications "that my life as Earl Brewster is about over and often I long for that ending to come" (EHB to Lucile Beckett 3/21/57). He had often expressed the hope to be reborn with the same parents, brother, wife, and daughter, as well as "some more wisdom and common sense added to my character." And not only that: "Next time I shall have sense enough to master my languages—English, French, Sanskrit and Greek" (EHB to HBP 8/22/42). In his last letter to Harwood, he wrestled with the problem of egoism ("What a hindrance it is!") as a barrier to achieving Oneness with Divine Reality (8/12/57).

Earl died in the hospital at Bareilly on September 19, 1957, two days before his seventy-ninth birthday. A close friend who was present wrote to Harwood the next day, "He seemed to know that he was leaving his body, and he waited only long enough to embrace one by one a handful of his friends who had come. And then he went, in a most wonderful way, as though his was really a spirit freed, freely choosing to go and very much at peace" (Jean Dhawan to HBP 9/20/57). Like Achsah, he was cremated near a river, his ashes scattered on the water.

EPILOGUE

As Earl traced the roots of his artistic sensibility in *L'oeuvre de E. H. Brewster et Achsah Barlow Brewster,* he was struck by the "persistence of a great uniformity of character" in the values that shaped his priorities and guided his career (Brewster 1923, 5). Such constancy held true no less in life than in art. To a remarkable degree, the moral and philosophic principles that the Brewsters had discussed so fervently throughout their courtship remained the bedrock of their lives for the next fifty years: work hard, live simply, do your best, don't judge others, seek knowledge and beauty, and above all, be true to yourself. A favorite passage from the *Bhagavad Gita* enjoined, "Better one's own Dharma, though destitute of merit than the Dharma of another, well discharged" (EHB to ABB 9/11/13; *BG* 3:35).

Even during the hard times, the Brewsters asked little of the world, much of themselves. Several years before his death, Earl wrote to Lucile, "I believe that the best method I have found for a happy life, is to be intensely interested in how I meet what comes to me and not so much interested in what that something is which comes. . . . Thus I try to treat the day somewhat as though it were a picture I were painting. On one side are my ideals; I am trying to express them in the life of the day, I must also use them in the way which seems best to meet the unforeseen events of the day" (12/27/51). Outwardly, such detachment led to poverty and exile, but the inward journey was ecstatic: "I find it wonderful and thrilling to precipitate the fluid impressions of life into crystals of beauty," Achsah exclaimed, "to create art and music and literature out of heartaches and disappointments and joys! It is only a little Dance of Shiva on our own private stage, after all!" (9/29/31). Withdrawing from the conventional pressures and expectations of their milieu (husband as breadwinner; adherence to the traditional rhythm of Protestant American family life; the pursuit of material gains and societal recognition) granted them time and space to paint, study, and dream. "Father and I keep very busy, and we only hope we do grow into fuller, freer, deeper life" (10/7/36).

"By all American standards" the Brewsters would be "counted as . . . failure[s]" (Washburn 1968, 20), as they themselves well knew. In the letters and memoirs are occasional hints that their illustrious circle of acquaintance provided a certain reassuring validation in the face of their own obscurity. Still, those many distinguished and lesser figures "gravitate[d]" (20) to the Brewsters—to their sincerity, modesty, intelligence, and joie de vivre, and to their uncompromising aspiration "to be happy and free, to live gloriously, full of light and reality" (AHB to HBP 1/11/36). Theirs was a self-sufficient, even self- "abolishing" (20), world of their own creation. Few of their company made the same choices, yet all readily helped the Brewsters keep body together while the soul continued its search for Oneness.

At the close of "The Child," Achsah turned to Emerson's Poet, whose inheritance of the earth—"Thou true land-lord! sea-lord! air-lord!"—she claimed as their own (Emerson 1983, 468; A. Brewster 1942, 436). The natural beauty, calm, and remoteness of their final home mirrored the distance traveled into their collective artistic and spiritual consciousness, as if they had finally found harbor within a Puvis de Chavannes mural. For Earl, who continually measured his progress toward an inner goal, their physical surroundings functioned as a signpost to what was hidden. Near the end of his life he wrote to Lucile, "Is not the world as we know it an expression of ourselves, and really of our own making? . . . How slowly but ever increasingly the realization dawns upon us that subject and object are one" (8/31/53). Achsah, as ever, took the beauty around them as another expression of Earl's luster, wisdom, and goodness. Writing to Harwood a year before her death, she described their earthly and spiritual home in terms of a modern-day Eden: "We have good lives together as if the whole world had been made for us to enjoy" (2/8/44).

2. Achsah Brewster and Edith Lewis, Ravello, Summer 1914. Courtesy of Frances Picard Holt.

3. **Achsah and Earl Brewster, Paris, 1922 or 1923. Courtesy of Frances Picard Holt.**

4. **Harwood, Achsah, and Earl Brewster, Capri, ca. 1927. Courtesy of Frances Picard Holt.**

farming regions and forests of the lower country, to the sylvan embedded Carthusian monastery of Montrieux-le-Jeune, near
a swift flowing stream, (founded in the 12th century,)
where at one time Petrarch is supposed to have resided, or was
it his brother? (!) As women are not allowed to enter the
monastery, and as I had previously had the privilege of doing
so, we remained content with viewing the place from outside
and with the pleasure of the drive and the surrounding country.

Willa told us of her chance meeting in Aix-les-Bains (perhaps in a previous visit there) with Madame Grout, the favorite
neice of Flaubert, with whom he lived, the Caroline of his
letters. This meeting, so sensitively and vividly recorded in
Willa's book "Literary Encounter," must have been a very important and gratifying event for both Willa and Madame Grout.

When I was with Willa - due to my own self consciousness-
I was aware of that lack of the classical discipline in language
and literature, which I am regretting that my youth had not provided me. I had heard Willa express her strong disapproval of
those who regard writing as an art for anybody to pursue, and
who indulge in it without having any genius for it. However,
I found Willa to be free from the natural prejudice which hinders
the professional writer from giving consideration to the work
of the inexperienced. A few years before Willa's visit, my
wife and I, at the request of Frieda Lawrence, had published a
book containing the letters to us from our friend D.H. Lawrence,
and also including our reminiscences of him. I was touched and
somewhat surprised when Willa could say to us, that of the considerable number of books written on Lawrence, she considered
ours the best, nor did she limit her encouragement with reference to that work alone.

It seems to me that I never have known a person who
found it so painful to endure falsity, shallowness and superficiality in human nature, especially in the bore and "lion
hunter", as Willa did. Instead of accepting such as the inevitable in life she inexorably rebelled against them. Yet
how tender and considerate she was toward simple and sincere
people. Nor did she consider those forms and conventions
which dignify and beautify life to be of an insignificant or
superficial character.

Somewhat coinciding with Edith's and Willa's presence with
us, we had two other guests, my wife's sister, Alpha Barlow,
whom I think both Willa and Edith much appreciated, and Mrs.
Rhys Davids to whom I was deeply in debt for years of guidance
in my study of Pāli and the Buddhist canonical scriptures,
concerning which she was the leading authority in the Western
world. She was then an old lady, near the end of a somewhat,
isolated, strenuous and brave life, devoted to her special
line of scholarship. She was much attracted by Willa and
gave her an important translation she had made of the
psalms in which the Sisters of the Order, in Buddha's own time,
had recorded their experiences - a charming gift, I thought,
from one woman, so eminent in her line of writing, to another
woman as eminent as Willa in a different line ---- This gift
of the earliest known anthology by women of ancient times.
Willa's delicate consideration and appreciation of our friend
was to be expected, yet so many people absorbed in their own
interests, impatient of interruption, would have failed to
appreciate this brave old scholar.

Soon after this Willa returned to America and I did not
see her again. It is evident from Willa's latest writing, it
seems to me, that those realizations of certain spiritual
values, which generally cannot come until late in life (and
then how rarely) were greatly achieved by her, and crown the
splendid collection of her work. For all of which she has my
love and gratitude.

**5. Earl Brewster. "For the book Willa Cather-living," [1949], p. 3.
Courtesy of University of Nebraska-Lincoln Libraries.**

2

"Happy Working Days":
Willa Cather and the Brewsters

DAVID PORTER

INTRODUCTION

As THE FIRST CHAPTER REPEATEDLY SUGGESTS, ONE OF THE
Brewsters' most remarkable qualities was their penchant for
making friends with people of great distinction. Wherever they
went—Italy, France, India—these modestly successful and oft-
impecunious artists quickly established warm and apparently
mutually satisfying relationships with leading figures, connections that the Brewsters clearly relished for their own sake but
that also not infrequently opened further doors to them and
helped them in times of need. Within this circle of friends writers loom large, among them Vachel Lindsay, Aldous Huxley,
D. H. Lawrence, and Willa Cather.

Of those named, it is Cather whose acquaintance with the
Brewsters spanned by far the most years, and Cather whom
many would now judge the greatest writer. It is accordingly the
more extraordinary that only now—more than one hundred
years after Cather and Achsah Barlow met, and more than sixty
after Cather's death—are the opening chapters of this book in-
troducing the Brewsters to the Cather community. But such is
indeed the case: until recently the Brewsters' presence in Cather's life had virtually vanished. James Woodress's comprehen-
sive Cather biography mentions Earl alone, and that but once
and with reference to the Lawrences' visits with Cather and
Lewis in 1924 (Woodress 1987, 353). Even Edith Lewis, who had
known Achsah since her college days and was the link between
the Brewsters and Cather, mentions them by name only once in
Willa Cather Living (138–39), and that too in connection with
the 1924 Lawrence visit. Only through the materials that are

now available at Drew University can we begin to understand this long friendship and its significance to both Cather and the Brewsters.

FROM GREENWICH VILLAGE TO INDIA

Although Willa Cather's direct communications with the Brewsters cluster around the period 1920–24, her friendship with them began well before then—and extended long after. Between 1904 and 1910 both Achsah Barlow and Willa Cather visited Edith Lewis at 60 South Washington Square, and Achsah visited Lewis at 82 Washington Place in 1910 when Lewis and Cather were living there together.[1] Through their common friendship with Lewis, Achsah and Willa inevitably crossed paths upon occasion during these years, and one of the most memorable vignettes in the Drew archive is the picture Achsah paints of the still-young Willa in her unpublished memoir, "The Child." Achsah's full description, from a chapter aptly entitled "April Twilights," will be found in part 2 of this book, but the following excerpt suggests something of its flavor:

> I remember the first time I saw Willa, rustling out to a dinner party in a shimmering rose charmeuse satin and an opera cloak. We hung over the bannister to watch her sweep down the hall majestically— that dingy hall of 60 South Washington Square that she describes in "Coming, Aphrodite." Willa's eyes were like jewels, clear moss agates of grey and olive edged with gold, the cornea of crystalline clearness and lighted from within. She spoke slowly, hesitating for the word she wanted because she would not be satisfied with a makeshift, but sought to capture some hidden truth. One listened for every significant word. (A. Brewster 1942, 317–18)[2]

Achsah's painterly eye seizes upon both Cather's external stylishness and her inner strength, both her élan and her seriousness. Achsah's allusion to Cather's "Coming, Aphrodite!" is also apt in its implicit association of Cather with the ambitious and socially adept heroine of that story, Eden Bower, whom in fact the Cather of those early New York years resembled far more than she did the story's other major character, the high-principled but scruffy artist, Don Hedger.[3]

In 1949, some seven years after Achsah wrote this passage in "The Child," and some four years after Achsah's death, Earl Brewster at the invitation of Edith Lewis put on paper his recollection of first meeting Willa Cather in 1910. Since Earl's full essay appears in part 2, we again include here only a brief excerpt: "I found her both genial and reserved, quiet, not eager to express herself, but, when speaking, doing so with force and conviction. One was quickly aware of her sympathies with the genuine, with the sincerely worthwhile in life and art. I at once realized that I was in the presence of an unusually sensitive person of deep reflection and of wide experience of the world" (E. Brewster [1949], 1).

That both Achsah and Earl, each writing close to forty years after their initial meetings with Cather, retain such vivid—and complementary—impressions suggests both the force of Cather's own personality in her early New York years and also how much she continued to mean to the Brewsters even near the ends of their lives. The occasion that Earl describes was not only his first but probably also his only meeting with Willa Cather before he and Achsah sailed for Italy two days after their December 1, 1910, wedding in New Haven, and even Achsah's meetings with Cather in her New York years were at most intermittent, a consequence more of her visits with Edith Lewis than of any close acquaintance with Willa Cather herself. [4]

It was not until 1920, ten years after the Brewsters' wedding and their departure from the States, that Cather came to know them well, when she and Lewis met them in Naples for a short but warm visit at the end of their 1920 European trip. The friendship deepened during Cather's own 1923 trip to France, when she saw the Brewsters frequently at both the beginning and the end of her stay abroad. Lewis and Cather visited the Brewsters in France again in 1930, this time at Château Brun, their home near the Côte d'Azur. Characteristically, Edith Lewis glosses over this visit in her account of the 1930 trip, and other sources refer only to "visiting friends in Marseilles."[5] But the Brewsters' daughter Harwood specifically mentions that Cather and Lewis stayed at a nearby hotel when they came to see her parents in south France (Picard 1977, 54); Achsah writes Harwood on September 27, 1930, that "Aunt Edith and Aunt Willa . . . sail [today] for America"; and Achsah refers back to this 1930 visit when she reads Cather's "A Chance Meeting" in the *Atlantic* three years later (ABB to HBP 2/15/33). This visit turned out to be the last time that Cather saw the Brewsters. In a 1934 letter in the Drew archive Cather mentions her hope for another visit, but it is clear that on their 1935 trip to Europe Lewis alone was able to see them.[6]

It is also clear, however, that Cather's friendship with the Brewsters remained very much alive in the years after her last meeting with them, spanning distances that became yet greater when the Brewsters moved to India in 1935, and feeding the vivid and fond recollections both Brewsters record in the memoirs they wrote in the 1940s. One of the most telling indices of the length and vitality of this friendship is the large and ever-expanding trove of books by Willa Cather that the Brewsters owned and carried with them as they moved from place to place—and that they clearly continued to read. The Drew archives contain no less than fourteen books that Lewis or Cather inscribed by hand and either sent or presented in person to the Brewsters, and two more came to them from Cather's publisher with notes indicating that they were sent with the compliments of the author. The warmly inscribed copies from Lewis date from *O Pioneers!* in 1913 through *Willa Cather on Writing* in 1956, nine years after Cather's death. Those that came directly from Cather extend from *Youth and the Bright Medusa* in 1920 through *Lucy Gayheart* in 1935, with the copies from 1920–24 often inscribed in highly personal ways (of her books written from 1920 to 1927, the only one she did not herself inscribe for the Brewsters was *The Professor's House,* an omission that Lewis remedied). In addition, the Drew archive contains several copies of Cather books that are signed by the Brewsters, and one suspects that these too were probably sent them by Lewis or Cather. In all, the Brewsters owned copies of all of Cather's book-length works except for *Alexander's Bridge.*[7]

Even without their autographs and inscriptions, the books themselves have their own story to tell. That the copies sent are not always first editions suggests that Cather knew the Brewsters would value them as books to read, not as artifacts to display on their bookshelves. The books' appearance and condition justify her expectations. Almost without exception they look used: covers and corners are worn, the spines well flexed so that the volumes lie open easily, and pictures and clippings are folded or pasted into some of them. The letters the Brewsters write each other through the years document the place Cather and her books continued to play in their lives long after they last saw her in 1930.

On October 1, 1931, Achsah writes Harwood, "Since tea I have been reading from Sarah Orne Jewett's 'Land of the Pointed Firs.'[8] It is written with so much sincerity and beauty. Every time I reread it I am amazed to find how wonderful it is. Certainly, Aunt Willa caught her first inspiration there and I feel her last book bears the stamp of that same noble quality." The "last book" to which Achsah refers is *Shadows on the Rock,* of which Cather had sent her a copy just a few months earlier (ABB to HBP 7/8/31). About a year later, on September 19, 1932, Achsah writes Harwood that Cather's *Obscure Destinies* has arrived. Two days later Earl describes his birthday celebration that morning, at which Achsah included the Cather volume among his birthday gifts. That same day Achsah writes that she too is now reading it, singling out "Old Mrs. Harris" for special praise; by September 24 both have finished the book (letters dated 9/19–9/24, 1932). On February 15, 1933, Achsah mentions to Harwood that they have just read in the *Atlantic* "A Chance Meeting," the story Cather wrote "after she left us here" (i.e., following the 1930 visit); on December 13, 1937, she writes that she has just reread this same story and is savoring the memories it brings back of Aix-les-Bains, where the story is set. Early in 1941 Achsah writes from India that she has seen a notice of Cather's new novel *Sapphira and the Slave Girl.* Two months later she notes that the book has arrived, apparently sent by Edith Lewis, and within a week she has read it.[9] Early the following year she is reading the inscribed copy of *April Twilights and Other Poems* that Cather gave them in 1923, and in her letter to Harwood she copies out both "Recognition" and the inscription in which Cather indicated that this poem had been composed with the Brewsters in mind (2/14/42). Late in 1943 Achsah writes, "Daddy and I have enjoyed re-reading Willa's 'Obscure Destinies,'" noting that "Neighbour Rosicky [is] really tender and lovely" (10/25/43). Apparently rereading these stories led the Brewsters to want more, for in January and February 1944, just a year before Achsah's death, they have what Achsah describes as a "bout of Willa's books," beginning with *Youth and the Bright Medusa* in mid-January ("a volume of stories about art aspirants") and continuing with *The Song of the Lark* ("with great pleasure and admiration. It is lovelier than we remembered even"), *My Ántonia* ("a wonderful writing"), and *O Pioneers!*—all read within the space of a month.[10] During the same period Achsah urges Harwood to read *The Song of the Lark* ("you would love it" [1/31/44]). The reading continues after both Achsah's and Willa's deaths: in 1955, Earl writes Harwood that he has been rereading *Death Comes for the Archbishop:* "It is a beautiful book" (2/1/55); and two years later his friend Haridas reads to him *My Mortal Enemy,* which, along with "Neighbour

Rosicky," they rank with Cather's greatest writing: it is a poignant pairing, given that both works end with death—and that
Earl himself was failing and would die soon.[11]

Harwood had married in 1936 and lived from then on largely
in the United States, and letters to her parents show that she
continued to keep in touch with Cather and Lewis and to see
them from time to time in New York.[12] A copy of *Sapphira and
the Slave Girl* with her name in it, presumably given her by
Cather or Lewis, suggests her ongoing interest in Cather's
books, and in 1946, the year after her mother's death, and a year
before Cather's, she too apparently had a "bout" of Cather, for a
letter from Earl expresses his pleasure in hearing that she has
been reading Willa Cather's works (11/22/46). A book in the
Brewster archive also contains a touching indication that via
Harwood the relationship long outlived Cather, Lewis, and both
Earl and Achsah Brewster. On the page where Earl has apparently inscribed Achsah's name in what had been their copy of
Obscure Destinies, a spray of delicate leaves and flowers, the latter still with a trace of their bluish-purple color, has been taped
to the page. Next to it, in Harwood's hand, is the following inscription: "From the Cemetery at Jaffrey, N. H. where Willa
Cather & Edith Lewis are buried 5/22/1983." More than thirty-
five years after Cather's death, Harwood visited the Jaffrey cemetery and picked these flowers in memory of a friendship that
had meant so much to her parents and herself. That she placed
them in her mother's copy of *Obscure Destinies,* now become her
own, fits both the elegiac cast of that book, with the losses
wrought by time prominent in all three of its stories, and the fact
that Jaffrey, where her mother had spent time in the summers,
held its own memories for her.[13] Harwood may also have recalled
the spate of warm letters she had received from her parents
when this particular copy arrived in India in time for Earl's 1932
birthday.

If the presence of Willa Cather's books in the Brewster household attests to how much she was a part of their lives from the
early teens until the time of their deaths, another set of artifacts
exemplifies how much the Brewsters were a part of the New
York lives of Willa Cather and Edith Lewis from a similar time
onward: the Brewsters' paintings. In Cather's first note to the
Brewsters, written in 1917 to accompany a letter to them from
Lewis, and at a time when Cather still addresses them as "Mr.
and Mrs. Brewster," she refers to the pleasure she and Edith
take in the Brewster paintings they own. Lewis may have picked

up some of these on a 1914 trip to see the Brewsters, something she and Cather regularly did on later trips. In a May 14, 1914, letter to her Houghton Mifflin editor, Ferris Greenslet, Cather mentions that Lewis is sailing for Naples at the end of May to visit friends who live near Ravello, and an early chapter in "The Child" confirms that Lewis did indeed visit the Brewsters there at that time (23).

The painting that Cather singles out in her 1917 note to the Brewsters, however, was a more recent acquisition. In 1916 Earl Brewster and his New York dealer, William Macbeth, parted ways, and Earl asked Macbeth to invite Edith to choose whatever she wished from the paintings still at the gallery, with the remainder to go to Achsah's sister Lola in New Haven. Among the paintings Lewis chose was *The Family by the Sea*,[14] and in Cather's note to the Brewsters she writes that she's never had the good fortune of living within four walls with anything more lovely. Her very language suggests her warm feelings for the painting, for it carries unmistakable overtones of a passage that held special meaning for her, and that she would cite in 1922 at the end of her essay "The Novel Démeublé": "The elder Dumas enunciated a great principle when he said that to make a drama, a man needed one passion, and four walls" (Cather 1949, 43).[15]

The second Cather letter in the Drew archive, dated February 21, 1923, and this time addressed to "Earl and Achsah," mentions that she and Lewis had brought back additional Brewster paintings from their 1920 Naples visit with the Brewsters and that she herself especially likes *The Three Scalops*.[16] And in his 1949 memoir Earl Brewster recalls that Cather herself purchased from the Brewster's 1923 Paris exhibition "one of the most purely imaginative paintings I have ever done" (E. Brewster [1949], 2).[17] Given these and other references, we can now for the first time fully identify an oft-mentioned feature of the Cather-Lewis home. In *Willa Cather. A Memoir*, Elizabeth Sergeant describes visiting the Park Avenue apartment to which Cather and Lewis moved in 1932 and feeling great relief at finding amidst "the new tables and chairs, more formal than those in Bank Street," some familiar items: "the orange tree, the freesias, the George Sand engraving, the head of Keats, and *the charming little paintings of the Mediterranean shore by a friend of Miss Lewis who lived in Capri*" (252; italics mine). As with virtually all other writers on Cather, Sergeant does not name the Brewsters, but it is clear from what she writes that she understood the place of their paintings not just in Cather's home

but in her life—paintings that, as we can now see, Cather lived
with probably from 1914 on. Letters from Earl to Harwood show
that Cather and Lewis added to their collection of Brewster
paintings in the 1930s and that Lewis purchased yet another
shortly before Cather's death in 1947 (4/18/36 and 5/30/47).

As the preceding paragraphs suggest, the numerous letters in
the Brewster archives at Drew University are a major source for
reconstructing both the outlines of the friendship between
Cather and the Brewsters and its meaning to the parties concerned. Of the 1,700 letters written by the Brewsters, more than
100 speak of Willa Cather. Many of these references are but
passing mentions, but even these can be significant. Among
them, for instance, are a number of allusions to letters they have
received from Cather herself,[18] and Cather's usual designation
in the Brewsters' letters, "Aunt Willa," itself suggests the degree
to which, like Lewis, she was almost a member of the family
(e.g., 3/1/33 to Harwood: Achsah has "been writing . . . Aunt
Willa and Aunt Edith long letters"). Other letters, however, reveal how much Cather and her books were regularly on the
Brewsters' minds—e.g., the series of letters that cluster around
Earl's 1932 birthday, and the place of *Obscure Destinies* in that
occasion, or the several letters in the 1940s that chart the Brewsters' frequent reading and rereading of Cather's novels. Typical
in tone and character is a passage from a letter Achsah writes
Harwood on April 30, 1933, enclosing a clipping about Cather
and commenting that Harwood will "grin over the awful picture
of Aunt Willa being once more decorated with honours, under
which she will be utterly submerged by now, I should think."
(The "honour" in question was the Prix Femina Américain,
which Cather received in February 1933.) Achsah's description
of the picture reveals her acute understanding of the mixture of
annoyance and delight that Willa would have felt in being "submerged" by such recognition. The same sort of close acquaintance and insight is implicit in a cryptic comment that Achsah
makes to Harwood in a letter written on July 9, 1944, less than
a year before her death. Noting that Harwood's children have recently been to the circus, Achsah wonders how they liked it and
adds, "Ask Aunt Willa to tell about the 'lion-faced' boy." Also tes-
tifying to the Brewsters' feelings toward Cather are those letters
they write Harwood about news they have recently received
from Edith Lewis. On July 15, 1937, Achsah writes that "Aunt
Willa and Aunt Edith find Mabel Luhan and Tony full of loveliness and visit there from time to time," on October 5, 1938, that

she has just received "the most lovely letter from Aunt Edith" reporting that she and Willa are "enjoying a breath of air" in Grand Manan. Two months later, on December 19, her news is darker: "Such a dear letter came today from Aunt Edith. She says that dear Isabel[19] Hambourg died in October at the Cocumella in Sorrento. Poor Willa has lost her favourite brother and Isabel both within a few months, and the shape of earthly life is much changed for her. She is writing at the Shattuck Inn at Jaffrey New Hampshire." On August 8, 1941, she has just heard that Edith and Willa "[are] enjoying San Francisco and Willa [is] really better." Two years later she passes along to Harwood Edith's encouraging comment, directed again at Willa, that "Maine can be a lovely place and full of health" (8/20/43), and poignantly, a year later, as her own health continues to fail, Achsah comments that "[i]t is good news that Willa is writing again and I hope the depths of her will shine out" (9/3/44). She then mentions that in response to her complaints that morning "of the vanity and meanness of most people" Earl had "named off a list of our personal saints and friends, good to remember," with the clear implication that Cather was on that list.

Of even greater interest are the five letters in the Drew archive from Cather to the Brewsters (how one wishes that we had as well the additional letters the Brewsters mention receiving from her!). Three of these five, including the one that is by far the longest and most revealing, cluster around the 1920 and 1923 visits with the Brewsters, and we shall look at them in detail in the next sections of this chapter. But the two outliers of the group, the first from 1917, the last from 1934, also contain much of interest. There is, to begin with, the very fact that in 1917 Cather feels close enough to the Brewsters to add her own postscript to Edith's letter. Her acquaintance with them from their premarriage years in New York is now distant, and she addresses them formally, but she nonetheless expresses her pleasure in their paintings in a manner that is deeply personal. In 1934 it is four years since Cather has last seen the Brewsters, but her warm letter looks back on the friendship that has developed over the past two decades with nostalgia and real feeling, and her closing wish that they may soon see each other again feels very much from the heart. It is clear too that Cather has kept in touch with the Brewsters in the years since this 1930 visit. In July 1931 she had sent them a copy of the newly published *Shadows on the Rocks* with a personal note to the three Brewsters enclosed. On September 13, 1931, Achsah writes Har-

wood that a letter from "Aunt Willa" has informed them that
"[h]er mother has just died in California where she has been in
a sanatorium for the last three years" (Cather's mother died on
August 31), and the "long letter" that Achsah is writing Aunt
Willa on 3/1/33 is presumably in response to yet another letter
she has received from her.

Cather's 1917 and 1934 letters also sound themes that run
throughout Cather's relationship with the Brewsters—the happiness of working hard, devotion to one's artistic calling, honesty. Even in her brief 1917 note Cather treats the Brewsters
not just as friends but as fellow artists. Not only does the core of
her note focus on their paintings, but her concluding wish that
the new year may bring splendid working hours, the first statement of a leitmotif that will later become familiar, reveals that
even at this early stage of the friendship Cather saw the Brewsters as colleagues who, like her, were passionately devoted to
their work and their art. Implicit in the 1934 letter is the same
relationship. It begins with the D. H. Lawrence book the Brewsters have just published—and ends with the book Cather has
just completed (*Lucy Gayheart*). We may take as sincere the
praise she lavishes on the Brewsters' book—anyone who has
read Cather's letters to other writers knows that she does not
pull punches in such situations: she praises what she likes but
does not hesitate to pillory what she finds weak.[20] That she singles out the honesty of the Brewsters' portrait of Lawrence both
reflects the weight she always placed on this quality[21] and also
foreshadows her own candid comments later in the letter about
her own latest novel: had hand problems not intervened, that
book would probably be better. We shall see in subsequent sections that these same themes shape and define the relationship
during the years when it was most active, the decade of the
1920s.

The 1920 and 1923 Visits with the Brewsters

Just as materials in the Brewster archive expand our knowledge of the trip Cather and Lewis took to Europe in 1930—and
reveal that this trip included time spent with the Brewsters—so
the Brewster papers fill out numerous details of the European
trips taken by Cather and Lewis in 1920, by Cather herself in
1923, and show that both of these too included visits with the
Brewsters.

The basic outlines of these two trips are familiar. Cather and Lewis sailed for France on May 19, 1920, the express purpose being to enable Cather to explore French locations associated with her novel *One of Ours*.[22] Cather stayed in Paris at the Hôtel Quai de Voltaire well into July, with Lewis leaving in late June "to visit friends" in Italy.[23] In July, in company with Isabelle Hambourg, Cather traveled to Cantigny to visit the grave of G. P. Cather, the cousin whose death in combat was the catalyst for her new novel, then set out with the Hambourgs for the south of France.[24] Cather had planned to go to Sorrento for the fall, but she changed this plan both because of Lewis's warning of food shortages in Italy and because she herself fell ill during the trip with the Hambourgs.[25] In late August Lewis joined her in the south of France, and from there they made their way slowly back to Paris, where they again stayed for a time at the Quai de Voltaire. They sailed home from Marseilles, arriving in mid-November after a stormy crossing.[26]

Cather's 1923 trip began soon after she completed *A Lost Lady* and stretched from April through November. During her first weeks in France she spent much of her time with the Hambourgs at Ville d'Avray. They had fitted up a study for her, and her initial plan had been to spend most of her visit with them. She found, however, that she was unable to write there, and from late May through most of July she was in Paris, "hoping to achieve a working state of mind" (Woodress 1987, 338) and staying once again at the Quai de Voltaire, which she had found so conducive to her needs during the 1920 trip. After spending late August and most of September in Aix-les-Bains, she returned to Paris, among other things to sit for a portrait by Leon Bakst, before visiting the Hambourgs again in early November and sailing for home on November 17.[27]

Materials in the Brewster archives fill in and flesh out the 1920 trip at a number of points:

- The choice to stay at the Hôtel Quai de Voltaire at the start of this trip, a choice repeated on subsequent returns to Paris, was no doubt made on the Brewsters' recommendation. Lewis and Cather had clearly been in touch with the Brewsters prior to their 1920 trip; the Brewsters knew Paris well; and the Quai de Voltaire was a hotel they frequented, as is evident both from the memoirs Achsah, Harwood, and Earl wrote and from numerous Brewster letters.[28]
- Not only do Edith Lewis's long ties to Achsah themselves

suggest that the "friends" she visited in Italy in June 1920 were the Brewsters, but in "The Child" Achsah writes, "Edith . . . was coming for a visit with us while Willa Cather was with the Hambourgs in France" (163). And on April 23, 1944, she writes Harwood and quotes from a recent letter in which Lewis recalls Harwood reciting Euripides during that same visit: "How well I remember [Harwood] in Sorrento—reciting for me at your behest—'What else is Wisdom . . . ?'"

- Cather had originally hoped to join Lewis and the Brewsters in Sorrento; in a June 20 letter to Ferris Greenslet she refers to these plans, not mentioning the Brewsters by name but describing their "Villa Daphnis" and its location in detail.

- Although that plan fell through, Cather saw the Brewsters at the end of the trip, for between their October departure from Paris and their November sailing from Marseilles, Cather and Lewis met the Brewsters in Naples. In his 1949 memoir about Cather, Earl writes that the first time he saw Willa after meeting her in New York in 1910 was in "1920, when Edith, my wife and I joined her in Naples, just before she and Edith were to sail for New York" (E. Brewster [1949], 1).[29]

- It was during that visit that Cather gave the Brewsters their inscribed copy of *Youth and the Bright Medusa,* dating it "Naples, October 29 1920."

- Almost two years later, she sent them from Grand Manan a prepublication copy of *One of Ours* with an inscription that recalls the Naples stopover: "To Earl and Achsa [*sic*][30] Brewster I send a copy of the novel they carried off from the Pa‗tria in a little boat for me. It was then all in manuscript except the last books, which were not yet written. Willa Sibert Cather Whale Cove Grand Manan N. B. August 29th 1922." Her description of how far she had progressed in the writing of *One of Ours* precisely fits the state of the novel at the time of the 1920 trip.[31]

- When Cather writes the Brewsters in February 1923 prior to her upcoming trip to France, she again recalls with pleasure the time Edith and she had spent with them in Naples, and mentions the new Brewster paintings they had acquired.

- In the same February 1923 letter Cather expresses delight that the Hambourgs have chosen Earl Brewster's *Le Négre bleu,* that this painting will be in her room at Ville d'Avray during her upcoming visit, and that she will accordingly have the pleasure of rooming with it *again*. Apparently Cather invited the Hambourgs to choose one of the Brewsters' paintings as a gift from her, and they chose this one (perhaps after attending the Brewsters' 1922 show in Paris, in which this painting was included). The "*again*" suggests that Cather had somehow come to know this painting during her 1920 visit to the Brewsters, and it appears that Isabelle, understanding, as did Elizabeth Sergeant, how much Cather liked the Brewsters' art—and perhaps this painting in particular—placed it in Cather's room for her upcoming stay at Ville d'Avray.

- The opening line of Cather's essay on Katherine Mansfield in *Not Under Forty* takes on new meaning in light of the 1920 stopover in Naples: "Late in the autumn of 1920, on my way home from Naples, I had a glimpse of Katherine Mansfield through the eyes of a fellow passenger" (123). Whether the conversation that follows between Cather and "Mr. J——" is fact or fiction remains unclear, but the start of the essay is based on fact: as we have seen, Cather and Lewis sailed from Naples to Marseilles before continuing on to New York in early November 1920.[32] It must have been on the same trip home that Cather, sailing along the south coast of Spain, saw "the ranges of the Sierra Nevadas tower[ing] on their right, snow peak after snow peak, high beyond the flight of fancy, gleaming like crystal and topaz," the sight that suggests to Professor St. Peter the design for his great history in *The Professor's House,* which Cather began soon after returning from her 1923 trip to France (Cather 1925, 106).

Between the time of the Cather-Lewis trip in 1920 and Cather's own trip in 1923, the Brewsters were very much on the move—en route to Ceylon in late 1921; there until May 1922, with a visit from D. H. and Frieda Lawrence in March and April; back in Europe in June 1922, first in Switzerland, then in Paris for a show in December 1922. Shortly after their return to Europe Cather sent them the inscribed copy of *One of Ours,* and on February 21, 1923, she wrote them a long letter in response to their comments on this novel and in anticipation of their upcoming trip to the States, and her own to Europe.

As with the 1920 Cather-Lewis trip, the Brewster archive tells

us much about Cather's 1923 trip to France, as well as about the
Brewsters' trip home that same year:

- Cather's February 1923 letter mentions her hope to see the
  Brewsters in Paris, and this hope was realized not long after
  Cather arrived in April (she had sailed on April 1). Prior to
  their one return to the States, the Brewsters came from
  Capri to Paris in early May, with a stopover in Rome en
  route, and spent a week there before heading for Le Havre
  and the voyage home. Achsah writes in "The Child" that
  Cather had come to France to see Isabelle and that "to be in
  the heart of Paris they stayed at Quai Voltaire. We saw much
  of them to our joy" (271).
- "As we were sailing for home," writes Achsah, again in "The
  Child," "[Cather] gave us her 'April Twilights and Other
  Poems' inscribed: 'To accompany The Brewsters on the long
  Voyage home—they do not know how long it is! The verse on
  Page 65 is theirs already, for they were both very much in
  my mind on the afternoon last summer when I wrote it.
  Willa Cather, Ville d'Avray. May 16th, 1923'" (318). That
  close to twenty years later Achsah copies out both Cather's
  inscription and the poem itself—as we have seen her do also
  in a letter to Harwood the same year, and as Earl will do in
  the memoir he writes in 1949—suggests how much Cather's
  gift and inscription meant to all of them.[33]
- Cather's hope that the Brewsters would spend time with
  Edith Lewis during their American sojourn was also fulfilled. They arrived in New York shortly before Decoration
  Day. Lewis was waiting at the dock, and they drove at once
  to 5 Bank Street where, in Achsah's words, "[w]e were only
  too often mutually exclusive, tucking in where Willa had left
  for the time."[34] Achsah goes on to tell of exploring places familiar from earlier days—60 and 42 South Washington
  Square, where Edith and Earl respectively had lived—and
  delighting in the peaceful ambience of the Cather-Lewis
  apartment, with "pictures painted by Earl and me on the
  walls," treasures from Annie Fields and Sarah Orne Jewett
  adorning the book-lined rooms, and the oft-mentioned drawing of George Sand over the fireplace (A. Brewster 1942,
  316–17).
- The Brewsters were back in Paris by late September. They
  had sailed from New York on September 8, and on October
  17 D. H. Lawrence writes Earl that he has just received let-

ters from him and Achsah—"yours from the sea, Achsah's from Quai Voltaire" (*LL* 4 #2937). Cather too was back in Paris, completing her sittings for the Bakst portrait, and also staying at the Quai Voltaire. It was during this period that she gave Achsah a copy of *A Lost Lady,* which had just appeared in the States, inscribing it "For Achsah from Willa Cather Paris October 1923."

- Though the chronology of Achsah's account in "The Child" is confused, it was also probably during this period rather than in May that Cather and Isabelle Hambourg took Harwood to a matinee performance of Ibsen's *Peer Gynt* that sent Harwood home filled with images of Anitra's dance, as Achsah describes in vivid detail in chapter 130 of "The Child" (see chapter 6). In the same chapter Achsah also speaks poetically about evensongs attended together at Nôtre Dame, with the lights twinkling on the altars, the sound of the organ rolling through the arches above, and the last glow fading from its rose windows, services she later describes as "full of the essential quality of the Willa Cather to whom I pay homage" (271, 318). Given the proximity of Quai Voltaire to Nôtre Dame, one suspects that attendance at such services began in May and resumed when the Brewsters returned to Paris in the early fall.

- Before she left Paris, Cather saw the Brewsters' 1923 show, which she praises in the November 29 letter she sends Achsah soon after her return to New York, making special mention of the Ceylon pictures, and of the delight Dorothy Canfield had taken in Achsah's triptych. A letter she wrote Canfield that same day covers similar ground: the easy crossing, her pleasure in the company of novelist Frank Swinnerton, Canfield's seeing her off on the boat train.[35] Achsah's account of the show in "The Child" also mentions Canfield, though she evokes Canfield's admiration for a sketch by Earl rather than for her own triptych: "Dorothy . . . was full of appreciation. She knelt down before the picture, and wept, saying: 'And such beauty was born from the U.S.!'" (316).[36]

- Lawrence's reference to the letters he had received from the Brewsters—Achsah's from Paris, Earl's "from the sea"— might seem to suggest that Achsah had returned before Earl, but it is clear that the three Brewsters sailed together.[37] Once they were back in Paris, however, it was Achsah with whom Cather spent the most time, and with whom

she developed a particularly close friendship. She mentions
Earl warmly in both her November 1923 and February 1924
letters (and in both sends greetings to Harwood as well), but
both of these letters are addressed to Achsah alone. Other
details as well point to the special bond the two women
forged during this time in Paris: the "Dearest" with which
Cather addresses Achsah in both letters, the "Lovingly" with
which she signs off in both; her mention in the February
1924 letter of the vaporizer Achsah had given her, and of her
daily delight in using it in New York; and, most notably, the
copy of *A Lost Lady* that Cather inscribed to Achsah alone
during their days in Paris.

CATHER, LEWIS, AND THE BREWSTERS

The Brewster papers at Drew also cast new light on several
larger issues. Perhaps most obviously, they broaden our understanding of Willa Cather's relationship with Edith Lewis, in
which Lewis's role is often undervalued. It is, of course, a misun-
derstanding to which Lewis herself contributed by keeping so
low a profile, a fact dramatically exemplified by the contrast
between what she tells us about the Brewsters in *Willa Cather
Living* (one brief mention in the whole book) and what we now
learn from the Drew archive: that this was a friendship which
involved both Lewis and Cather, probably from the time of Cather's early contacts with Lewis in New York; that it was important to Cather in a variety of ways; and that it owed its inception
entirely to Edith Lewis.[38]

What one senses from the Drew papers, and especially from
Cather's five letters to the Brewsters, is that the Cather-Lewis
relationship had in it much more equality, and much more concern for her friend on Cather's part, than is usually suggested.[39]
Many details in the archive contribute to this picture: the sub-
sidiary role Cather initially adopts in her 1917 letter; the mention in her February 1923 letter—omitted in the paraphrase
later in this book—that she hopes the Brewsters have received
Edith's box, on which she lavished such care, just as she did with
a similar box she'd sent Cather in Nebraska the previous Christmas; Cather's description in her November 1923 letter of her efforts to give Edith a full understanding of the paintings in the
Brewsters' Paris show and, on a different level, her comment
that she'd saved many of Earl's cigarettes for Lewis—and, in

deference to Edith's love for French sweets, *all* of the Brewsters' chocolates; in the February 1924 letter, her obvious pride in the recognition Lewis has received from her company—recognition she knows will especially please Edith's former roommate. Not least is a feature of all five letters that is hard to convey in paraphrases—the profusion of first person plurals: the pleasure *we* take in the pictures (1917), the good winter *we* are having and *our* pleasure in the cards from Harwood (1924), *our* plans for heading to Grand Manan, and how much *we* talk about you and long to see you (1934). Though all these touches owe something to Cather's recognition that the Brewster friendship began with Lewis, not herself, they also clearly reflect a warm, caring, and mutual relationship.

Cather's letter of February 21, 1923, is especially revealing. It is by far the longest of the five letters in the archive, and the most personal in tone, and its bulk is devoted to Lewis, for whom Cather feels keen concern as she looks ahead to her own long absence in Europe. She begs the Brewsters to write Edith often and hopes that they will see her frequently while they are in the States. Above all, there is Cather's remarkable insight into her companion's feelings about the Hambourgs: Edith has never liked them very much, they irritate her, she feels jealousy that the Hambourgs have now become the Brewsters' friends—the same sort of jealousy she feels toward Cather's own relationship with the Hambourgs.[40] It is a letter in which Cather clearly reads herself into Lewis's feelings, empathizing with her friend's emotional anguish and the way in which it darkens her life. Indeed, one cannot help sense Cather the novelist at work, exploring the complex workings of the human psyche, and dubbing as the most disheartening thing in life the way that love and envy, likes and dislikes, intertwine in our hearts against our will, especially with regard to those people to whom we feel the closest—precisely, of course, the sort of internal conflict she will limn so powerfully in her next two novels, *The Professor's House* and *My Mortal Enemy*. Cather understands that Edith is jealous now not only of Cather's close ties to the Hambourgs but also of the Brewsters's new friendship with them, and she betrays considerable relief, as she heads off on a trip in which she will see both couples, that Lewis will have the Brewsters to herself when they visit the States that summer. Edith enters into the final pages of the letter as well in the mention of the box she has sent the Brewsters and in Cather's concluding wish that Lewis too would be seeing the Brewsters in Europe. It is a letter one wishes one could quote rather than paraphrase, for in both tone and content it has much to tell us about Cather's feelings for Lewis, and—though more indirectly—about Lewis's feelings for her.

In the last decade of Cather's life Lewis becomes Cather's main conduit to the Brewsters. A comment by Achsah in an April 9, 1943, letter to Harwood, at a time when Lewis has been devoting the past months to caring for the seriously ill Cather, captures the way the Brewsters saw the relationship, and Lewis's devotion to her friend: "Dear Aunt Edith, her heart ever faithful, will always be serving those she loves." And in 1947, some two years after Achsah's death, a letter from Earl to Harwood suggests his sense of the closeness of the two women: "Edith Lewis cabled me of the death of Willa Cather. . . . It shocked me considerably for I had vividly pictured her and Edith continuing their lives together for years to come. I am very anxious to hear from Edith how she will adjust her life to this great change for her" (5/30/47).

"Integer Vitae"

The candid comments about Lewis that Cather shares with the Brewsters in her February 1923 letter bespeak the ease she felt with them, and the trust. Even her short first note to them in 1917 exudes warmth, even intimacy, in what she writes about living with their paintings, and this closeness grows once she spends time with the Brewsters at the end of the 1920 trip. That visit cannot have lasted more than a few days, but it leaves indelible traces: Cather's reference in her February 1923 letter to the twilight hours spent together in Naples; the poem in the revised *April Twilights* expressly inspired by the Brewsters—and with a setting that evokes the Naples area where they had met; and, not least, her comment in the inscribed *One of Ours* she sends them from Grand Manan, "a copy of the novel they carried off from the Patria in a little boat for me." The *Patria* was a Fabre Line steamer which frequently sailed between Marseilles and Naples, and it must have been the ship on which Cather and Lewis arrived in Naples. That in the process of disembarking Cather temporarily entrusted her unfinished manuscript to the Brewsters presupposes considerable faith in these friends she was just coming to know!

Whereas Lewis had known Achsah for years and had visited

the Brewsters in Italy in 1914, Cather had at best an acquaintance with Achsah in the years up to 1910 and did not come to know both Brewsters well until this visit with them in 1920. But the strong kinship established during those short days and materially enhanced during the time she spent in 1923 with the Brewsters, and especially with Achsah, was such as to bridge the ocean and to make up for the paucity of face-to-face meetings. The starting point was Cather's instinctive recognition that the Brewsters, like herself, were people whose lives resided in their work. Her very first note wishes them splendid working hours; her first dedication is to "friends and fellow-workers"; her closing wish in both 1923 letters is for happy working days and the satisfaction they bring—a wish mirrored in the description she gives of herself in early 1924: working steadily and productively, and finding life satisfying and peaceful. Matching the language is the content of her letters, all of which treat the Brewsters as fellow artists. Just how well Cather had read them is clear from what Achsah writes about Earl and herself in 1923: "We have lived intensely, we have studied with ardor and have spent in our work hours that were long and happy" (Brewster 1923, 16–17). Equally apropos is what Earl says to Achsah in an August 28, 1922, letter: "Life is very simple—all we have to do is our best!"

Other characteristics of the Brewsters also drew Cather to them—their honesty, for instance, a quality that she praises in their portrait of D. H. Lawrence, and that in her November 1923 letter to them she highlights in her comments about her recent shipboard companion, the novelist Frank Swinnerton. Once again, she has clearly read the Brewsters right: "Originality has always seemed to me," writes Achsah in 1923, "to consist only of sincerity, integrity, honesty, albeit, of course, in different degrees and with infinite nuances. Be sincere and you will show your individuality" (Brewster 1923, 15).[41] Cather also recognized that the Brewsters' honesty was rooted in their modesty: they could create a true portrait of Lawrence because, unlike others who had written about him, they were not really writing about themselves. She has again seized on a quality the Brewsters consciously sought. "To be an artist, one must be a child," writes Achsah in 1923 (16).[42] Elsewhere in the same essay Achsah notes that to tame egoism is to open the way to "the peace for which we always seek," and to beauty itself: "After having lived in the Orient, one comes to appreciate the values of life differently: one feels less interest in personal success, and has only the desire to see beauty manifested" (19, 20). The honesty and openness that Cather found in the Brewsters would, a decade later, draw her to another artist—the young Yehudi Menuhin; in turn, these were the very qualities that others, including the Brewsters, found and admired in Cather herself: "It seems to me that I never have known a person who found it so painful to endure falsity, shallowness and superficiality in human nature," commented Earl in 1949 as he looked back on his long acquaintance with Cather (E. Brewster [1949], 3).[43]

What Cather saw in the Brewsters others noted as well. Harwood describes her father as "very truthful, very humble" and mentions her parents' habit of reading religious and philosophical texts together regularly (Picard 1984, 205, 209). M. S. Randhawa, who knew the Brewsters during their later years in India, describes their "simple life in peaceful surroundings," the dominance of Buddhist and Hindu artifacts and books in their home (17–18). Even D. H. Lawrence, who at times mocked and became impatient with the Brewsters' naïveté,[44] appreciated their avoidance of the competitive rat race and respected the sincerity of their quest and the peace of mind it brought them: "The more I go around, the nearer I do come in a certain way, to your position. I am convinced that every man needs a bho tree of some sort in his life."[45]

Like Lawrence, Cather admired the Brewsters' success in creating a lifestyle that not only gave play to their passion for painting but also reflected their personal values; that they managed to combine unworldliness with a certain élan no doubt appealed to her as well—just as Earl praised Cather's appreciation of "those forms and conventions which dignify and beautify life" (E. Brewster [1949], 3). Above all, though, Cather felt in tune with the Brewsters' artistic principles, which mirrored the values she saw in their lives: simplicity, purity, honesty, the quest to strip away nonessentials and get at underlying essences.

In his 1923 essay Earl Brewster comments that in recent centuries the focus of art had shifted from inner reality to outer, a movement that climaxed in the impressionists' devotion to capturing on canvas the world we see. In what follows he describes how living amid the simple and pure peasant art of southern Italy had inspired him to move beyond this external world, to seek colors and forms that would capture what alone mattered— the human truths and emotions that lie beneath, and beside which all else is insignificant: "I would wish that that which is the most pure and essential in art should obtain in our consciousness, at a deeper level of our being, its rightful place. Then humanity will be able to become an artist again" (Brewster 1923, 13). He proposes to call what he seeks "character"—the ability to capture through art the underlying human reality, and to communicate that reality from one human being to another (13–14). Achsah seeks a similar reality: "As unpopular as it is among contemporary painters, Plato's theory of beauty is the one which satisfies me the most. Only these proper proportions, this 'beauty of holiness,' or whatever other name one gives it, only that which is essential, that which is truly in its place—that alone can be beautiful" (18–19).[46]

In their art as in their lifestyle the Brewsters put their principles into practice. Critics note their search for "a purity in their art," their goal of "eliminat[ing] . . . 19th century 'realistic, romantic, sentimental, literary, and scientific' accretions in painting" (Cushman and Sagar 1991, 193) and describe their art as "austere, formal, understated," as "communicat[ing] . . . a tranquil harmony that strives for a spiritual dimension" (Cushman 1992, 47). M. S. Randhawa finds "[s]implicity of composition . . . the key-note" of Earl's Buddhist paintings. "By simplifying the subject matter, by eliminating the non-essentials, and by emphasizing the essentials by skilful use of colours he tries to abstract the real value of objects or persons" (30).

The conclusion of Cather's February 1924 letter to the Brewsters acquires new meaning in light of these artistic goals: how fine life can be if one does not fret about silly things. On one level she is reiterating what she has written about herself in this letter—that she is happily at work again, untroubled by distractions. But her words look also toward the Brewsters, for whom moving beyond the "silly things," rising above the minutiae, was a central tenet. We do not know whether Cather had read their 1923 book,[47] but she had certainly absorbed its principles from time spent with them in Paris, from the 1923 show she had recently seen there, and from living for years with their art. Surely when she ends her 1924 letter with "not getting caught up in silly things," she is alluding to the Brewsters' success in focusing on what is essential and rising above the merely peripheral.

In addition, this letter comes during a period when rising above the minutiae, whether in one's life or one's art, was becoming an ever more pressing concern to Willa Cather. The early 1920s brought home to her that to write well she had to protect herself from the clutter of life—to hold at bay the bother and fatigue that came with the success of One of Ours, for instance, as

she writes the Brewsters in early 1923; to find the happy working hours she so often wishes for them, and that she is so relish-
ing for herself when she writes them a year later, in early 1924.[48]
At the same time, her fiction itself, and her thinking about it,
were moving in similar directions—toward a focus on essentials,
an avoidance of clutter. Just the year before her 1923 European
trip she had in "The Novel Démeublé" articulated such a vision:
"Out of the teeming, gleaming stream of the present [the novel]
must select the eternal material of art. . . . The higher processes
of art are all processes of simplification. The novelist must learn
to write, and then he must unlearn it; just as the modern painter
learns to draw, and then learns when utterly to disregard his
accomplishment, when to subordinate it to a higher and truer
effect" (Cather 1949, 40).

The similarities between her language and that found in the
Brewsters' 1923 essays, especially Earl's, are striking. Cather
comments that the modern novel has become "over-furnished"
and seeks an alternative to the realism that has become its dom-
inant mode (35); Earl notes that art has been moving toward a
focus on the external world and proposes an art that reaches beyond either realism or impressionism (Brewster 1923, 8–14).
Both stress that art must select, with Cather longing to "leave
the scene bare for the play of emotions" (43), Brewster wishing
to restore "that which is the most pure and essential in art . . .
to its rightful place" (13). Cather speaks of capturing "the inex-
plicable presence of the thing not named, of the overtone divined
by the ear but not heard by it" (41), while Brewster speaks of
using the materials of his art "to evoke certain emotions," with
the resulting creations being as free of any literal reference as is
music (10). And as we have seen, Cather compares the novelist's
art with that of the modern painter, while Brewster borrows the
term "character" to describe his artistic goals.

Though it is not impossible that Earl had read "The Novel Démeublé" before he wrote his 1923 essay, it seems better to explain these similarities simply as reflecting a convergence of
parallel ideas. By the time Cather and the Brewsters saw each
other in 1920, the Brewsters' art had long been moving toward
the principles they would articulate in 1923, while in her earlier
novels Cather was already working toward the "heroic simplification"[49] that would find theoretical expression in "The Novel
Démeublé." Indeed, just before she and Lewis left for Europe in
1920, she published a short essay, "On the Art of Fiction," which
shows her well on the way toward that longer essay of 1922:

"Art, it seems to me, should simplify. That, indeed, is very nearly the whole of the higher artistic process; finding what conventions of form and what detail one can do without and yet preserve the spirit of the whole—so that all that one has suppressed and cut away is there to the reader's consciousness as much as if it were in type on the page" (Cather 1949, 102). How ready Cather and the Brewsters were for each other when they met in 1920, how many sympathetic vibrations they must soon have felt!

Among other things, they would certainly have discovered that similar experiences had helped shape their thinking about their art: exposure to the native people and primitive art of southern Italy had been the catalyst that led the Brewsters toward an art that was simpler, more rooted in the basic realities of human existence—just as Cather's 1912 and 1915 encounters with the people and indigenous art of the American Southwest had led her back toward archetypal reality, "toward abstraction in her handling of character."[50] When Cather in 1923 gives Achsah *A Lost Lady,* the gift feels like a retrospective thank-you for the resonances they had discovered in their time together, for it is a novel in which—again to quote Phyllis Rose— "the inner expresses itself in the outer," a phrase that in turn captures what the Brewsters so sought in their paintings.[51]

In 1920 Cather could feel quickly in tune with the Brewsters also because she had for years lived with their pictures, and her 1917 letter suggests how much those pictures meant to her. One reason she responded so warmly to their art, and one to which we will return later in this chapter, may have been that it reflected the Brewsters' enthusiasm for an artist whom Cather herself had admired ever since her first visit to Paris in 1902: Puvis de Chavannes. In his 1923 essay Earl Brewster tells of his strong attraction to this artist, which he traces to his childhood; Achsah does not name Puvis in her essay for the 1923 book, but she stresses the role of muralists such as Puvis: "Mural decoration is essential to life, at least to life that is such as it should be" (17). And anyone familiar with Puvis will at once sense the affinity between his art and that of both Brewsters—the predilection for mural-like scenes, the predominance of religious subjects, the focus on heroic and statuesque figures.[52] Given Cather's long interest in Puvis, it is hard to believe that she would not have picked up the Brewsters' debt to him as she lived with their paintings—and that their common admiration for Puvis would not have emerged early on as one more bond between them. Moreover, Puvis' own words suggest how close his artistic credo was to those the Brewsters and Cather were espousing in the early 1920s, for he too speaks of selecting and simplifying, of rejecting what is not essential: "It is necessary to cut away from nature everything that is ineffective and accidental, everything that for the moment is without force. Art completes what nature roughly sketches. How does one succeed when helping nature in her efforts toward speech? By abbreviation and simplification. Be careful to express the important facts, and leave the rest out. That is the secret of composition, of design, and even of eloquence and wit."[53]

"On the Art of Fiction" and "The Novel Démeublé" touch as well on more personal issues that also drew Cather to the Brewsters during this same period. "On the Art of Fiction" begins with the plight of young writers as Cather saw it in 1920—and with the choice they must make between popular success and genuine art: "A good workman can't be a cheap workman; he can't be stingy about wasting material, and he cannot compromise. Writing ought either to be the manufacture of stories for which there is a market demand—a business as safe and commendable as making soap or breakfast foods—or it should be an art" (Cather 1949, 103). She develops the theme in "The Novel Démeublé," where she applies the metaphor of her title ("The Unfurnished Novel") to the clutter she finds in so much modern fiction: "The novel manufactured to entertain great multitudes of people must be considered exactly like a cheap soap or a cheap perfume, or cheap furniture. Fine quality is a distinct disadvantage in articles made for great numbers of people who do not want quality but quantity" (36).

Similar themes are focal in *Youth and the Bright Medusa,* published in the same year as "On the Art of Fiction," where story after story focuses on the tension between quality and quantity, between artistic excellence and commercial success.[54] In the very first story, "Coming, Aphrodite," Cather brings together the gleaming Eden Bower and the scruffy Don Hedger, the one irresistibly drawn to the brilliant but ultimately facile pursuit of public success, the other attracted by this model—as he is by Eden herself—but in the end holding fast to his antipopularizing artistic principles. "The Diamond Mine" explores the career of Cressida Garnet, a talented singer who is ultimately reduced to being a "diamond mine" for the men who court her and use her; and the two subsequent stories, "The Gold Slipper" and "Scandal," focus on another singer, Kitty Ayrshire, who despite her

talent, charm, and wit has been sucked into the rat race of court-
ing public success. As for the stories reprised from Cather's earlier collection, *The Troll Garden,* the hero of "Paul's Case" ends
up destroying himself by his craving for the accoutrements of
success and glamour, while "The Sculptor's Funeral" sets the
world which spawned Harvey Merrick, a world of "raw, biting
ugliness" (Cather 1920, 261), of "money and knavery" (268),[55]
against the "eternal wonder" (259) of his artistic vision.

Similar preoccupations surface in the four novels that follow
Youth and the Bright Medusa. The hero of *One of Ours* ends up
fighting in France less out of patriotic sentiments than out of a
youthful yearning—reminiscent of that of the title character in
"Paul's Case"—to find something in life more permanent, more
worthwhile, more intrinsic than the grasping dullness by which
he is surrounded in Nebraska. *A Lost Lady* revolves around a
heroine who, for all her loveliness, warmth, and fineness, ends
up selling her better self for comfort and company.[56] Central to
The Professor's House is the tension between the intangible principles that have governed Godfrey St. Peter's life and the more
material interests that motivate other members of his family, a
tension reflected in the contrast between the mundane world of
Hamilton, where St. Peter lives, and the pure air and ambience
of the Blue Mesa that Tom Outland discovers. The theme cli-
maxes in the Myra Henshawe of *My Mortal Enemy,* a woman
whose whole life has been torn between her instinctive appreciation of what is intrinsically worthy and her longing for a life that
is comfortable, surrounded by good things—"well furnished," if
you will.

The conflicts Cather explores in the fiction of these years were
ones she herself was experiencing, and that, ironically, came
home to her perhaps most clearly through the very success of
One of Ours—its booming sales, its winning of the Pulitzer
Prize.[57] It is a point she makes in her February 1923 letter to the
Brewsters, where she contrasts the commercial success of the
novel with the bother and fatigue it has brought to her life. Lee
notes the prevalence in Cather's 1920s essays of "sour references
to the 'tawdry' cheapness of the present, to the 'ugliness of the
world'" (Lee 1989, 183), while Skaggs comments on how Cather
herself was torn by the very conflict she writes into her books of
this time, and into their heroes and heroines: "[W]hile Cather by
1922 had long since outgrown a willingness to compromise her
talents in order to appease public taste, she had not outgrown—

Does anyone?—her desire for public approval" (Skaggs 1992, 6–7). This last is a point to which we shall return shortly.

In 1940 Cather wrote that in *The Professor's House* she had "tried to make Professor St. Peter's house rather overcrowded and stuffy with new things; American proprieties, clothes, furs, petty ambitions, quivering jealousies—until one got rather stifled. Then I wanted to open the square window and let in the fresh air that blew off the Blue Mesa, and the fine disregard of trivialities which was in Tom Outland's face and in his behaviour" (Cather 1949, 31–32). It is a passage that feels wrung from Cather's own experience in the early 1920s, the years that led up to the publication of this novel, and a time in which Cather's own life, as she herself attests, had felt overcrowded and stuffy with new things, "petty ambitions" and "quivering jealousies" among them. Under these circumstances, it is easy to understand why she would find in the Brewsters precisely the open window that she was seeking. Here were two artists who exemplified Tom Outland's "fine disregard for trivialities," the ability not to fret about silly things; who had retained their commitment to honesty, simplicity, purity; who had sought in both their lives and their art to limit clutter, to push beyond what was external and passing to what was real and important; and who, despite their passionate pursuit of artistic excellence, had remained largely free of egoism and ambition—and had shaped a life-style that insulated them from the rat race.[58] In her prefatory note to *Not Under Forty* Cather wrote, "The world broke in two in 1922 or thereabouts," a comment that echoed what she had written Dorothy Canfield Fisher that same year—that they seemed to be living in a different world than the one they used to know (Cather 2002, #601). We have seen reflections of this broken world both in the books Cather writes beginning in 1920 and in her expressed feelings about her own life.

This sense of fracture carries over even to Cather's relationship with the Brewsters themselves. Despite her admiration for them and for the life they had forged for themselves, Cather must have recognized that in certain respects they lived in a world she could never fully enter. In her 1923 essay Achsah cites Horace's famous Ode I.22, "Integer Vitae": "To be an artist, one must be a child. The work of one who has purity of heart—*integer vitae*—is a new vision of God" (16). Whether or not Cather had read these words in the Brewsters' book—one suspects she had, given how often she saw the Brewsters in 1923—she clearly understood their implications. Acute reader of character that she was—both of others and of herself—Cather must have seen that the wholeness of life, *integritas vitae,* that the Brewsters had achieved was inextricably intertwined with a childlike innocence unlike anything she saw in herself. And given how different her personal background and artistic career had been from theirs, she must have realized that there were gulfs between their lives and hers that were ultimately unbridgeable.

In the first chapter of this book, Lucy Marks comments on the lasting impact on Earl and Achsah of the childhoods they both had experienced:

> Earl and Achsah were thirty-two years old when they married, had traveled abroad and lived apart from their families. Yet each was still very much under the protection of parents and siblings, both financially and emotionally; each was still the classic indulged youngest child, creative, largely freed from conventional responsibilities, accustomed to being taken care of, and ultimately interested more in inquiry than achievement. . . . There was a childlike unworldliness and naïveté about Earl and Achsah, a sense of their "sitting upon rosy clouds," as Lawrence put it (Brewster 1934, 245), above the fray, concerned with matters spiritual and cerebral, rather than corporeal.[59]

At almost every point, Willa Cather differed markedly from the Achsah and Earl here described. The oldest rather than the youngest child in her family, she had grown up with a strong sense of responsibility for her siblings and a clear understanding of the financial realities and constraints under which her family lived. If indeed her parents indulged this talented daughter in certain respects, it was not in being overprotective but rather in granting her freer rein to find and make her own way, something that she, like her alter ego Thea Kronborg in *The Song of the Lark,* was doing by the time she was seventeen. Although, like all great artists, Cather throughout her life retained a youthful freshness of vision, it had little in common with the Brewsters' "childlike unworldliness and naïveté." To the contrary, as I argue in a recent book,[60] Cather was from early on consumed not only by ambition to write books worthy of what she called "The Kingdom of Art" but also by ambition to win recognition and worldly success: as mentioned earlier, Achsah captures a very real part of Willa Cather when she associates her with the aggressively on-the-make Eden Bower in the verbal portrait with which this chapter began. From early in her career Cather devoted time and energy to helping and hectoring her publishers in their publicity efforts, even to writing—usually anonymously—advertising copy for her own books. If one side of Cather unceasingly sought the seclusion from the world that would enable her to write, another worked with equal persistence to assure that the world took due notice of her achievements. When in her ghostwritten biography of Mary Baker Eddy Cather commented that Eddy had through her advertising genius achieved annual royalties that put "all other American authors to financial shame," she was clearly numbering herself among the shamed.[61] Contrast what Earl Brewster writes of the Tibetan-Chinese artist Ram Jor in a March 13, 1946, letter to Ralph Ruzicka: "I . . . admire him for his devotion to his art, so apparently free from all desires for recognition or money."[62]

While at their best these two sides of Cather's character complemented each other, their very existence entailed a division of mind and soul which Cather wrote into a number of her fictional characters—most obviously Thea Kronborg—and which differentiated her sharply from the Brewsters, and from the wholeness and harmony of life they had found. When in 1923 Cather spent so much time with them in France, she cannot have failed to mark this divide, knowing herself as she did—and reading her friends with her characteristic penetration: that she could never achieve the Brewsters' childlike unworldiness, live as they lived, she must have recognized. Perhaps still more, she must also have noted the vast gulf that existed between her accomplishments and theirs. By the time she saw the Brewsters in 1923, she had written several novels that had won broad acclaim—one thinks particularly of *O Pioneers!* and *My Ántonia*—and her most recent novel, *One of Ours,* had not only been a huge commercial success but would that very year win the Pulitzer Prize, with the announcement coming while Cather was still in France. In contrast, the Brewsters' art had at best garnered some critical praise—and the occasional purchase—from a limited audience. Between the magnitude of Cather's accomplishments, and the fierce determination with which she had worked to win recognition for them, and the Brewsters' far more modest achievements, and their dilatory efforts to promote them, there was an unmistakable divide.[63] Cather could still look through the window and, albeit vicariously, enjoy—and no doubt often envy—the Brewsters' ability largely to rise above ambition such as her own, and to escape its attendant tensions and turmoil, but at the same time she could not but realize that these very tensions and turmoil were integrally related to what she, in contrast to the Brewsters, had managed to achieve. This separation did not, however, rule out a strong sense of kinship in other respects. Both she and the Brewsters scorned specious compromise and sought to create work that probed beyond mere particulars to a more permanent, essential realm; both she and they found their deepest joy in their work as artists—in the "happy working hours" she is so savoring when she writes Achsah early in 1924. Despite the divisions in her soul, and those between herself and the Brewsters, she could, with them, find a measure of wholeness in the principle which Earl had articulated in his August 1922 letter to Achsah: "Life is very simple—all we have to do is our best."

THE BREWSTERS AND THREE LATER CATHER WORKS

Although in the decade that followed their extensive time together in 1923 Cather and the Brewsters saw each other again only once—in 1930—the Brewsters' impact on Cather's writing if anything became more significant. To begin with, Cather's friendship with the Brewsters contributed materially to what many consider Cather's greatest novel, *Death Comes for the Archbishop*. The clearest connection is one mentioned earlier, Puvis de Chavannes, whom Cather expressly associated with this novel, and whom both she and the Brewsters had long admired. "When I was almost eight years old," wrote Earl in 1923, "someone gave me an art review that reproduced the works of Puvis de Chavannes; I felt immediately a powerful attraction for this great master, an attraction which has only grown" (Brewster 1923, 6). Achsah too had long known Puvis, and admiration for him was one of many ties she and Earl discovered during their courtship in 1910. In a letter written from Maine that August, Earl tells Achsah of his love of Italy, speaking of "[f]air islands of the sea where life is as simple as true and as beautiful as in a canvas by Puvis de Chavannes" (8/14/10). A month later Achsah, writing him from Deer Island in Maine, responds in kind: "You would rejoice to see your Camden town from here. It is the silver blue line of hills beyond the sea that Puvis de Chavannes painted in the Pantheon" (9/12/10).

Just as a shared enthusiasm for Puvis helped draw Earl and Achsah together in 1910, so it must have drawn Willa and Achsah to each other during the time they spent together in Paris in 1923. Indeed, when in her September 1910 letter Achsah men-

tions Puvis' paintings "in the Pantheon," she names the location
of the very paintings to which Cather traces her interest in
Puvis, and which she expressly associates with what she sought
to achieve in *Death Comes for the Archbishop:* "I had all my life
wanted to do something in the style of legend, which is absolutely the reverse of dramatic treatment. Since I first saw the
Puvis de Chavannes frescoes of the life of Saint Geneviève in my
student days, I have wished that I could try something a little
like that in prose; something without accent, with none of the
artificial elements of composition" (Cather 1949, 9).[64] Given the
sympathetic vibrations between this passage and the Brewster
excerpts quoted earlier, one suspects that during their weeks together in 1923 Willa and Achsah must at some point have
walked together from the Quai de Voltaire to the Pantheon—
about a mile—to see the Puvis murals that both of them had
known for so long. This seems the more likely in that in the novel
Cather would begin soon after her return from Paris, *The Professor's House,* Godfrey St. Peter recalls walking in this very area—
"along the Rue St. Jacques and Rue Sufflot" and thence to the
Pantheon (Cather 1925, 102–3). That Achsah and Willa took a
similar walk we can only surmise, but we know that in 1923
Cather spent much time with two artists whose book, published
that very year, identified Puvis de Chavannes as an influence on
their work, and whose show, which Cather saw before her return, was filled with paintings which showed that very influence.[65] In the years following, Puvis emerges as an important
model for the distinctive style Cather develops in *Archbishop;*
though she had long known Puvis, at the very least her time
with the Brewsters in 1923 helped inspire a renewed interest in
him.

In the same essay on *Death Comes for the Archbishop* Cather
mentions another enthusiasm that fed into her novel: "The
longer I stayed in the Southwest, the more I felt that the story
of the Catholic Church in that country was the most interesting
of all its stories. The old mission churches, even those which
were abandoned and in ruins, had a moving reality about them;
the hand-carved beams and joists, the utterly unconventional
frescoes, the countless fanciful figures of the saints, no two of
them alike, seemed a direct expression of some very real and
lively human feeling. They were all fresh, individual, first-hand"
(Cather 1949, 5). The Brewsters too had been deeply impressed
by ancient Catholic churches. "In the Italian province of Salerno," writes Earl in his 1923 essay, "one sees today a peasant

art replete with richness, abundance, and beauty. I know, in their mountains, a chapel they have constructed where, from the first glance, one recognizes perfection" (Brewster 1923, 12). A few pages later Achsah comments that the art in the convents and other dwellings near which they lived in Italy exemplified the role art should play in life—something essential, not a mere luxury (17). Cather's interest in the old churches of the Southwest went back to her 1912 and 1915 trips there, and it can only have been rekindled by her 1920 and 1923 visits with the Brewsters, the more so in that she herself had long associated these churches of the Southwest with those she had seen in France.[66] The evensong services at Nôtre Dame which Achsah and Cather attended in 1923, and which Achsah associated with "the essential spirit" of Willa Cather, seem of a piece with the radiant, reverent faith that Cather's two French priests will bring to the churches of the Southwest a few years later in *Death Comes for the Archbishop*.

These ancient churches lead easily to another interest shared with the Brewsters, again one that Cather explicitly associates with *Archbishop*. Cather prefaces her comments on Puvis by mentioning her longstanding wish "to do something in the style of legend," and she returns to the same theme a bit later: "In the Golden Legend the martyrdoms of the saints are no more dwelt upon than are the trivial incidents of their lives; it is as though all human experiences, measured against one supreme spiritual experience, were of about the same importance" (Cather 1949, 9). An interest in traditional legend had long shaped the Brewsters' art—the paintings in their 1923 book, for instance, repeatedly draw on the legendary subjects both of Buddhism and of Christianity. In addition, the style adopted by both Brewsters throughout their paintings closely resembles the distanced, "unaccented," two-dimensional style that Cather found in *The Golden Legend* and sought in *Archbishop*—a style similar, in turn, to that of Puvis, in whose works also human life feels "measured against one supreme spiritual experience."

The esthetic Cather articulates in these last words was one she would have felt at work in both the Brewsters' lives and their art, an esthetic rooted in their study of Asian religion. In an early letter to Achsah Earl had written, "If the lessons from the Gita could be put into a few words it seems to me it is working for the sake of work and leaving the results in the hands of God. We ought to be happy and peaceful if we would renounce the fruit of our actions—for we act the best that we know how to

act—how can one do more?" (EHB to ABB 5/15/10, language that
in turn throws light on what Earl means by "doing one's best").
One thinks too of Achsah's comment, quoted earlier, that "after
having lived in the Orient, one comes to appreciate differently
the values of life: each one feels less interest in personal success,
and has only the desire to see beauty manifested." And in a letter of November 9, 1930, to Harwood, Earl describes how Buddhism and Hinduism enable us to "look upon our ordinary
intelligence and our ordinary consciousness as but a limitation
or a reflection of a higher reality—an absolute reality." The state
of mind Earl describes is close to that which Cather evokes in
Bishop Latour when we first meet him in *Archbishop*, lost and
wandering in the desert: "Empowered by long training, the
young priest blotted himself out of his own consciousness and
meditated upon the anguish of his Lord. The Passion of Jesus
became for him the only reality; the need of his own body was
but a part of that conception" (Cather 1927, 17).[67] It is not sur-
prising that when in 1955 Earl returns to Willa Cather, the book
he reads, and finds very beautiful, is *Death Comes for the Archbishop*.

At a still deeper level, both the centrality of religion in the
Brewsters' lives and the character of their faith complemented
and reinforced the steady shift in Cather's attitudes toward religion that began in the early 1920s and culminates in *Archbishop*. Religion had always been part of her life, beginning with
the place of *Pilgrim's Progress* and the Bible in her childhood.
Religious experiences figure prominently in her account of her
first trip to Europe in 1902—the peace she found in the cloister
of Chester Cathedral, her awed response to the rose windows
she saw in Rouen, her pleasure at being welcomed, outsider
though she was, into a Catholic communion service in an Italian
part of London. Her early trips to the Southwest evoked similar
feelings as she visited villages clustered around "cathedrals
built in the time of Elizabeth I," came to know missionary
priests and to hear tales of their predecessors, and responded to
a spiritual element in the land itself.[68] In contrast, much of what
Cather saw and felt in organized religion struck her as narrow-
minded and hypocritical, and her negative feelings come out
strongly in many early works—one thinks, for instance, of the
Christianity that smothers the talented heroine in "The Joy of
Nelly Deane," or of Jim Laird's savage retort to his self-righ-
teous, judgmental fellow citizens in "The Sculptor's Funeral":

"Oh, you're a discriminating lot of Christians!" (Cather 1920, 270).

This negative side remains very much alive in Cather's 1922 novel, *One of Ours,* in the first part of which her hero, Claude Wheeler, finds "Christian theology . . . too full of evasions and sophistries to be reasoned about" (Cather 1922, 50). In the novel's second half, however, the rose window in Rouen's St. Ouen evokes in him a response similar to what Cather herself had felt when she visited that city in 1902, an experience that, as John Murphy writes, heralds "an attitude toward religion and art made manifest in Cather's confirmation in Red Cloud's Episcopal Church in 1922" (Cather 1999, 335). In the following years Cather's interest in religion becomes ever more apparent. The deep-rooted Catholic faith of Augusta, St. Peter's seamstress in *The Professor's House,* runs throughout the novel and undergirds the solace she brings the professor in the final chapters. In Cather's next novel, *My Mortal Enemy,* Myra Henshawe's embrace of the Catholicism she had once rejected becomes an anchor in her final months, and she dies looking out over the Pacific, her crucifix clutched in her hands. The profound religious feeling that shapes every level of *Archbishop* is the natural and glorious next step.

Many factors, both internal and external, contributed to this progression, but Cather's contact with the Brewsters was certainly among them. For in them she came to know people whose religious commitment was not only deep but also open armed. Like Cather, the Brewsters resisted the narrower, judgmental forms that religion can take. Of a puritanical Waldensian they met in Rome, Achsah comments, "Lina moved from a sense of duty, she did everything because she felt she ought to, never because it was fun. She unconsciously taught me to admire hedonism" (A. Brewster 1942, 111). In contrast, the Brewsters took active pleasure in their wide-ranging religious observances. "[T]hey felt that all religions were aiming at the same goals. . . . [T]hey used to spend every evening reading aloud, taking turns, and they read a great deal of philosophy, Plato—they read Plato every Sunday—and the Eastern philosophy too," as Harwood recalled in 1977, commenting on the role that Christianity, Buddhism, Vedanta, and other spiritual exercise played in her parents' lives (Picard 1984, 209). The same eclectic spirit comes through in Achsah's description of the Brewsters' studio in Rome, with her mural of Gethsemane and her painting of Earl and Harwood as St. Antonio and the baby Jesus complementing

Earl's paintings of the Buddha.[69] A few years later Cather would in *Death Comes for the Archbishop* breathe a similar openness into Bishops Latour and Vaillant who, in contrast to some of the other priests in the novel, follow something akin to the Buddhist Middle Path—firm in their beliefs, but not so rigid as not to appreciate or find beauty and meaning in local beliefs and customs, and in their personal lives avoiding extremes of both self-indulgence and self-mortification.[70]

Perhaps most important, in the Brewsters Cather found colleagues for whom religion and art were inextricably related—one thinks again of the prominence of religious subjects in their art. Indeed, a familiar comment that Godfrey St. Peter makes as he lectures in *The Professor's House* calls the Brewsters very much to mind: "Art and religion (they are the same thing, in the end, of course) have given man the only happiness he has ever had" (Cather 1925, 69). St. Peter's linking of religion to art, and of both to happiness, is apt for the spirituality that energized both the Brewsters' lives and their art. It is apt also for the religion that became increasingly part of Cather's life in the 1920s and that increasingly left its mark on the fiction that leads up to and includes *Death Comes for the Archbishop*. Cather's friendship with the Brewsters, and especially her time with them in Paris in 1923, culminating as it did in her exposure to the religious art that dominated their 1923 show, surely contributed to this progression.

Finally, though I will not push the point, I cannot resist noting that the two central figures of *Death Comes for the Archbishop*, Fathers Latour and Vaillant, themselves have much in common with the Brewsters, starting with the centrality of religion in their lives and extending to their openness to forms of spirituality outside their own faith; to their purity of heart, honesty, and integrity; to their happiness in working hard; to their understanding of what is important, and what is not; to their strong ties to France and the Old World, including the distinctly French delight in fine food and wine with which they season their spirituality. They too have left their homes for a lifelong pilgrimage in foreign lands, and even the complementarity of the very different Latour and Vaillant has its similarities to the partnership of opposites that Cather would not have failed to see in Earl and Achsah.[71] It is in *Death Comes for the Archibishop* that I believe Cather comes closest to articulating the wholeness of life she perceived in the Brewsters at their best. In Latour and Vaillant she has transformed the Brewsters' spirituality into an *integri-*

tas vitae that is mature, radiant, and profound, as if in writing this novel Willa Cather herself for a time found a way to step through that square window into a new world where the air blows fresh off the Blue Mesa.

🕉️

I believe that Cather's friendship with the Brewsters also contributed to another of her greatest works, "Old Mrs. Harris," the autobiographical short story that she made the centerpiece of *Obscure Destinies* when she published this collection in 1932. And here we turn to the time Cather spent with the Brewsters in 1930 in southern France.

In "The Child" Achsah comments on the warm ties that developed between her daughter Harwood and Cather during this period: "The visits on the terraces of Château Brun, St. Cyr, were precious revelations of the depth and sincerity of her nature, which was the reason that Harwood and she understood each other so well.[72] It has seemed to me that some fragrance of the Child, Harwood, exhales from the child, Cécile, in 'Shadows on the Rock'" (A. Brewster 1942, 318). Achsah's association of Harwood with Cather's portrayal of Cécile in *Shadows* is touching, and it reflects the delight Achsah took in this novel, of which Cather sent her a copy shortly after it appeared in 1931.[73] Moreover, the novel clearly sustains and builds upon Cather's interest in religious faith and the refuge it offers—an interest which, as we have seen, Cather's contact with the Brewsters had helped kindle. Cather later wrote that in *Shadows* she focused her attention on the activities of an "orderly little French household that went on trying to live decently" (Cather 1949, 16). Given Cather's habit of drawing on her memories of people she had encountered,[74] one cannot doubt that the Brewster family with whom she spent time in Paris in 1923 made its contribution to this novel, especially since that family lived a life infused by strong religious and spiritual feeling, as do the Auclairs of *Shadows,* and included a young woman who at that time was eleven— close to the age of Cécile in the body of the novel. Harwood herself recalls that during this period in Paris Cather "once or twice came and stayed in my room while I was in school. She left six beautiful handkerchiefs with my initials on them" (Picard 1926, 38 [third series]). Harwood's delight in this gift, and her pleasure in wearing Isabelle Hambourg's silk negligee and dainty slippers in visits to Ville d'Avray, recall Cécile's surprised elation over the grown-up clothes she receives from family members in France. In turn, Cécile's ready responsiveness to stories is of a piece with Harwood's delight in the Tolstoy tales Achsah read to her as a child, or with her mimicking of Anitra's dance after seeing *Peer Gynt* with Willa Cather and Isabelle Hambourg in 1923: "In her nightgown she whirled and pirouetted, frisking out her legs and pointing her pink toes in a twirl of ecstasy."[75]

In contrast, the link that Achsah suggests between the Harwood Cather came to know in 1930 and the Cécile of *Shadows* is more problematic. For one thing, by the time Cather visited the Brewsters in 1930 that novel was nearly finished. Cather began writing *Shadows* in the summer of 1928 and worked on it throughout 1929 and into the early part of 1930; the only portion of its creation that follows her 1930 stay with the Brewsters falls between her return in early October and the completion of the novel on December 27; to put it differently, by the time Cather visited the Brewsters in the summer of 1930, she had already largely shaped the character of the young Cécile.[76] In addition, the Harwood Cather spent time with in 1930 was very different from the Harwood she had known in 1923—and from the Cécile we meet in the bulk of *Shadows*. At the time of Cather's St. Cyr visit, Harwood was approaching eighteen—several years older than Cécile. She had just completed her first year at the progressive Dartington Hall in Devonshire, from which she was home for the summer when Cather saw her; in 1931 she would finish her studies there and apply for entry to university, again in England. To judge by letters and journals in the Brewster archive, Harwood was also, again in sharp contrast to Cécile, showing the headstrong willfulness of late adolescence. Following graduation from Dartington she would battle her parents, and prevail, as to what course of study she would pursue at university. For now, her very enrollment at Dartington had for the first time given her a measure of independence—which she exerted, during her second year, in her decision to play field hockey despite her parents' opposition![77]

Letters from D. H. Lawrence to the Brewsters in 1929, the year before Cather's visit, make clear that he thought this break had come none too soon. On June 2, 1929, he responded to word that Harwood was thinking of becoming a doctor: "[I]f she *wants* to, let her—and if she's going to, then it's high time she began some regular work in preparation, at some regular school or college. If it's not going to be America, let it be England. But for God's sake do *something,* about it—another year has gone by, she's going to be seventeen, and the muddle only deepens" (*LL* 7 #5122).[78] On September 5 he wrote, "As for the child, so she's not going to be a doctor. Well, she's not a child any more either, so it'll be quite a vocation being a woman: God help us all" (7 #5305). Three weeks later, on September 27, he wrote Harwood directly, asking how she liked Dartington: "It will seem strange at first, but I'm sure after a while you'll love it. And I do hope you'll get a footing in the world among other people, and independent of your father and mother. Thank goodness it is not too late. Then you can come back to Earl and Achsah with a new outlook, and a new energy, and give them a share of a new Harwood" (7 #5345). The following January 15 he reported on Harwood's return to Dartington after Christmas vacation: "I think she loves escaping her parents" (7 #5481).

Behind Lawrence's comments one senses Achsah's and Earl's reluctance to recognize that Harwood was growing up—a natural outgrowth, one suspects, of the early experiences and conditions that had imbued both of them with such childlike innocence and naïveté toward the world, had in some ways even prevented them from ever fully growing up themselves. We recall, for instance, that Earl had struggled with how he could leave his mother to marry Achsah and had even for a time considered having his mother join him and his new wife on their honeymoon. As for Achsah, Lucy Marks comments, "When Achsah (John Barlow's 'dear baby girl' into her late twenties) paid homage to the aunts who had raised her, she singled out those characteristics with which she also clearly identified: 'crystalline purity, a flavour of goodness' and 'white, immaculate soul, unsmirched with any worldliness.' She habitually dressed in white, the color of childhood innocence."[79]

The language Lawrence uses in his September 5 letter points especially toward Achsah: "As for the child . . . Well, so she's not a child any more." Though Achsah comments on how Earl and she had always tried to treat Harwood as an adult,[80] the very title of her memoir, and her regular use of "the child" in referring to Harwood, confirm what Lawrence implies—her unwillingness, even inability, to see Harwood not as a child but as someone approaching womanhood.[81] Even when Achsah near the end of "The Child" recognizes the great happiness that Harwood found at Dartington, her language suggests the pain of letting go: "We were at Dartington now. Harwood was leaving us. Like the 'Departure of the Prodigal Son,'" this last a reference to a Rilke poem, which Achsah then quotes at length, ending,

> And to depart: why? Impulse, generation,
> Impatience, obscure hope and desperation
> Not to be understood or understand:
> To take all this upon you, and in strife
> To lose perhaps, all that you had, to die
> Alone and destitute, not knowing why—
> Is this the entrance into some new life . . . ?
>
> (A. Brewster 1942, 433–34)

The bright optimism of Achsah's immediate comment on this passage is as astonishing as it is characteristic: "For me, Dartington Hall is a radiant rainbow shining from earth to heaven." Achsah's words are more than just a reflection of her perennial inclination to seize on the bright side of things. From the full chapter on Dartington Hall, much of it quoted in chapter 6, it is clear that Achsah was genuinely excited by Dartington Hall itself and that from the retrospect of 1942 one side of her fully appreciated how much the school had meant to Harwood. But that she should at this climactic moment—the very end of her memoir—cite at such length from Rilke's dark poem bespeaks the conflicting sense of loss, loneliness, and desolation that she still felt as she thought back on, and wrote about, what would prove to be Harwood's definitive and defining departure from home and from childhood. Indeed, one wonders if Achsah's feelings about Harwood and Dartington are not infused with the despair that she herself was feeling in 1942 as she looked back at the impulsive departures that had marked her own life, and had led her to India where she would three years later die "alone and destitute."

In 1977 Harwood would comment that the happiest days of her life, a period when she and her parents could and did talk with each other about anything, were at St. Cyr-sur-Mer—the period that *followed* the decisive break of Dartington (Picard 1977, 57). In contrast, Achsah ends "The Child" at the point when Harwood *enters* Dartington—and says nothing about these subsequent years when "the child" was becoming an adult. Indeed, even in letters written well after Harwood's departure from home, Achsah continued to address her as "little daughter of my heart" (e.g., 9/9/36, when Harwood is almost twenty-four, and married: compare the way Achsah's father addressed her into *her* twenties!). In this same 1936 letter Achsah even protests the fact that children do grow up: she has read that "the Himalayas are growing taller from year to year" and comments,

"It seems strange that like unruly children those mighty mountains should be visibly growing before our eyes."

Given this background, that Achsah in "The Child" associates the almost eighteen-year-old Harwood of 1930 with the preadolescent Cécile of *Shadows* is exactly what we would expect—as if Harwood were still the Cécile-like girl of Cather's 1923 visit. The picture that emerges of the actual Harwood Cather came to know in 1930, however, suggests instead a quite different Cather heroine of the same period, the Vickie of "Old Mrs. Harris." Vickie at fifteen is closer to Harwood in age than is Cécile, and she shows the same willful determination to set her own course that Lawrence had sensed in Harwood. Just as Harwood attained a new independence when she headed off to school in England, so Vickie's focus in the story is above all on getting away to the university, a goal she pursues on her own—and that sets her at odds with her parents. Her mother sees Vickie's efforts to win a scholarship as "overdoing it," an instance of her daughter's tendency to "run to extremes" (Cather 1932, 149).[82] As for Vickie's father, when Mrs. Rosen reminds him that Vickie has finished school "and should be getting training of some sort; she is growing up," both her words and Mr. Templeton's response recall the dynamics, and even the language, of the debate over Harwood's attending Dartington, and the Brewsters' resistance to the shattering of the tight "trinity" of their family: "Oh, don't remind me, Mrs. Rosen!" he says. "I just pretend to myself she isn't. I want to keep my little daughter as long as I can" (109). Finally, the suggestion that the time Cather spent with Harwood in 1930 helped shape the character not of Cécile but of Vickie also fits the chronology far better: while *Shadows* was largely completed by the time Cather returned in 1930 from her visit with the Brewsters, "Old Mrs. Harris" dates from the following summer.[83]

We know that Vickie is in large part Cather's portrait of her teenage self, and it is but a short step further to suggest that in Harwood Brewster Cather met a young woman who reminded her of this teenage self—independent, ambitious, university-bound—and that this meeting helped catalyze and shape her subsequent portrait of Vickie. That Harwood had been seventeen when she left for Dartington in 1929 makes the connection the more likely: Cather was seventeen when she left Red Cloud for the university in 1890, and in *The Song of the Lark* she makes Thea—another alter ego—"barely seventeen" when she heads off to study music in Chicago (Cather 1915, 151). There is also a clear continuity among the three mother-daughter pairs. A picture dating from the late twenties shows Harwood as stocky, plainly dressed, and with her hair severely parted in the middle (see fig. 3); and recalling an occasion when D. H. and Frieda Lawrence tried to buy her a dress, Harwood once commented, "I was fifteen and must have been very awkward, ungracious and unappreciative" (Picard 1982, 15). Vickie has a "sturdy build" and wears her hair in "a single braid down her back"; she is not unattractive, but she is also not "pretty" (Cather 1932, 107). Cather herself as an adolescent was sturdy in build, eschewed traditional feminine dress, and cropped her hair short. In contrast, all three mothers, Achsah Brewster, Victoria Templeton, and Virginia Cather, are svelte, dress elegantly, and carry themselves with style.[84]

If I am correct in suggesting that in Harwood Brewster Cather found herself face to face with her own teenage self—and wrote what she saw into Vickie—it was a turning point of some significance. Strong-willed, full-blooded young women of Vickie's sort are common in Cather's early fiction—most obviously Thea, but also Clara Vavrika in "The Bohemian Girl," both Alexandra and Marie in *O Pioneers!,* and the title character of *My Ántonia*—but the type is largely absent in her fiction of the late twenties. There are hints of it in the younger Myra Henshawe we occasionally glimpse in *My Mortal Enemy,* but it is virtually absent from *Death Comes for the Archbishop* and appears in *Shadows on the Rocks* mainly in Jeanne Le Ber—who, significantly, has chosen to stifle this side of herself in a life of chastity, obedience, and seclusion. In contrast, in "Old Mrs. Harris" Cather places a figure of this ilk front and center, and in interaction with other women—her mother, her grandmother, Mrs. Rosen. It is a huge step toward the central role that female figures will play in Cather's last two novels, and especially toward the complex dynamics that obtain among the women of *Sapphira and the Slave Girl.*

D. H. Lawrence and others had, despite their affection for the Brewsters, found in them a good bit to satirize, not least their mix of childlike unworldliness with a quite adult love for the finer things of life. If our surmises about "Old Mrs. Harris" are correct, Cather's perceptions of the Brewsters in 1930 had a clear-eyed, even critical edge that is not apparent in her earlier relationship with them, at least in documents we possess. If in 1923 Cather could see their innocence as admirable, something she might even envy, albeit from the distance of her own very

different life, by 1930 she could no longer ignore its liabilities
and limitations, especially as these related to Harwood. In particular, she too, like D. H. Lawrence, must have been struck by
the gulf between the strong-minded young woman Harwood had
become and "the child" to whom her parents still clung. One can
also not doubt that as she came to know Harwood, and to see
ways in which Harwood resembled herself at that age, she applauded the ambition and independence by which this tenacious
young woman was finding her way into a world more mature and
less sheltered than that in which her parents had lived their
lives. A letter that Earl wrote to Harwood two years later, when
she was studying medicine in London and living on her own, dramatically exemplifies where her quest for independence would
soon lead. In the first part of this October 1932 letter Earl treats
his twenty-year-old daughter as still a child, pressing her for detailed accounts of her daily schedule and counseling her never to
allow a man into her room without the presence of a chaperon.[85]
At the end, however, in implicit acknowledgement that Harwood
is already making her way in the adult world, he asks her to
send him and Achsah some badly needed money, adding,
"Maybe I can even return the sum to you some day. But you
know I am not good at that."[86] Earl wrote this letter about a
month after he and Achsah had built the celebration of Earl's
1932 birthday around the arrival of Cather's *Obscure Destinies.*
One wonders whether as they read the book, and as Achsah singled out "Old Mrs. Harris" for special praise, they sensed how
the emotional dynamics of their own family had helped shape
this remarkable story.

※

A third instance of the Brewsters' continuing impact on Cather's writing goes less deep but is even more demonstrable. We
have mentioned that Cather's meeting with Madame Grout, recounted in "A Chance Meeting," occurred during the visit to Aix-
les-Bains that Cather made after leaving the Brewsters in 1930.
That same encounter provided the starting point as well for
Cather's short story, "The Old Beauty," written in 1936 but not
published until 1948 in the posthumous *The Old Beauty and
Others.*[87] Like "A Chance Meeting," this story is set in Aix-les-
Bains and begins with an encounter with an elderly woman, this
time not between Cather and Madame Grout but between her
male lead, a Mr. Seabury, and an older woman who attracts his

curiosity at dinner and who looks vaguely familiar. The climactic episode of the story is a drive from Aix-les-Bains into the neighboring mountains to visit a Carthusian monastery. The story describes the road winding "higher and higher toward the heights" (Cather 1948, 62); the accident that the party experiences on the return trip near "one of those sharp curves, with a steep wall on their right and an open gulf on the left" (65), an accident that precipitates the heroine's death the next morning; and, most memorably, the arrival at the monastery itself: "At last, beyond a sharp turn in the road, the monastery came into view; acres of slate roof, of many heights and pitches, turrets and steep slopes. The terrifying white mountain crags overhung it from behind. . . . The monastery, superb and solitary among the lonely mountains, was after all a destination" (63).

In his 1949 memoir Earl recalls a day trip the Brewsters took during the time when Cather and Lewis were visiting them in 1930: "To give Edith and Willa a view of the surrounding country, we attempted a drive to the virgin forest of beech wood in which is the grotto of Ste. Baume, where, according to tradition, Mary Magdalen retired to end her days. But the narrow ledges of the great heights over which the road ascended made Willa fearful, and perhaps the view was too grandiose for her enjoyment. I imagine that, like myself, she preferred the gentler regions, graced by man's habitation, but not such as are marred by the monstrous outcroppings characteristic of the shores of the Riviera. So we retreated, to drive through the farming regions and forests of the lower country, to the sylvan embedded Carthusian monastery of Montrieux-le-Jeune" (E. Brewster [1949], 2–3). This perhaps too memorable outing clearly played a role in the genesis of "The Old Beauty." Artist that she was, Cather transposed this episode from the French Riviera to the area near Aix-les-Bains, grafted it into a plot that owes much to her meeting with Madame Grout, and changed a number of details (in the story, for instance, the monastery they visit is deserted, and the party explores its grounds, while in Earl's account the monastery they visit is active, and open only to men). But the coincidence of motifs—the day trip into the mountains, the awe and terror the drive inspires, the Carthusian monastery as destination—is unmistakable. That Cather in her story has conflated this episode from her Brewster visit with the meeting with Madame Grout that occurred soon after in Aix-les-Bains is a telling instance of the alchemy of her imagination—the way in which she repeatedly took the ephemeral events of her daily life and transmuted them into the lasting reality of her fiction.

That Earl in his 1949 essay does not link this story to Cather's 1930 visit suggests to me that "The Old Beauty" was one Cather work he had not read, and the fact that, unlike the books sent the Brewsters during Cather's lifetime, *The Old Beauty and Others* retains its dust jacket (as do the other two posthumous volumes sent to Earl by Edith Lewis) may point the same way. Achsah would probably have read the book upon its arrival from Edith Lewis in the late summer of 1948, but she had died three years earlier.

EPILOGUE

The three examples explored in the previous section suggest the many ways in which Cather's contact with the Brewsters enriched that repertoire of past people, places, situations, and ideas upon which she drew for her novels and short stories.[88] More could be said about each of these examples, especially the first two, and other works of Cather seem ripe for exploration. In what ways, for instance, does the time Cather spent in Paris with the Brewsters in 1923 feed into the French portions of *The Professor's House,* the novel she began soon after her return? Although Myra and Oswald Henshawe in *My Mortal Enemy* are very different from Earl and Achsah Brewster, are there—as I suspect is the case—significant resonances between the two couples? Although we have argued that Achsah mistakenly associates the Cécile of *Shadows on the Rock* with the Harwood Brewster Cather came to know in St-Cyr, are there other ways in which that novel reflects Cather's exposure to the Brewsters, not least given her description of *Shadows* as an effort to capture "a kind of feeling about life and human fate that I could not accept, wholly, but which I could not but admire" (Cather 1949, 15)?

We conclude, however, with "Recognition," the 1922 poem Cather herself explicitly links to the Brewsters, and a poem that in its eight short lines captures so much of what the Brewsters meant to Willa Cather as both writer and human being. Indeed, even to focus, as we have been doing, on anything so specific as the Brewsters' influence on one Cather work or another risks obscuring the most important thing they gave her, a vision of wholeness in a world that felt fractured. It was a gift that had special meaning for Cather in the years when she first came really to know them, 1920–23, a period she herself identified as one of cosmic fracture, and a gift that points the way to the serene and sublime integrity of the novel she would write a few years later, *Death Comes for the Archbishop*. It is this gift which Cather honors in the poem that, as she notes in the copy she sent to the Brewsters, was composed with them expressly in mind:

> *Recognition*
> The old volcanic mountains
> That slope up from the sea—
> They dream and dream a thousand years
> And watch what-is-to-be.
>
> What gladness shines upon them
> When, white as white sea-foam,
> To the old, old ports of Beauty
> A new sail comes home!
>
> (Cather 1923, 65)

The landscape of this poem is the Gulf of Naples, where Lewis and Cather had visited the Brewsters in 1920—a landscape central to many Brewster paintings, including some of those in the Cather-Lewis home.[89] In the "new sail [that] comes home" Cather no doubt wanted the Brewsters to recognize themselves, knowing as she did their sense that in the ancient beauty of southern Italy they had discovered the living roots of their own art, had found their own true home.[90] The Brewsters themselves clearly read the poem this way. Achsah comments in "The Child" that the poem was "something to live up to in the fullness of heart," and in his 1949 essay Earl speaks of it as symbolically "referring to our life as artists" (A. Brewster 1942, 318; E. Brewster [1949], 1). But Cather's poem is even more about herself and her own homecoming. In her friendship with the Brewsters she caught glimpses of—recognized, if you will—something beyond the tawdry, driven, greedy world that so pressed upon her in the early 1920s, and what above all she celebrates in this poem is how the Brewsters had helped lead her back to "the old, old ports of Beauty" which meant so much to both them and her.[91] If our surmises are correct about *Death Comes for the Archbishop* and "Old Mrs. Harris," works that many would identify as Cather's greatest novel and greatest short story, the Brewsters also helped point Cather's sail toward new and significant "ports of Beauty" in the future.

II

3

Checklist of Materials in the Brewster Archive, Drew University

Brewster, Achsah Barlow. "The Child: Harwood Barlow Brewster." Typescript. 1942.

Brewster, Achsah Barlow and Earl Brewster. Ca. 1,700 Autograph Letters signed, Typed Letters signed, and postcards between Achsah and Earl Brewster, and to their daughter, Harwood Brewster Picard. 1910–57.

Brewster, Earl. 63 A.L.s to Lucile Beckett. 1931–57.

Cather, Willa. 4 A.L.s and 1 T.L.s to Achsah Barlow Brewster and Earl Brewster. Jan. 7, 1917; Feb. 21, [1923]; Nov. 29, [1923]; Feb. 16, [1924]; July 1, 1934.

Lewis, Edith. 2 A.L.s to Achsah Barlow Brewster and Earl Brewster. "Thanksgiving Day" [Nov. 23, 1923]; [spring 1934].

———. 13 A.L.s to Harwood Brewster Picard and 1 A.L.s to Picard from Helen Lewis Morgan, Edith Lewis's sister. [1938]–72.

Picard, Harwood Brewster. "To Frances and Claire Some Memories of Your Grandparents Earl Henry Brewster and Achsah Barlow Brewster." Typescript. 1977.

Brewster, Achsah Barlow and Earl Brewster. *L'oeuvre de E.H. et Achsah Barlow Brewster: 32 reproductions en phototypie précedées d'essais autobiographiques.* Rome: Par les Soins de "Valori Plastici," [1923].

Lawrence, D. H. *D. H. Lawrence: Reminiscences and Correspon-*

dence. [Ed.] Earl and Achsah Brewster. London: M. Secker, 1934.

PRINTED MATERIALS: WILLA CATHER

April Twilights: Poems. Boston: Richard G. Badger, 1903. [1st ed.] Crane A1.a

The Troll Garden. New York: McClure, Phillips, 1905. [1st ed., 1st issue] Crane A4.a

O Pioneers! Boston: Houghton Mifflin, 1913. [1st ed., 1st print., 3rd binding variant] Crane A6.a.i.c

The Song of the Lark. Boston: Houghton Mifflin, 1915. [1st ed., 1st print., 1st issue] Crane A8.a.i.a

My Ántonia. Boston: Houghton Mifflin, 1918. [1st ed., 1st print., 2nd state] Crane A9.a.i

Youth and the Bright Medusa. New York: Knopf, 1920. [1st ed., 1st print., trade issue] Crane A10.a.i

One of Ours. New York: Knopf, 1922. [1st ed., 2nd print.] Crane A11.a.ii

April Twilights and Other Poems. New York: Knopf, 1923. [2nd ed., 1st print., trade issue] Crane A2.b.i

A Lost Lady. New York: Knopf, 1923. [1st ed., 1st print., trade issue state "A"] Crane A13.a.i.a

The Professor's House. New York: Knopf, 1925. [1st ed., 1st print., trade issue] Crane A14.a.i

My Mortal Enemy. New York: Knopf, 1926. [1st ed., 3rd print.] Crane A15.a.iii

Death Comes for the Archbishop. New York: Knopf, 1927. [1st ed., 2nd print., trade issue] Crane A16.a.ii

Shadows on the Rock. New York: Knopf, 1931. [1st ed., 1st print., trade issue] Crane A17.a.i

Obscure Destinies. New York: Knopf, 1932. [1st ed., 1st print., trade issue] Crane A19.a.i

Lucy Gayheart. New York: Knopf, 1935. [1st ed., 2nd print.] Crane A20.a.ii

Not Under Forty. New York: Knopf, 1936. [1st ed., 2nd print.] Crane A21.a.ii

The Autograph Edition of the Novels and Stories of Willa Cather. [New York: Houghton Mifflin, 1937?] [prospectus] Crane AA1 (note on prospectus)

Sapphira and the Slave Girl. New York: Knopf, 1940. [1st ed., 1st print., trade issue] Crane A22.a.i

The Old Beauty and Others. New York: Knopf, 1948. [1st ed., 1st print.] Crane A23.a.i

On Writing: Critical Studies on Writing as an Art. Foreword by Stephen Tennant. New York: Knopf, 1949. [1st ed., 1st print.] Crane AA2.a.i

Willa Cather in Europe: Her Own Story of the First Journey. Introd. and incidental notes by George N. Kates. New York: Knopf, 1956. [1st ed., 1st print.] Crane AA5.a

4

Cather Books and Letters
in the Brewster Archive

Two groups of material in the drew university archives are of particular importance to understanding Cather's relationship to the Brewsters—the books by Willa Cather that are from the Brewsters' library (many of them inscribed), and the letters that Willa Cather wrote to the Brewsters. For ease of reference, this chapter focuses on these two groups and offers additional information not contained in the checklist of chapter 3. Part 1 reviews the Cather books owned by the Brewsters and cites any inscriptions contained in them, dividing them into three sections: (A) books inscribed to the Brewsters by Willa Cather herself; (B) books inscribed to the Brewsters by Edith Lewis; and (C) books owned (and often signed) by the Brewsters themselves, but without other inscriptions. Part 2 brings together and paraphrases the five letters in the collection that Cather wrote to the Brewsters, the earliest dating from 1917, the last from 1934.

I. Books by Willa Cather Owned by the Brewsters

(A) Books inscribed by Willa Cather

Youth and the Bright Medusa: inscribed, "For my friends and fellow- / workers, The Brewsters, / from Willa Cather / Naples, October 29 / 1920." First edition.[1]

One of Ours: inscribed, "To / Earl and Achsa [*sic*] Brewster / I send a copy of the novel / they carried off from the / <u>Patria</u> in a little boat / for me. It was then all / in manuscript except / the last books, which / were not yet written. / Willa Sibert Cather / Whale Cove / Grand Manan N. B. / August 29th 1922." Second printing.

April Twilights and Other Poems: inscribed, "To accompany The Brewsters / on the long voyage home—they / do not know how long it is! / The verse on page 65 is theirs / already, for they were both / very much in my mind / on the afternoon last sum- / mer when I wrote it. / Willa Cather / Ville D'Avray / May 16, 1923." Copy has small cross-hatching added in ink on page containing this poem. 1923 trade edition.

A Lost Lady: inscribed, "For Achsah / from / Willa Cather / Paris / October 1923." First edition.

My Mortal Enemy: inscribed, "Autographed for / Earl and Achsah / Willa Cather." First and second printings before publication, with remains of the original box in which the book was published.

Death Comes for the Archbishop: inscribed, "For / Earl and Achsah / and Harwood, / from Willa Cather / July 4th / 1927." First and second printings before publication.

Shadows on the Rock: This first edition is not signed, but a July 8, 1931, letter from Achsah to Harwood indicates that Cather has sent them a copy of this novel "dedicated/rather inscribed/[2] to 'The Brewsters—all three, with my love.'" One suspects that this copy originally contained a slip, now lost, with Cather's inscription.

Lucy Gayheart: Unsigned, but contains card inscribed, "With the compliments of Miss Willa Cather." The handwriting on the card appears to be neither Cather's nor Lewis's. First and second printings before publication.

The copy of *Death Comes for the Archbishop* is the one that Earl Brewster rereads in 1955 in India (see chapter 2). "Do you have a copy of it?" he writes Harwood on February 1, 1955. "Any way I had better send to you the copy I have. It is inscribed by Willa's hand-writing to us in these words." He then quotes the inscription, noting that it was Cather herself who underlined "and Harwood."

(B) Books inscribed by Edith Lewis

O Pioneers!: inscribed, "To my dearest Achsah / from / E. L. / July 9, 1913." First edition.

The Song of the Lark: inscribed, "Achsah Barlow Brewster / from / E. L. / November, 1915." First edition, first issue, with cutout picture of Cather slipped in.

My Ántonia: inscribed, "Achsah Barlow Brewster / from her loving / E. L. / November 11, 1918 / (fin de la guerre)." Although the second numeral of the date is badly smudged, Lewis's allusion to the end of the war points to November 11. First edition.

The Professor's House: inscribed, "Achsah, from her loving / E. L." First edition, with cutout picture of Cather pasted in.

Not Under Forty: inscribed, "For Earl Henry Brewster / from his loving friend / Edith Lewis / November 29, 1936." First and second printings before publication.

The Old Beauty and Others: inscribed, "For my dear friend / Earl Brewster / from / Edith Lewis / August 9th, 1948." First edition.

Willa Cather on Writing: inscribed, "For / Earl Henry Brewster / with love from Edith Lewis / October 1949." First edition.

Willa Cather in Europe: inscribed, "For / Earl Henry Brewster / from his devoted friend / Edith Lewis / October 23d 1956." First edition.[3]

These eight volumes, dating as they do from 1913 through 1956, nine years after Cather's death, underscore the length of the relationship between the two households. Although Lewis sent the first two volumes on her own, one assumes that she did so with Cather's approval. That Lewis sends the three posthumous volumes to Earl in India bespeaks her wish to sustain the connection after both Achsah's and Willa's deaths.

(C) Books owned and signed by members of the Brewster Family

April Twilights: signed, "Earl Brewster" (but in Achsah's hand). First edition.

The Troll Garden: signed, "Earl H. Brewster." First edition, first issue.

Obscure Destinies: signed, "Achsah Barlow Brewster" (but in Earl's hand). First edition. With note added by Harwood along with spray of dried flowers: "From the / Cemetery at / Jaffrey, N.H. / where Willa Cather / & Edith Lewis are / buried 5/22/ 1983."

Sapphira and the Slave Girl: signed, "Harwood Picard." First edition. Tucked into the book are a review of *Sapphira* by Aubrey L. Thomas and a March 14, 1953, editorial from the *Washington Post* on Edith Lewis's and E. K. Brown's books on Cather.

We may assume that the copy of *Obscure Destinies* is the one which both Achsah and Earl report receiving in France—and reading immediately—in September 1932, soon after its August publication (see chapter 2). In contrast, the first-edition copies of *April Twilights* (1903) and *The Troll Garden* (1905) must have come to the Brewsters as gifts well after their publication dates, since neither Cather nor Lewis seems to have had a close acquaintance with Earl until after his marriage to Achsah.[4]

II. LETTERS FROM WILLA CATHER TO THE BREWSTERS

In accordance with the restriction in Cather's will that prohibits direct quotation of her letters, the five letters in the archive from Cather to the Brewsters are here paraphrased.

To Earl and Achsah Brewster. January 7, 1917; one page handwritten.
Is adding her postscript to Edith's letter with thanks for the pleasure they take in Mr. Brewster's paintings. Has never lived with anything lovelier or more satisfying than "The Family by the Sea."[5] Wishes the Brewsters splendid working hours in the new year. Willa Cather.

To Earl and Achsah Brewster. February 21, [1923]; four and one-fourth pages handwritten.
Has been unable to respond to their letter about "One of Ours" because she was at home for her parents' fiftieth anniversary. Has found this book a new experience: critics fault its sentimentality, but ex-service men like it and buy it[6]—as does the general public. Has had to hire a secretary to deal with correspondence she receives about the book; is glad not to have had this sort of success before—it brings bother and fatigue. Is pleased the Hambourgs have chosen "Le Négre bleu"—and that she will room with it again.[7] Takes pleasure in the photograph of it that the Brewsters sent but misses the color. She and Edith love the paintings they brought back from the last trip; she herself likes "The Three Scalops" best of all.[8] Will sail for France around April 1 and hopes to see the Brewsters in Paris. In her absence please write Edith often. Confides that Edith doesn't care for the Hambourgs—never has. They irritate her, Isabelle especially. Has been hard for Edith to know the Hambourgs were seeing the Brewsters this winter, just as she finds it hard when Cather is with them. Nothing Edith can help—just an example of how love and jealousy interweave. Hopes Brewsters and Edith can spend much time together when they are in America this summer—she does not have many friends, and she's had a hard winter. Expects Brewsters will have a show during their time here; she and Edith were pleased with the reviews from last fall's Paris show. There's much she'd like

to say—about painting, writing, ourselves, life itself; hopes there will be more times such as the twilight hours they spent together in Naples. Except for golden wedding and Christmas at home, has been a hard winter, with constant interruptions of work, for which nothing can compensate. Both send wishes for happy working days and the satisfaction that attends them. Both wish they could be with them next year—we could all help each other. Love and happy memories. Willa Cather.

To Achsah Brewster. November 29, [1923]; two pages handwritten.
Had lovely crossing. Enjoyed Frank Swinnerton as table companion—he's charming, honest, and kind.[9] She smokes little at sea, so has saved plenty of Earl's cigarettes—and all of Achsah's chocolates—for Edith, who so likes French candy. Has told her about the Paris show but can't find words to describe the Brewsters' Ceylon pictures. Dorothy Canfield saw her off at the boat train; she too was moved by the Brewsters' show, and found Achsah's triptych beautiful and uplifting. Love to you both, and happy working days. Willa. P.S. Sends big hug to Harwood.

To Achsah Brewster. February 16, [1924]; one and one-third pages handwritten.
Are having happy and stimulating winter. Is working with joy, is healthy and not troubled as she was most of the time in Paris. Edith's company gave her $1,000 for Christmas and raised her salary again; this sort of thing happens at a New York firm only when one is really performing well. Claude and Lost Lady continue to sell, so she and Edith are indulging themselves in modest luxuries. Is good to be home—knows Achsah must feel the same way. Uses the vaporizer Achsah gave her every day—just the thing for the New York climate, as it is for Paris. Greetings to Earl and Harwood; they love Harwood's cards. Life is good when one doesn't fret about silly things. W. S. C.

To Earl and Achsah Brewster. July 1, 1934; one page typed.
Hand problems have delayed her response to receipt of their D. H. Lawrence book. Thinks letters in the book show a better side of Lawrence than appears in other collections, and likes the honesty of what they have written about him. Most who write about Lawrence do so to talk about themselves—Brett's book is the one exception.[10] Isabelle has recently written saying she has learned more about Lawrence from your book than from any other. We hope to get to Grand Manan by second week of July. Have been kept in town by business affairs and Cather's insistence on finishing book.[11] Missed

three months of work because of her hand; book would have been better without this interruption. Edith and she think often of Brewsters and wish they could see them. Had planned to go abroad this spring, but hand changed those plans. One day they will get together—God speed the time. Willa Cather.

5

"For the book Willa Cather-living" by Earl Brewster

INTRODUCTION

THOUGH FAR SHORTER THAN ACHSAH'S AND HARWOOD'S MEMOIRS, Earl Brewster's brief essay, an unpublished draft in the Robert and Doris Kurth Collection at the University of Nebraska, contains fascinating information and insights on the Brewsters and their relationship with Willa Cather. Earl's heading, "For the book Willa Cather-living," makes clear its connection to the book about Cather that Edith Lewis would publish in 1953, and an April 9, 1949, letter from Earl to Harwood refers to "a request from Edith that I write an article on Willa Cather for a book to be prepared by more than a dozen eminent people in America. At first I thought decidedly no I could not: then my creative impulse over came my reluctance and I have written such an article and sent it off, very doubtful if it will be found worthy of the book." Apparently Lewis decided against the book of essays that Earl describes and wrote instead her own memoir under the same title, but at some point she gave serious consideration to including Earl's essay, for the typescript at Lincoln contains numerous editorial changes in her hand (see fig. 4).

Written some seven years after Achsah completed "The Child," Earl's essay contains the same sorts of memory slips we find there—his recollection that the Brewsters had seen Cather receive her Yale honorary degree in 1923, for instance, or his confusion over the year of her visit with them in St. Cyr. Given its explicit focus on Cather, however, it identifies perhaps even more cogently than does Achsah's book-length memoir those qualities that so drew the Brewsters to Cather—her candor and sincerity, her directness, her appreciation both of the refinements of life and of its simple pleasures, her warmth and receptiveness to them and to their art. It also contains information

140

that we do not get as clearly, or at all, elsewhere—his specific reference to the Brewsters' 1920 rendezvous with Cather and Lewis in Naples, for instance, or his description of the otherwise unknown 1930 meeting in St. Cyr between Willa Cather and the Brewsters' revered friend and colleague Mrs. Rhys Davids. And as we saw in chapter 2, Earl's vivid account of the 1930 drive through the mountains to the monastery of Montrieux-le-Jeune provides new insight into Cather's 1936 story, "The Old Beauty."

Edith Lewis's revisions are of interest in themselves, and we comment on them in a brief appendix to this chapter. The essay as printed here, however, omits these revisions and reproduces Earl's original version with only minor changes of spelling, punctuation, and the like. His prose is awkward at times, and in need of editing, but as a long-considered and deeply felt retrospective memoir by one of Cather's close friends and colleagues, it deserves to be read as Earl Brewster wrote it. In addition, Earl's language at times attains great eloquence, as when he describes the nostalgia he feels when—now in India, many years later—he reads Cather's evocation of southern Italy in "Recognition," the poem she wrote for the Brewsters in 1922, or when he applies to himself what she had in 1923 inscribed in their copy of *April Twilights* as to the impending "long voyage home."

For the book
Willa Cather-living.
E. H. Brewster.
   My first acquaintance with Willa Cather was made through her short story "Paul's Case," when it appeared in McClure's Magazine.[1] This writing, which greatly impressed me at the time, after a lapse of many years I admire no less. It appeals to me as written with deep psychological insight and sympathy, and with an artist's keen response to the visible and invisible world. In those days I was a young artist living at 42 Washington Square, New York City. Somewhat later in 1910, my artist friend, Achsah Barlow, whom I was soon to marry, took me to make my first call upon her friends Edith Lewis and Willa Cather, who then had an apartment not far from Washington square.

   What I recall of our conversation upon that occasion with Willa is that she spoke at some length of her admiration for Sarah Orne Jewett, which greatly interested me, since both my mother and I had delighted in Miss Jewett's writing from my early boyhood.[2] Willa's appearance in itself was suggestive of her character, rich in bodily form, with fine features, splendid eyes and a full sensitive mouth. Her laugh was low and pleasant to hear. The sense of humor, which Buddhist psychology so discerningly bases upon the aesthetic sense of proportion, was from her seldom absent. Her garments, one felt, were chosen from her feeling for beauty and appropriateness, rather than from the trivial dictates of mere fashion, and were worn with a refreshing indifference. I found her both genial and reserved, quiet, not eager to express herself, but, when speaking, doing so with force and conviction. One was quickly aware of her sympathies with the genuine, with the sincerely worthwhile in life and art. I at once realized that I was in the presence of an unusually sensitive person of deep reflection and of wide experience of the world.

Soon after this meeting Achsah and I were married and went to live in Sicily and then in Italy and France. I did not see Willa again until 1920, when Edith, my wife and I joined her in Naples, just before she and Edith were to sail for New York. The scene of departure from that Italian coast was in Willa's thought when she wrote her poem "Recognition." In the copy of "April Twilights and other Poems" which she afterwards gave to Achsah and me, she wrote—relating to our visit to America after thirteen years' absence, but more symbolically, I believe, referring to our life as artists—"To accompany the Brewsters on the long voyage home—they do not know how long it is! The verse on page 65 ("Recognition") is theirs already, for they were both much in my mind on the afternoon last summer when I wrote it."

> Recognition.
> The old volcanic mountains
> That slope up from the sea—
> They dream and dream a thousand years
> And watch what is to be.
>
> What gladness shines upon them
> When white as white sea foam,
> To the old, old ports of Beauty
> A new sail comes home!

Poignant indeed are those lines to me, describing a scene before my eyes for many happy years, but now only so in nostalgic memory. Now instead, for thirteen years I have lived facing the inaccessible, heavenly Himalayas, and my "long voyage home" still continues, long indeed!

In the same volume, the preceding poem is followed by one entitled "Going Home," describing Willa's journey by train beyond the Missouri, to the Western home of her earlier years. It especially appeals to me as rarely sensitive and beautiful.

When we made our brief visit to America we had only a glimpse of Willa, which was at Yale where we happened to be when that University conferred a degree upon her.[3]

But not long afterward Willa was in Paris where we were then holding an exhibition of our paintings. Willa was staying much of the time with friends at a charming house and garden near St. Cloud.[4] Delightful were the splendid concerts we attended in the beautiful salon of that house. Willa's much pleased host and hostess hoped that she would long remain with them. It is amusing to recall how her hostess, to make her place as accommodating as possible, arranged off Willa's bed-room a small cubicle, in which it was intended Willa was to write! My memory is that it was not larger than a clothes-cupboard! Her hostess, however, thought that it would provide protection from interruption and encourage such concentration as the monk finds in his cell; but how well one can understand its inappropriateness and disharmony with Willa's love of freedom, space and air.

We were staying at the Hôtel Quai de Voltaire, where sometimes Willa would come for a few days, and we often dined out together with a few friends. Willa did not have that casual indifference to food which seems to me generally characteristic of women. Instead she properly appreciated the preparation and serving of food as the art which it truly is, and was keenly aware of the quality of the food and wine which were served to her.

I remember going with her to an exhibition of Gauguin's paintings and her interest in his work and her sympathetic response to at least certain aspects of it. She purchased from our exhibition one of the most purely imaginative paintings I have ever done.[5] She always made us feel her sympathy for our attempt at painting, and she and Edith honored and encouraged us by hanging on their walls in New York several of our works. Her attitude toward painting seemed to me sensitive and remarkably open minded, contemplative, neither hastening to accept nor to reject the ventures into modern forms, but giving her sympathy to what genuinely appealed to her.

We did not see Willa again until 1935, when she and Edith came down from Aix-les-Bains to join us for a short time in Southern France, where we were living in an old chateau somewhat removed from the tourist section of the Riviera.[6] To give Edith and Willa a view of the surrounding country, we attempted a drive to the virgin forest of beech wood in which is the grotto of Ste. Baume, where, according to tradition, Mary Magdalen retired to end her days. But the narrow ledges of the great heights over which the road ascended made Willa fearful, and perhaps the view was too grandiose for her enjoyment. I imagine that, like myself, she preferred the gentler regions, graced by man's habitation, but not such as are marred by the monstrous outcroppings characteristic of the shores of the Riviera. So we retreated, to drive through the farming regions and forests of the lower country, to the sylvan embedded Carthusian monastery of Montrieux-le-Jeune, near a swift flowing stream, founded in the 12th century, where at one time Petrarch is supposed to have re-

sided, or was it his brother? (!)[7] As women are not allowed to enter
the monastery, and as I had previously had the privilege of doing so,
we remained content with viewing the place from outside and with
the pleasure of the drive and the surrounding country.[8]

Willa told us of her chance meeting in Aix-les-Bains (perhaps in a
previous visit there) with Madame Grout, the favorite niece of Flaubert, with whom he lived, the Caroline of his letters. This meeting,
so sensitively and vividly recorded in Willa's book "Literary Encounter,"[9] must have been a very important and gratifying event for both
Willa and Madame Grout.

When I was with Willa—due to my own self-consciousness—I was
aware of that lack of the classical discipline in language and literature, which I am ever regretting that my youth had not provided me.
I had heard Willa express her strong disapproval of those who regard writing as an art for anybody to pursue, and who indulge in it
without having any genius for it. However, I found Willa to be free
from the natural prejudice which hinders the professional writer
from giving consideration to the work of the inexperienced. A few
years before Willa's visit, my wife and I, at the request of Frieda
Lawrence, had published a book containing the letters to us from our
friend D. H. Lawrence, and also including our reminiscences of
him.[10] I was touched and somewhat surprised when Willa could say
to us, that of the considerable number of books written on Lawrence,
she considered ours the best,[11] nor did she limit her encouragement
with reference to that work alone.

It seems to me that I never have known a person who found it so
painful to endure falsity, shallowness and superficiality in human
nature, especially in the bore and "lion hunter," as Willa did. Instead
of accepting such as the inevitable in life, she inexorably rebelled
against them. Yet how tender and considerate she was toward simple and sincere people. Nor did she consider those forms and conventions which dignify and beautify life to be of an insignificant or
superficial character.

Somewhat coinciding with Edith's and Willa's presence with us,
we had two other guests, my wife's sister, Alpha Barlow, whom I
think both Willa and Edith much appreciated, and Mrs. Rhys Davids, to whom I was deeply in debt for years of guidance in my study
of Pali and the Buddhist canonical scriptures, concerning which she
was the leading authority in the Western world.[12] She was then an
old lady, near the end of a somewhat isolated, strenuous and brave
life, devoted to her special line of scholarship. She was much attracted by Willa and gave to her an important translation she had
made of the psalms in which the Sisters of the Order, in Buddha's
own time, had recorded their experiences—a charming gift, I
thought, from one woman, so eminent in her line of writing, to another woman as eminent as Willa in a different line—this gift of the

earliest known anthology by women of ancient times. Willa's delicate consideration and appreciation of our friend was to be expected, yet so many people absorbed in their own interests, impatient of interruption, would have failed to appreciate this brave old scholar.

Soon after this Willa returned to America and I did not see her again. It is evident from Willa's latest writing, it seems to me, that those realizations of certain spiritual values, which generally cannot come until late in life (and then how rarely), were greatly achieved by her, and crown the splendid collection of her work.[13] For all of which she has my love and gratitude.

APPENDIX: EDITH LEWIS'S REVISIONS

Edith Lewis was herself a skilled writer, and a number of the corrections she makes in Earl's manuscript are of the sort that any experienced editor would make in the interest of clarity, flow, and precision. On several occasions she also corrects obvious errors—e.g., Earl's reference to Cather's 1936 book of essays as "Literary Encounter" rather than *Not Under Forty*. It is accordingly the more interesting that she does not correct some far more glaring errors—e.g., Earl's mistaken reference to having been present when Cather received an honorary degree at Yale in 1923, or to his having last seen Cather in 1935 in southern France: perhaps it was errors of this sort, which Lewis must surely have noticed, that decided her against using Earl's essay in her book.

The great majority of Lewis's editorial changes, however, go beyond merely emending Earl's text. These changes fall into two categories, both of which are revealing in terms of the mind-set Lewis brought to this project. One group of changes reflects her clear intention always to maintain an element of dignity and even distance in the picture drawn of Willa Cather. Thus when, as often, Earl speaks of Cather as "Willa," Lewis has invariably changed the name to "Willa Cather" or replaced it with a pronoun. She has also eliminated both Earl's description of Cather as "rich in bodily form" and his reference to her bedroom as adjoining the writing nook prepared for Cather at Ville d'Avray. Perhaps of greatest interest is that she has crossed out Earl's entire description of the drive into the mountains and thence to the Carthusian monastery, presumably because of its reference to the anxiety this drive evoked in Cather (for Lewis's corrections to this portion of the typescript, see fig. 4).

A second group of changes reflects Lewis's determination to

exclude herself from this account of Willa Cather. Thus, for instance, she crosses out the reference to herself in Earl's mention of the visit Achsah and he made to see Lewis and Cather in 1910, edits herself out of both the 1920 rendezvous in Naples and the later visit to the Brewsters in St. Cyr, and crosses out her name in Earl's reference to the Brewster paintings that hung in the Cather-Lewis home in New York. Her effort even extends to the occasional elimination of specific mentions of Achsah, Lewis's Smith College roommate (see, e.g., the brief comparison below of one passage as it appears in Earl Brewster's original and in Lewis's edited version). Lewis's consistent and unremitting elimination of herself from this account is, of course, of a piece with the way in which she subordinates her role throughout *Willa Cather Living*—not least in her virtual exclusion of the Brewsters themselves, those close and long-cherished friends abroad who had meant so much to both Cather and Lewis, and whom Cather had come to know entirely through Lewis.

An excerpt from the third paragraph of the essay, here presented in its two forms, aptly suggests the sorts of changes Lewis makes throughout Earl's typescript.

Earl Brewster's original version:
Soon after this meeting Achsah and I were married and went to live in Sicily and then in Italy and France. I did not see Willa again until 1920, when Edith, my wife and I joined her in Naples, just before she and Edith were to sail for New York.

Edith Lewis's edited version:
Soon after this meeting I married and went to live in Sicily and then in Italy and France. I did not see Willa Cather again until 1920, when my wife and I joined her in Naples, just before she was to sail for New York.

Lewis's determined efforts to place the spotlight on Willa Cather clearly reflect the affection and admiration she felt for her friend, but they make sense also in terms of her profession. As a highly skilled advertiser, Lewis saw her role as that of drawing attention to her subject—and of rendering herself invisible in the process, even when, as in this case, it was through her efforts that the spotlight shone so brightly on that subject.

6

Selections from "The Child" by Achsah Barlow Brewster

INTRODUCTION

Aᴄʜsᴀʜ ʙᴀʀʟᴏᴡ ʙʀᴇᴡsᴛᴇʀ's ᴍᴇᴍᴏɪʀ, "ᴛʜᴇ ᴄʜɪʟᴅ," ɪs ᴀ ᴜɴɪᴏ̨ᴜᴇ legacy of a unique woman. Originally intended as "some memories of Harwood for Frances and Claire,"[1] it eventually grew into a 436-page family history, covering the seventeen years from Harwood's birth up to the time that she left for Dartington Hall. Achsah began work on "The Child" at Almora in late June 1941, when treatment for her pernicious anemia was finally proving beneficial, enabling her again to walk, paint, and hold a pen. Although this "maze of memories,"[2] completed in July 1942, was not her first attempt to order and record the past,[3] the result was on an entirely different scale from anything she had yet undertaken, and remarkable in view of her poor health. As an artist, Achsah had often worked on an outsized canvas; with "The Child," she produced in effect the largest painting of her career, as full of "experiments and exaltations" (A. Brewster 1942, 409), as colorful and programmatic, as her sprawling murals.

Her memoir was written "to the child's children," Harwood's daughters Claire and Frances, who are occasionally addressed directly in the text (e.g., 108), but Achsah clearly was writing for herself as well. By June 1941 she had been away from Harwood for almost six years, and from her sisters many more, and surely realized she would never see them again. "There is an ache of longing in every direction at once," she told Harwood.[4] In addition, the wartime post was slow and irregular, with letters often taking more than a month to arrive.[5] Writing was a way both to transmit and relive the legacy of the past (to "keep its splendor gleaming around us always"),[6] and to channel the energy of her love and longing. "The Child" served to introduce her granddaughters to those "elect souls" (100), her husband and daughter, to their impressive circle of friends, their homes and travels, and, not incidentally, to Achsah herself.[7] By invoking Emerson's "The Poet" at the close of her memoir, she seems to come full circle, epitomizing Harwood's youth in the same words with which she had declared her love for Earl thirty-two years before: "And this is the reward, that the ideal shall become real to thee" (436; Schreiner 1987, 147)— her hope for her granddaughters as well.

In addition to its saga of an unusual family, "The Child" offers a vignette of a type that was to become common in the years after World War I: the American individual or family that combined a measure of financial independence with artistic and literary ambitions, social skills, and background, and the willingness—even the thirst—not only to emigrate from the States but also to move freely about Europe—and beyond. What emerges from "The Child" is a story both exemplary of a generation of American expatriates and also particular enough in its details to defy any typecasting: for in the distinctive character of their artistic quest and achievement, and in the extraordinary range of their friendships and experiences, the Brewsters remain originals.

As will be clear from our notes, "The Child" is uneven in quality and reliability: at many points Achsah's memory falters, especially when it comes to names and chronology, and her writing can become overwrought. At other times, however, her recollection of details is extraordinary, her writing as evocative, eloquent, and sardonic as it elsewhere can be precious. In the text printed here we have, as elsewhere in this book, corrected obvious minor errors and inconsistencies but have retained or specifically noted anomalies that seem of particular interest. Harwood at some point went through the entire typescript carefully, correcting errors where she saw them, revising sentences that were flawed, and in some cases filling out details that Achsah had omitted. Except in the case of routine corrections (typing, spelling, etc.), we have noted those passages in which we have accepted Harwood's emendations.

TO THE CHILD'S CHILDREN.

THE CHILD.

HARWOOD BARLOW BREWSTER:

A direct descendant of Elder William Brewster, scholar and leader of the Pilgrim Fathers, Harwood bore the Brewster look. Her character fulfilled the family motto:

VERITE SOYET MA GARDE

CHAPTER I.
[p. 3–4][8]

T H E   C H I L D

For who could live or breathe, if there were not this
delight of existence as the ether in which we dwell?
From Delight all these beings are born, by Delight they exist
and grow, to Delight they return.

—Taittiriya Upanishad.

Château Neuilly-sur-Seine.

The first time we, her parents, saw the Child she lay cuddled
on the scales, a round, dimpled rosiness with a smile, a rampant
tuft of gold hair and dark pencilings of nitrate of silver under her
round eyes.[9] Only the day before, Earl her father had said:

"If he is a boy, I shall have charge of him, but if it is a girl, she
is in your hands."

We gazed, the baby smiled enigmatically.

"She is like my Father," said her delighted mother.

"I think she looks like H. P. Blavatsky.[10] She already is a full-
blown personality," rejoined her father exultantly. So small, just
6 1/4 lbs. of round endimplement, so complete, so happy she
looked. During the month of waiting, to both her father and
mother, she had grown to be 'William Henry,' a puritan, scholar,
and leader, but here the Child was, a lovely rose, feminine and
sweet. We wanted to share her with her Grandfather Barlow
who had died four months earlier in Venice.[11]

Jean, Jeanne, Giovanna were discarded for names, but looking
out into the tall chestnut trees in the garden, I exclaimed:

"Harwood, her grandfather's middle name given for his
mother, Mary Harwood! How do you like that? Harwood Barlow
Brewster. It is sylvan and fresh, like the woods. She seems to
belong to the sunrise and green trees." Both of us felt that Harwood was her name.

Nurses and doctors dropped in frequently.

"What a lovely child, and you did not utter a sound!" said Dr.
Robert Turner, with pride.

"That's because we were reading Marcus Aurelius," and I
drew out a small blue volume from under my pillow. "This was
in my father's breast-pocket when he died, a gift from my husband Earl, marked with bits of rosemary. The baby would like
to give a copy of it to the Hospital library, for convalescents to
read."

When she was eight days old, her mother began to write a story for her, "The little Princess." The first person to call on her was her Aunt Persis Parker, visiting in Paris, who said:

"I dreaded seeing that baby, for I knew you'd expect me to admire it, but I really do, she's lovely!"

Aunt Villa Page[12] visiting Paris from New York came with Uncle Fred, Earl's old roommate, to see the new baby.[13]

Days went on. The baby knew perfectly how to find food when pressed to her mother's breast. The chateau garden swayed majestically; cool shadows and bright shafts of sun gave strength to mother and child.

CHAPTER II.
[p. 5]

16 Quai de Béthune.

The Child and her parents lived on the Ile St. Louis, 16 Quai de Béthune, on the top floor under a sky-light. Down below flowed the Seine with its fishermen; across the stream Pont Sully led into the Boulevard St. Germain. On the north end was a large studio window, showing roof pots and the Bastille. Wide was the view over Paris. Can it be that the Child has no memory of those wide, low skies of Paris, of the way in front of the grey buildings inscribed, "In this house lived Abelard and Heloise," the dark morgue, the open place before Nôtre Dame and the garden of Nôtre Dame where she lay in her white perambulator? It must have stirred some depth in her heart to cross from the Ile St. Louis under the plane trees and sycamores. Surely the immaculate red velvet carpets, the glistening white balustrade, mahogany rails and brass knobs of the hall forbidden to "service," sacred to gentlefolk, must linger in a crevice of the Child's mind! So, surely, the wattled basket worthy of Moses, with its dark green cover—she must remember still where she slept more quietly than a pet dog, a part of the beauty of that spacious studio with its carved Gothic chairs, richly cushioned in gold braided peacock silk, and the pomegranate crepe silk curtains which dragged gracefully on the floor in the sun, but rose two feet above when damp; and the gold screen, the mirror so high over the fire-place that it reflected the feet of people on the Boulevard St. Germain.

If a pin scratched her, and she cried, her mother played the

1st movement of Beethoven's Moonlight Sonata which soothed her instantly, without fail. . . .

CHAPTER VII.
[p. 19–21]

Carosiello.

Sometimes the Child sat on a tiny cane foot-rest, pensively nursing Betty, her calm eyes of grey like a moss agate jewel, with a gold band edging the pupil and the translucent cornea. Her eyes were quiet and deep-seeing, as if from the beginning she were aware that vision was a gift not dependent upon her searching, but upon her receiving truthfully.[14]

For the first night at Carosiello, she was restless and gnashed her teeth. We were anxious that she was nervous, but in the morning eight new teeth in one swoop showed in her gums. She never did things by half, not even teething. She was given a room for her own, and left to sleep in a bed alone, not a crib. For two nights there was a dull thud followed by a wail and quick comforting—then her room was her room. Her privacy and individuality were her birthright. The sense of self sufficiency was fostered in every way. One night we stole into her room and could not find her, until looking up, we saw she clung like a monkey to the top of the green blinds leading in from the balcony. . . .

Nina was like her father, with his same gentle, quiet deliberation and concentration. From the beginning, she knew wisdom and truth. If I really wished to know, I asked her and her response was always true for me. What she felt was clear and right, according to her nature and the eternal verities. Yes, she was like her father and that Elder Brewster from whom he sprang, a seeker and lover of the truth.

Earl Henry filled the house with good sounds. As he painted, he whistled and hummed, singing, "Our hearts are light, our skies are sunny, our pathway lies through fairyland." And truly it did, both the inward and outward path. His life was one following, rejoicing in and manifesting of beauty; the world was resplendent for him—changing—its loveliness inexhaustible. To look at sea, sky, mountains, to walk through the manifold glories of the scene held enough, a fulfillment of joy not only for him but for the little Harwood, like him. A boy, he was lithe and trim, with the grace of the sure gesture, the significant articulation, the balanced body on firm feet, those beautiful feet that never stumbled, but seemed to have a consciousness of their own as they lightly sprang up goat paths in the dark. At this time Earl was an ardent student of Buddhism, a stark Hinayanist. He was memorizing the Buddhistic psychology, the Abbhidammata San-gaha, and I would listen as he recited that section about "the Calm and Insight of the Holy Life," defining each lovely quality with the precision of the oriental psychologist.[15]

The days were happy, full of painting, communing with nature, studying, meditating and swimming. He was like the sea, wide, deep, open, clear and pure; so calm and tranquil, sensitive to every breeze. Unresistant apparently, yet carving everything into shape, even his wife. All three of us, Earl, Harwood and I were aimable [sic] by nature, preferring consent to dissent, acquiescing easily on minor issues, but strike rock bottom, neither Earl, Harwood nor I could be budged. Little things did not matter, but basic principles were unshaken by heaven or earth. . . .

CHAPTER VIII.
[p. 23–24]

Carosiello.

Shortly after our arrival at Carosiello, Uncle Fred Shaler joined us from Paris. He had two and sometimes three rooms on the second floor, one for a studio, for we plunged deeply into painting. Every day there would be three pictures started, and each of us was inspired by the work of the other two. We were thrilled and rejoiced by each new, eager attempt. In my canvas, little Harwood danced in the arms of fisher-girls near the town of Atrani. Earl painted hieratic crucifixions like ebony malachite, ivory and gold. Fred painted women bathing by the sea. They were fresh and full of hope, these paintings.

The days flew on, and Aunt Edith Lewis, my sophomore roommate at the Hatfield House, Smith College, came to visit us.[16] Aunt Edith was slender as a willow-wand, with brown eyes and brown curls. She still lisped if embarrassed, and she forgot all about herself in enjoying everyone and everything else, and seeing it with humour and philosophy. She must have had the charm and detached wisdom of Aspasia. With the rest of us she took to the water like a duck. She and I actually wore long black stockings, skirted bathing suits over bloomers and bathing caps—ducks though we were! Aunt Edith and I took the steamer from Amalfi for Capri, which did not return until the next day—my first night away from Nina. We loved every minute dashing over the sea past Capo Campanella, and the Isles of the Sirens, jolting uphill to Anacapri in our "carozza," and stopping at Eden Molari Hotel, looking over a vast view. . . .

We drove, walked, visited historical sites, read learned discourses and talked over all the girls in our class at Smith, and why they did as they did, and admired everything altogether, and loved it all tremendously, especially "Nina bella". . . .

CHAPTER XXI.
[p. 55–57]

Tolstoi.

Often I read to little Nina after her supper served on a tray in bed.[17] She and I both enjoyed a book of Tolstoi's short tales and fables. One evening, I had been reading about a girl, Marincha, who rescued a baby from the water and brought it up as her own child.[18] Harwood listened intently, and when we returned after dinner, she was not asleep as usual, but sitting up, her cheeks very red, reciting dramatically the story that she was repeating to herself:

"She was walking by the sea, and off on the water she saw something, so she went nearer and saw it was a basket, but could not see what was in the basket, so she waded into the water, and lifted the clothes and—there was a LITTLE BABY!" Harwood's voice broke with emotion, she clasped her hands ecstatically. Tolstoi had swept her away!

Francesco Franchetti brought his little son to see Harwood; also the Sfornis called and invited us there. They were living in their home on Piazza Donatello where Gustavo had his studio, and a collection of objets d'art, among them the finest Van Goghs and Cézannes, a Chinese statue of a red-lacquered Bodhisat, and all the paintings done by a certain friend. There were fabulous tales told of Gustavo's whims, such as his having a pet giraffe and cutting a hole through the roof so that the giraffe could hold his neck straight. Nina, his sister, came often to see us. We called her "Big Nina" to Harwood's "Little Nina." She was clear, simple, sincere and candid. We loved the Sfornis.

Franchetti also introduced us to a modern painter, Alberto Magnelli, who had a house down by the railroad. He was ultra modern, a friend of Picasso and Max Jacob, Giorgio di Chirico and one of the Italian "Valori Plastici" group. From him we

bought "Blast," Gaudier-Breszka's life by Ezra Pound, many
copies of the magazine "Valori Plastici," coloured stenciled papers which we pasted on to portfolios. Magnelli had the lower
part of his house filled with his paintings, while the upper rooms
held his beautiful carved Madonnas, old paintings, rare furniture, personal objects of exquisite workmanship. Magnelli had a
white English bull-dog, Ben. His brown hair hung in a round
bang across his broad brow. He was the Florentine craftsman,
and made Florence live for one. Many and vivid were his theo-
ries of art. He was always ahead of himself, so that he exhibited
last year's work and no criticism could sting, for he knew he had
already passed beyond that point in his development.[19]

At Smith College we had used Bernard Berenson's books on
art. Bernard Berenson's sister Rachel was in my class, and married our history of philosophy professor, Ralph Barton Perry,
while his sisters, Senda and Bessie, both taught Swedish gym-
nastics to the Smith girls. Here in Florence his villa, I Tatti, in
the direction of Settignano near Ponte a Mensola, held his choice
collection of art, which was generously opened to us. The beautiful villa amidst woods and wild country was spacious and comfortable, cheery with all its splendour, yet a real home with its
true heart in the library, a rarely complete one which made one
wish to linger in the arm-chairs by the open stone fireplace,
where ancient stone crocodiles once worshipped in Egypt long
ago were now used as fire-dogs. Above the fireplace was a grey
stone head of Buddha of great tranquility. Geoffrey Scott was
the private secretary and librarian. The Berensons gave us
many photographs by Andersen and Alinari of the masterpieces
in the Berenson collection. They were cordial, generously showing us the treasures all over the house, from Mrs. Berenson's
boudoir with its Titian Madonna, the drawing-rooms and long
hallways with Sienese altars by Verrocchio and Francia, to a
squat Chinese figure of a woman carved in pink stone, which
Mrs. Berenson pointed out as a likeness to Gertrude Stein.
Large, sweet and wholesome, Mrs. Berenson as a girl had been
invited by Walt Whitman for his joy: "Laugh, Mary, Laugh!" and
she never failed to do it, bubbling forth happily.[20]

We lunched by Sienese altars and tea-ed in the groves. Harwood came to play with Ursula and Stella, Mrs. Berenson's
grandchildren, and to their Christmas tree. Our life was enriched by them.

Low, Babylonian glass dishes were full of tea roses. The sun
caressed the marbles carved by Maillot in the hall. On a chest

near the entrance was an Egyptian cat, sculptured, slender and sleek, with lithe body and small head. In some bedrooms were high-keyed paintings by modern artists. When viewing these pictures, we were advised to go and see the Charles Loeser collection, especially his Cézannes.

CHAPTER XXXV.
[p. 90–91]

O, Rome, City of the Soul!

. . . Once in Rome,[21] we had our usual luck and found a studio, 54 Via Margutta, in the garden of the Circolo Artistico, where Maurice Sterne[22] had lived before us. We climbed up to the second story and out upon a balcony facing over the playground of a boys' school. All day their shouts burst out as football, basketball and other sports were enjoyed. Nina and I would hang over our iron-railed balcony watching them. We also could see into the school and watch the bright-eyed boys crossing the hall. Sometimes they smiled at us.

Oh, that beautiful studio, large, golden, with one wall opening in a great window over the Circolo garden; with a skylight, a high window gazing upon Villa Medici, residence for the French school for the Prix de Rome students, and spurting fountain where the sunset lingered, and the world turned to gold. Never could a window picture a more precious view! Earl exclaimed: "All it needs for that setting is a statue of the Buddha in meditation. I shall make one." And so he set to work, using mounds of plasticine which began to smile beneficently, at once blessing our studio. He knew from within what he wished to do, but desired to check it up from a model, yet found no one in Rome who could take the pose, as all the models had knees muscle bound. Earl, Harwood and I could sit for hours balanced cross-legged, and Earl and Harwood folded their feet back in a perfect "lotus asana."

Semprebene, a famous model exempted from military service because of his classic figure, could pose only one leg at a time, and that at an angle instead of lying flat.

Meanwhile, we were settled in our golden studio with a Bechstein upright piano and a brown majolica stove with an open grate, our books lining the walls and all ungainly objects concealed behind natural linen coloured curtains, black velvet couches, golden screen, our Bolognese refectory table in front of the wide window, a long nut chest below the Medici window where the Buddha eventually smiled down upon us, nut benches fastened by bolts in the manner of the table, and used for seats or tables. The chairs were upholstered by Earl and me, a papal chair in rose brocade, two armchairs in gold brocade and the cushion covers from Florence. On one wall hung a six-foot mural of Gethsemane I had painted after visiting San Domenico's sacred grotto. There was a painting of Earl holding baby Nina, as St. Antonio and the Christ Child. Paintings by Earl of the Buddha, afterwards with Marjorie Wise at 118 Grosvenor Road, and an upright Buddha with a pool and gazelles now owned by Mr. Randhawa, I. C. S., hung over the couches.[23] Some black majolica bowls with handles, and large jars were beautiful in the gold room. Flowers from the Spanish stairs brightened all. It was a joyful surprise to enter that large, welcoming studio.

The entrance from the balcony where wraps and fuel were kept, in the hall, was curtained off, and there was a room where Harwood and Giuseppina slept, Harwood in a lovely brass bedstead supplied by Theodora Synge,[24] and Giuseppina in a trundle-bed pulled out by night.

That was where we ostensibly lived, but Rome was truly the city of our soul, and our friends were the heart of our heart, "cor cordium."[25]

CHAPTER XLVI.
[p. 111–12]

Fifi.

. . . When we first came to our studio in Rome, we brought with us from Villa Pestellini Lina, reliable, honest, religious. . . . She was a Waldensian by persuasion, the stuff from which martyrs are made. Her brother was also Waldensian, "a god-fearing man and preacher of the gospel," as were his wife and little daughter. Their self respect bordered on spiritual pride. Lina moved from a sense of duty, she did everything because she felt she ought to, never because it was fun. She unconsciously taught me to admire hedonism. She looked so grave and determined to be good however difficult it might be. One day, firmer than ever, she announced that she felt it her duty to marry a certain Waldensian clergyman, although she had not seen him. He was a widower with nine children who needed a mother. So we gave her some silver spoons and our blessings. Life was much lighter and gayer after she left. Shortly, she called to say that after seeing her clergyman he had changed his mind and found another mother for his dear children—but she kept her wedding spoons![26] Yet Lina was a mystic, and taught Harwood that "Jesus was in her heart." Harwood seemed to visualise a full-grown man in a white shirt, standing up in her heart.

It was shortly before Theodora moved to the Strohferni that I was engaged in painting a small mural of the Baptism of Christ for which I had a nude model to correct my drawing. The Child, as always, walked freely and unconcernedly, playing about. In the afternoon, we were all invited for tea at Theodora's, especially Harwood was asked, who was a favourite. After tea, when we were settled back for a chat, Theodora brought out a pad and some coloured chalks for Harwood to draw, and arranged a low table and chair where she at once became engrossed in drawing. No one paid any attention, until Theodora finally picked up the picture to look. "No, it goes the other way. That's his head." Turning it about one could see the head, both full, front and in profile. The arms were folded over the breast as in the pose I had been studying. There was a neat dot for the navel. Below it, something dangled down.

"What's that?" asked Theodora.

"Oh I don't know. That was how it went on Mother's model." Theodora laid down the drawing and changed the subject.

CHAPTER LXI.
[p. 145–46]

The Six-year-old.

Harwood's cheerfulness was the gift of the sunlight. The air sufficed for her inspiration. She was her father's daughter—that father who as a baby, when first shown to his grandfather Chapman, was scrutinized gravely and then the old man exclaimed: "Shiner!" Earl has lived up to that name, and the shine has gleamed around him always.

Harwood was staunchly truthful with an honour of the mind, who "listens to the Eternal Voice is delivered from many an opinion." She was not glib, but she knew as a small child the great effort and patient renewal of effort, day after day, to learn to read. She knew instinctively, as every unspoiled child does, the best in contradistinction to the mediocre. Annotations and explanations are superfluous to some minds, the axiom being a self-evident fact, the answer to a question implicit in asking it. One never felt like talking down to Harwood. In the first place, she did not say "Yes" if she meant "No," or if she had a shadow of doubt.

She was fearless and full of courage. She trusted everyone, and she responded to the truth; no false glitter deceived her.

Sincerity and simplicity and a recognition of truth were distinguishing traits already in our six-year-old. It gave her an integrity of character that sat well with her square shoulders and firmly planted feet. . . .[27]

CHAPTER CXXVIII.
[p. 266]

Paris re-visited.

The gold plats of leaves lingered on the plane trees on the islands, knobs of brown buttons dangled from the spotted sycamores. The sun shone in a mellow glow. Out in the Tuileries, birds flocked around the old man who fed them, pecking up crumbs, perching on his head, his shoulder, eating from his hands. Harwood and I kept near him, like the twittering birds. Under our windows, on the top floor, Paris extended. Pont Neuf swung over the busy river. Bookstalls lined Quai de Voltaire. We were at Hôtel Quai de Voltaire, hanging out from our balconies, looking at the Louvre among gardens.

Up and down the river moved boats carrying cargoes, houseboats where curtains fluttered and pots of flowers bloomed and washing flapped on a line over tousled children. Horses were led to water, bathed, curried. Mattresses were freshly filled. Groups of people loitered at the bookstalls looking for treasures, but it needs wisdom to recognize worth. The old woman in her black knitted hood and hand warmer felt little thrilled by her junk.

A comfortable smell of the provinces pervaded the hotel, beeswax, in O-cedar polish mopped about by Louis, the "valet-de-chambre," moving silent in his black felt slippers and his green baize apron in the morning, until he changed to his smart red jacket. Madame herself, a rosy widow, sat at the "caisse" and kept her eye on those who came and went, on the fruit baskets with each pear counted, and a ribbon handle on the box. Probably anyone who ever tasted the joys of the hotel returned, at least until Madame had it done over "with all the comforts."[28]

Harwood always belonged in Paris. She had been born there

on a clear August day when horsechestnuts waved against a pure white sky. . . .[29]

CHAPTER CXXIX.
[p. 268–71]

Kidnapping Harwood.
    . . . What happy times we had with Harwood in Paris.[30] Our special joy was the Luxembourg where we sat with rows of children and heard Punch squeak and rant at Judy, and the children roar with laughter. We ate "gaufrettes," waffles browned for us while we waited, and sprinkled over with powdered sugar. We licked ice-cream cones. We looked at all the pictures in Paris, and held the Louvre as our own. Victory sailed over us every time we trudged upstairs, winged, flying. Black, mysterious Egyptians in basalt bent their heads on their knees, lost in unfathomable meditation. We walked through the Tuileries, under the Arc de Triomphe, on under the Eiffel Tower. The wind was blowing and it creaked and rocked. I suggested we take the elevator and go up. For the first time Harwood was frightened, something in her revolted against machinery, her lips quivered, tears came to her eyes. No, she did not want to go there.
    The Trocadero gardens and fountains were often favoured by us, and the ethnological museum with its villages and life portrayed in rich detail, its collections of utensils and costumes and works of art, we studied with pleasure. We went up to the Lion de Belfort and visited the Gobelin tapestry weavers.
    We enjoyed most of all going up the river in the little, churning boats, stopping at all the landings and finally getting down at the end to walk in the Bois de Boulogne.
    Sèvres, Ville d'Avray, and St. Cloud, Versailles, the chestnut trees and fountains, the gardens—we loved all of them. The great palace halls, crystal chandeliers and ceremonial pictures were pomp and circumstance. We liked the small, hidden private suites to which Marie Antoinette retired, and the theatre with its "mise-en-scène" piled there still. The Petit Trianon and the Moulin du Beurre where the poor, little shepherdesses played at playing among the flowers and trees, reminders of how little most people inherit the earth, forgetting to enjoy immortality.
    We were asked to call on Mr. and Mrs. Jan Hambourg who had bought an 18th century chateau at Ville d'Avray.
    Jan was a violinist, a pupil of Ysaye, and like Mozart, had

been an infant prodigy, delighting public audiences in his velvet suits and lace collars, and the sad thoughtful gaze of his gazelle eyes. Even his baby pictures looked like a stricken deer. Perhaps he had served music so arduously, so long, that he wished to be freed from compulsion, and public demands, to play only for the love of it on his rare violin. His father had a music conservatory. Mark, his eldest brother, was the pianist; Boris the 'cellist,[31] all famous musicians. His wife, Isabelle McClung, was Willa Sibert[32] Cather's beloved friend, whose sympathetic appreciation of Willa's genius kept it burning. As Willa often said:

"If there had been no Isabelle, I never would have continued writing."

Isabelle was the daughter of a doctor in Cherry Falls, near Pittsburgh.[33] She had deep, blue eyes of endless depth like the summer sky and sea, her cheeks were bright and her hair black, her voice tender. She made life lovely, full of beauty.

From Gare St. Lazare we set out, one evening, for Ville d'Avray, magic name, calling up the magnificence of Louis XIV and of "Les Jardies," the villa of Honoré Balzac. There was a fine rain and wisps of mist as we left the suburban station and plunged down onto the dark, muddy road between dripping banks. It seemed ages before we reached the chateau gates and were let into the garden where horsechestnuts waved to us, over a brook, the English waterway, as they called it grandiloquently. Giotto, the Alsatian pup, frisked down the path to welcome us, and we were in the lovely home, with its intense velvet blue carpets like Isabelle's tender eyes.

Sammy, a pupil studying under Jan, was living with them, a boy of twelve or thirteen, who had ability.

Our visits to the chateau were frequent and delightful. Harwood loved Isabelle and Jan, and liked to luxuriate over the "week-ends" in their exquisite appurtenances. Isabelle let Harwood wear her daffodil silk negligée with ruches of flower petals like chrysanthemums bordering it deliciously, and her dainty slippers edged with ostrich feathers. Harwood, who rejected all finery for herself, liked to have delicate underclothes and bedroom details. She loved Isabelle's brand of soap and bath salts. Yes, Isabelle was altogether sweet and lovely with Harwood.

Jan's warm, enthusiastic appreciations made everything worthwhile. His talk was quick with vision, his literary acumen delightful. He discoursed on Herman Melville at length, a foe to "Booby Dick," as he would call the white whale.

CHAPTER CXXX.
[p. 271–72]

Little Parisian.

Willa Cather came to see Isabelle, and to be in the heart of Paris they stayed at Quai Voltaire.³⁴ We saw much of them to our joy. At evensong we would go to Nôtre Dame while the lights twinkled on the altars, and the organ rolled through the high arches, and the last amethyst glow faded from the rose windows. Harwood felt especially drawn to St. Jeanne d'Arc on her prancing charger. She loved the little French Madonna, so chic and sweet.

Aunt Willa and Isabelle took Harwood to a matinée performance of Ibsen's Peer Gynt, her first taste of the theatre. She whirled back glowing with enthusiasm:

"Oh!" said Harwood, "You should have seen Anitra dancing!" In her nightgown she whirled and pirouetted, frisking out her legs and pointing her pink toes in a twirl of ecstasy, worthy of a dancing dervish. She could now visualize Grieg's music. . . .

CHAPTER CXXXI.
[p. 274–75]

The Hardens.

. . . After long debate, we decided to have an exhibition in Chéron's gallery One Rue de [la] Boetie, opposite the Salle Gaveau. The three galleries were well hung, and had many visitors. Elmer bought a black bronze of Earl's Buddha, and my painting of the Cowherd, and both were put into Pierre's studio. Earl gave him also a Buddha with deer and Hina, and I a Madonna done with Urbino setting. Willa Cather bought Earl's "Blue Nigger" for Jan and Isabelle Hambourg, and it was hung as the centre of the lovely salon at the Ville d'Avray chateau.³⁵

CHAPTER CLIV.
[p. 306]

Books.

Harwood had always inclined to science, or literature that showed epic character, not romantic fiction, but she enjoyed stoic and religious teachings. Thus it was that she was supplied with a complete French edition of Le Fabre which she prized, beginning with "Mon Oncle Paul." She was reading at that time George Sand's "Fanchon, the Cricket," and Daudet's autobiography, "Le Petit Chose." She had St. Francis' Fioretti[36] and "The Imitation of Christ." She steered clear of English novels. Later, she had told us because she believed we did not wish her to read them, which was not the case, unless she divined that we felt life itself and direct communing with nature was more than any book could open to her. She was like the child Samuel indeed, and heard the voice of God. She contemplated serenely.

CHAPTER CLXI.
[pp. 314–16]

Paris again.

Hôtel Quai de Voltaire had been garnished in our absence. Madame had added what she deemed modern conveniences, and had married again. In every room there were now set bowls for hot and cold water. Central heating gurgled and steamed through gilt pipes, but we cleaved to our fireplaces and baskets of fragrant wood.

There were Aunt Ida Harden, Elmer, Emily and Pierre, better than ever.[37] There were the Hambourgs at Ville d'Avray and even Willa Cather was once more in Paris with the returning horsechestnut blossoms.[38]

The little Harwood was pleased to return to Mlle. Marie and Mlle. Marguerite, to Grandmère and "petit Jacques," and the school on Rue de Lille. They made her feel welcome and she loved them all. Harwood was never so much the scholar and student. She never viewed life from the intellectual angle, but mystically, even mistily, she apprehended more than she attempted to explain. Like Keats, she stood in her shoes and she wondered, and that can be great fun, she found.

Aunt Willa spent some time at the hotel and some at the chateau with the Hambourgs, who had fitted a study for her in which to write, beautifully equipped, hung with long puce silk curtains in solemn folds.[39]

We had various feasts. Elmer gave a magnificent banquet at "La Perouse" for Willa and all, in the perfect way he knew, each detail a delight. Oh those beautiful Epicurean meals we enjoyed in Elmer's expansive generosity! Willa was having her portrait painted by the Russian ballet artist, Bakst, for a ladies' guild in Red Cloud, Nebraska,[40] where she had lived at one time. We were busy over our second art exhibition at Chéron's. Pierre's fine translation of our introduction was in front of our book of monographs. The pictures were well hung, and the galleries were full of appreciative people.

Earl's bronze Buddha smiled beneficently, and my mural of the Sermon on the Mount showed to advantage. Marie Leschetizky, the musician's widow,[41] brought the Archbishop of Paris to the exhibition, and he had the mural placed permanently at the beautiful 3rd century Gothic church of St. Georges at Crécy-en-Brie, the Venice of France with canals and waterways, where the Battle of the Marne ended.[42]

My altar painting of St. Jeanne d'Arc listening to angelic presences among her sheep was placed in a chapel.[43] The curé was a benign old gentleman with courtly grace, serving us a repast with wines and pâté de foie gras, giving us many pictures of the charming town and its historic church.

Admiral Edoard of the U. S. Navy, a grandson of Napoleon Buonaparte, bought a picture of a child in a tree, one of my paintings inspired by Harwood, the tree climber.

Dorothy Wilde, niece of Oscar Wilde, bought Earl's first sketch in oil for the moving picture of the crucifixion.

Dorothy Canfield[44] was full of appreciation. She knelt down before the picture, and wept, saying:

"And such beauty was born from the U. S. . . . . !"

CHAPTER CLXII
[p. 316–17]

All aboard for America.

Then off we sailed for our native land with the Hardens, delightful traveling companions.[45] We sat in a row on deck, and talked hours on end, and at every meal drank tisanes, camomile or Vervaine or "Tilleul" with lemon and sugar. Earl listened while Emily told David Garnett's "Lady into Fox"[46] in her silvery voice, her beautiful hands joining to its imagery, entrancing Earl.

We passed iridescent icebergs. At last through the mist we saw the Statue of Liberty rise from the waters, holding her torch. It was Decoration Day when we reached New York City. Aunt

Edith Lewis was at the landing, and off we drove waving au re-
voir to the Hardens, to Greenwich Village, 5 Bank Street, where
Edith and Willa lived. We were only too often mutually exclusive, tucking in where Willa had left for the time. This was near
old camping ground, 60 South Washington Square, where Edith
and Willa used to live, and close to 42 South Washington Square,
where Earl and Fred Shaler had their studio. From an open window a curtain blew out, and two youthful heads, a wavy brown
haired one, beside a straight, dark haired young man, leaned
over the sill, looking at the fountain in the park, and the people
thronging through the arch onto Fifth Avenue, this Decoration
Day. Changeless, change, the same boys still pursuing art in the
same old quarters, with the same ideals![47]

Edith and Willa's quiet upper apartment seemed remote and
full of peace. Bits of the past from our room in the Hatfield
House, Smith College, from South Washington Square, pictures
painted by Earl and me on the walls, and treasures from Mrs.
Fields's Boston home and Sarah Orne Jewett enriching the
book-lined rooms. A drawing of George[48] Sand looked out, wide-
eyed, over the fireplace. It all looked right to us. Harwood gazed
around contentedly. So this was America, she seemed to be
asking.

We had left our native land on our honeymoon, and here we
were back with a stalwart "Brewster buffalo."

Claude Washburn was in the city, and while Edith was occupied, we visited Chinatown, eating chop suey, buying Chinese
treasures and enjoying ourselves with him. Claude took us to the
theatre. We motored on top of buses and gazed at the gay, Babylonian throngs of the New York streets, struck dumb at the
transformations during our absence. Even the trees in Central
Park had shrunken after Versailles.

CHAPTER CLXIII.
[p. 317–19]

Willa. April Twilights.

It was not until the autumn of 1903 that I met Willa Cather.
She was a celebrity in my eyes, having published a novel, "Alexander's Bridge," poems, "April Twilights"[49] and a forthcoming
volume of Short Stories, "The Troll Garden."[50]

Edith had come to New York City to work on the Century Di-
rectory, and had taken a room at 60 South Washington Square

with her mother's friend, Willa Cather.[51] Weekends Edith and I spent together, usually one Sunday with me at 306 West 56th, the next Sunday at South Washington Square. Willa's pictures and photos were enthroned on Edith's chiffonière. In one, a vivid young person was perched on a table insouciantly, arranged carefully by the photographer in the prevailing fashion of looking "easy and off-hand." It was a fascinating picture to me, frank, thoughtful, forceful, young and eager.

I remember the first time I saw Willa, rustling out to a dinner party in a shimmering rose charmeuse satin and an opera cloak. We hung over the bannister to watch her sweep down the hall majestically—that dingy hall of 60 South Washington Square that she describes in "Coming, Aphrodite."[52] Willa's eyes were like jewels, clear moss agates of grey and olive edged with gold, the cornea of crystalline clearness and lighted from within. She spoke slowly, hesitating for the word she wanted because she would not be satisfied with a makeshift, but sought to capture some hidden truth. One listened for every significant word.

Those times in Paris when Harwood, Willa and I heard Vespers in Nôtre Dame cathedral, near the altar to the Virgin, where tapers flickered, are full of the essential quality of the Willa Cather to whom I pay homage. The visits on the terraces of Château Brun, St. Cyr,[53] were precious revelations of the depth and sincerity of her nature, which was the reason that Harwood and she understood each other so well.

It has seemed to me that some fragrance of the Child, Harwood, exhales from the child, Cécile, in "Shadows on the Rock."

As we were sailing for home, she gave us her "April Twilights and Other Poems," inscribed:

"To accompany the Brewsters on the long Voyage home—they do not know how long it is! The verse on Page 65 is theirs already, for they were both very much in my mind on the afternoon last summer when I wrote it.

Willa Cather.
Ville d'Avray.
May 16th. 1923."[54]

It seemed that the opinion of the Times Literary Supplement held this verse in highest esteem of all in the book, in which we wholly agreed. They were something to live up to in the fullness of heart.[55]

CHAPTER CCXIII.
[p. 433–36]

Dartington Hall.

Tantine,[56] Harwood and I set off for school together from Stratford-on-Avon.

I think back on that journey southwards to a brighter sky and bluer sea where white sails danced on the water.[57] The little daughter of my heart gazed out of the window onto the unknown world. Like "The Spirit Ariel," perhaps weeping too, "when you remember how he loved you, desired to leave you, always both at once."[58]

Past the red headlands and rocks jutting into the blue water of Torquay, the train puffed along, past children playing on the sands, on to Totnes on the Dart river, ancient bed of England's culture from where Drake and Raleigh turned "Westward Ho."

We were at Dartington Hall, and a new life! I was to go away alone from Dartmouth on my way back. In the glass-domed station of Berne while waiting for trains, a boy on military service came bare-headed, a knapsack on his back and friends around him. He threw back his head and sang in ringing tone, then pealed into a yodel that echoed through the arcade while everyone listened spellbound to his farewell.

We were at Dartington now. Harwood was leaving us. Like the "Departure of the Prodigal Son":

> Now to depart from all those hopes and fears,
> That we call ours, but which are not our own,
> Giving like water in the ancient weirs,
> A troubled urge by the breezes blown;
> From all that in our progress through the years
> Has clung to us like brambles, to depart
> And with a start
> To notice things that one had failed to see
> Familiarized through long habituation
> And then with tender reconciliation
> Close at the very source surmisingly
> To comprehend the whelming desolation,
> The inexorable impersonality
> Of all that grief the Child had to withstand:
> And then still to depart, hand out of hand,
> As though you tore a wound that had been healing,
> And to depart: whither? To unrevealing
> Instance, to some warm, unrelated land,

That back-clothwise, will stay without all feeling,
Behind all action, garden, sea or sand;
And to depart: why? Impulse, generation,
Impatience, obscure hope and desperation
Not to be understood or understand:
To take all this upon you, and in strife
To lose perhaps, all that you had, to die
Alone and destitute, not knowing why—
Is this the entrance into some new life . . . ?

Rainer Maria Rilke

For me, Dartington Hall is a radiant rainbow shining from earth to heaven, beautiful to behold, built on the beauty of selfless ideals.

Forests of beech trees flaunt silver feet into the hillsides, over the river where the birds fly and the children play. Rich farm lands are cultivated and experimented by the workers at "Dartiton 'All," who sing in the chorus when the music is not set to "Latin words and the Pope!"

The central quadrangle has the architectural beauty of Magdalen College, the Hall itself noble. Buildings dating from the 9th to the 14th century surround the green lawns.[59] The same gardens and jousting field of the same estate where Geoffrey Chaucer was once the clerk and secretary spread around the Hall. Splendid as it is, refreshing to the eye, it gladdens the heart still more to find altruism realizing its fondest dream of letting children grow freely.

And this was the school where Harwood was to spend two years of idyllic happiness; where she had dreaded going more than anything in her life, where she spent her happiest days. . . .

Emerson must have had youth in mind when he wrote "The Poet," so surely does it describe young things, particularly the Child, Harwood.

"And this is the reward, that the ideal shall be real to thee, and the impressions of the summer rain copious, but not troublesome to thy invulnerable essence. Thou shalt have the whole land for thy park and manor, the sea for thy bath and navigation, without tax and without envy; the woods and the rivers thou shalt own; and thou shalt possess that wherein others are only tenants and boarders.

Thou true landlord! Sea-lord! Air-Lord! Wherever snow falls or water flows, or birds fly, wherever day and night meet in twilight, wherever the blue heaven is hung by clouds, or sewn with stars, wherever are forms with transparent boundaries, wherever are outlets into celestial space, wherever is danger and awe and love, there is Beauty, plenteous as rain, shed for thee, and though thou shouldest walk the world over, thou shalt not be able to find a condition inopportune or ignoble."[60]

Achsah Barlow
Brewster [hand-
written]

7

Selections from "Fourteen Years of My Adventures" by Harwood Brewster Picard

INTRODUCTION

Harwood Brewster began writing her memoirs before the voyage home from India to Europe in December 1926. A diary entry from the second day aboard ship reads, "woke up breakfast meditated dressed wrote went up on deck heard daddys cretisem on Don Gopals book & wrote."[1] She had turned fourteen in Almora that August, and seemed to enjoy her family's lengthy sojourn in India far more than did either of her parents.[2] After nine months of visiting temples, bazaars, remote hilltowns, and crowded cities, studying Sanskrit with Earl and conducting scientific experiments with Boshi Sen, perhaps she felt an instinctive need to channel this excess of mental and sensory stimulation while confined to the ship. Her parents' disciplined schedule of study and painting, and their enthusiastic encouragement of all such activity, created an atmosphere in which artistic effort was simply a given. Already five years earlier, at age nine, Harwood had shared with D. H. Lawrence a small book filled with her one-page stories (Brewster 1934, 244; Picard 1926, 69 [1st series]); in addition, she and the Reynolds sisters had produced a weekly newsletter, "Genius Burning," since 1924. Her memoir, though, was a far more ambitious enterprise, which required a structure and ordering of the past reaching back to her earliest memories.

"Fourteen Years of My Adventures" is a straightforward chronological narrative, nearly 170 pages long, divided into more than two dozen chapters. Not surprisingly, in view of the Brewsters' peripatetic existence, each chapter is named for a house, street, or city (e.g., "Roccabella," "Via Margutta, Rome," "Chagrin Falls"), according to the sequence of her family's travels and relocation. For those periods when they were actually in transit,

169

she uses "Going Around Italy," "Voyage to Athens," or "S. S. Osterly."

Her buoyant self-confidence, independence, and good humor are evident throughout, beginning with the title page, signed "Harwood B. Brewster, L.D., B.B. Etc." She had Achsah's capacity to enjoy herself practically everywhere, with everyone; when she wasn't having fun, she was frank about that as well. Her detailed accounts of the studio on Via Margutta, the trips to Greece and the United States, and the layout of Quattro Venti enhance those in "The Child" (and illustrate her training-by-osmosis in acute observation), but also reflect the charming ease with which a teenager handles an abundance of material: simply include everything. She remembers the first tree she climbed (11) as clearly as her visits to Socrates's prison on the Acropolis (45). Earl and Achsah's adult voices are occasionally audible, as when Harwood seems to repeat comments that she probably heard from them: that the dentist in Sorrento was rude to Achsah (23); that the Neapolitan dukes and duchesses in their Sant' Agata hotel "were really very low class people who had bought their titles or something of the sort" (24); that their servant, Amabilia, "was rather rough and very much of a peasant" (31). There was the opportunity, too, for an occasional settling of accounts, as in her recollection of their friend Major Fraser, who "was always very nice to me and liked me better than the little girls that used to come to the hotel and that wore bows on their heads bigger than themselves" (23).

Sixteen years later, when Achsah was immersed in "The Child," Earl recalled Harwood's early memoir and inquired, "I hope no accident has befallen to your early memoirs written by yourself and that you keep them safely. I look forward to reading them again some day" (EHB to HBP 1/1/42). He would have delighted to hear in them once more the young voice of his cheerful, feisty, game daughter, equally conversant with playmates and Pallas Athena, and clearly enthralled with the daily adventure of their lives.

I. First Memorys
Carosciello
[March 1914–August 1916]
[p. 1–3 (1st series)]

The first memory I have is of having my picture taken with some other children.[3] We were bathing in the sea by a beach that belonged to the house where we were then living. The house overlooked the bay of Salerno and was [near] the village of Amolfi. The Father of these children was a man who called himself a pilgrim. He wore a white shirt. It made him look like some of the pictures of Christ. He would not bath in the sea because he wanted to go in naked as he said it was insulting the sea to go in with cloths on. But it was the rule not to go bathing without something on. The rocks out in the water seemed to me very far then. I also remember that on the way to the beach there was a little stone house where we changed our clothes. To go to the beach from the house one went through a small tunal and how I did enjoy going through it. Frinds often came to stay with us for visits. . . . I was only two or three when these things hapened. In the garden belonging to the house were orchards of lemons, oringes and also many grape vines. . . . The gardener and his wife had an old sarasenic tower to live in. There was also another grop of gardeners whos children came to my secound therd and fourth bithdays. I went to their house once. They sleeped four in one bed. Two at the bottom and two at the top! When they came to my birth day parties, they would bring me huge bunches of flowers. I never went out of the garden. There was no need to. Our garden was very big. The servants would take me about for walks in it. Just near the house in the garden was a beautiful big Caruba tree. Under it was a great stone table where we had our meals. My father had the carpenter make me some wooden blocks and then he painted them. On one side he painted a number, on another side a letter and colours on the other sides. There were some long shaped blocks some squar and some tringulare. The colours on them were lovely. Just to watch my father paint them gave me great pleausre. There was a window shaped like [a] cross in the house which I looked at very often.

Athens
[January 1920]
[p. 45–47 (1st series)]

We went to a very nice hotel that had many halls, all beautifully carpeted, with lovely Greek carpets.[4] We had one big room and I slept on a couch between two windows. It was there that one night I woke up when it was full moon and for the first time saw the face in the moon. We used to go to the Acropolis nearly every evening. I remember we went to what is said to be Socrates prison which is quite near the Acropolis.

We went through a woody walk to get there and a little dog kept barking at us. Another time, we went up a hill behind Socrates' prison and at the top, we found a column. It was so windy and cold that we went home quite soon that day. We also walked along the little river Lyssos where Socrates and Phaedrus once walked and to the stadium where I played hotel. That is, each seat was a room and I would run up the aisles and wait on imaginary people or Mother or Father. . . .

There was one shop where we bought many lovely post card[s]. One day, after they had just bought a good, big pile, the shop keeper showed me a post card of Pallas Athena, the goddess of wisdom and said, "If you can tell me who this is, I will give you the post card." Being my favourite goddess, I knew at once who the post card was of and told him, so he gave me the card very pleased that I had answered correctly. I even now have the card. . . .

We left in ten days because it was so cold, very expensive and we could not find a house to stay in. Another joke is that one day, after Mother and Father had been hunting very hard for a house and could not find one, I said, "I know we can live in the Parthenon!"

Kandy

[January–May 1922]

[p. 105 (1st series), p. 1–2 (2nd series)]

I went to school with Daddy early in the morning.[5] It used to be lovely then. We would be above the clouds and then walk down into the damp and mist. We would take a small bridge over the end of the lake and pass the tennis courts where all the English people would be playing tennis for their morning exercise. We would then climb up the hill and I would go to my school and Daddy to his. How I hated mine! I would arrive and have to stand in my place among all the other children in a huge hall. Then the head mistress would call our names and we would have to say that we were present. Then a teacher would look at our finger nails to see that they were clean because one day a little girl had said that she was so glad to be moving to another grade from the kindergarten because then she wouldn't have to clean her finger nails. That always made me mad that we should suffer because of that silly child.

We then all went to church and then lessons began and finally at half past eleven my ayah came for me. I say finally because all the teachers were horrid to me and told me that I ought to be ishamed not to read or spell better than all the Singhalese children being an American. But I didn't see it that way. I didn't see why children that had been learning how to spell from the age of two shouldn't spell better than myself who had never really studied spelling. . . .

Uncle David and Aunt Frieda, the Lawrences, came a short time after we had been in the house.[6] Aunt Frieda had Daddy's room, Uncle David the spare bed room and Daddy slept in Mother's room. We had straw beds or rather couches which we turned into beds. They were very uncomfortable and we decided then that we would never again economise on beds. One good thing about them was that we could move them about easily and so in the day time we would bring them out on to the veranda and have bright coloured cushions on them.

At night, it used to be quite terrifying to hear a great cocoanut leaf fall or a hard mango fall onto our tin roof. What a noise they did make! It was like a cannon going off! We had oil lamps which used to smoke a great deal. I used to have my supper in bed and Mother would read "Swiss Family Robinson"[7] to me. One day I gave my ayah the old doll Mother and Father had given me in Rome, Margheritucia. She was old and very much broken up but my ayah was delighted to have it for her little black baby. . . .

[Paris]
[October–December 1922]
[p. 15–16 (2nd series), p. 1 (3rd series)]

. . . [W]e went on to Paris, to the Hotel Quai Voltaire, a very quaint little place.[8] Our rooms were quite nice and looked over the river with the Louvre on the other side. We had very little and very simple food at this hotel but good. It generally consisted of fried potatoes, or potatoes done in some form or other, an omelet, some very good green salad and an apple or some fruit. The people were also quite nice and some we made friends with. . . .

On my free days, I went to the Louvre and other museums and

galleries and gardens, all of which I enjoyed very much. We also sometimes went to see the Hambourgs who lived outside of Paris at Ville d'Avray.[9] They had a very lovely house and garden. They had a beautiful police dog and also some cats. Mr. Hambourgh played the violin very beautifully. I always loved going there. There were bright blue carpets and sometimes Mother and I would rest in her room for a little before lunch and Mrs. Hambourg would lend me a darling neglige with a scolloped bottom. They had an Italian cook and were very fastidious about their food so that it was naturally very good.

Ville d'Avray was on the way to Versailles. I thought the palace and the gardens wonderful and loved going there. I particularly loved all the fountains and the ball room with all the mirrors.

Mother and Father gave an exhibition of their paintings which I enjoyed seeing very much. They certainly filled a large room with their work.

Paris
[September–November 1923]
[p. 38–39 (3rd series)]

I tried painting in oils and made a sketch of the Seine and the Louvre on a gray day.[10]

Willa Cather was in Paris. She was staying with the Hambourgs so once or twice she came and stayed in my room while I was in school. She left six beautiful handkerchiefs with my initials on them. We used to go out to Ville d'Avray quite often to see the Hambourgs and Aunt Willa.

Then I started to have some violin lessons with Sammy, a young boy of seventeen. Mr. Hambourg had been teaching him to play and he lived with him. Sam played very well and used to come on Thursdays to give me lessons.

One day Mother took me to [the] Eiffel Tower. I had never been up [and had] been longing to go. But when we came and stood right under that immense construction, I was terrified and said that I would rather not go. Mother was very surprised but we didn't go up and I haven't been even now.[11]

Mother and Father gave another exhibition of their work in the same gallery they had the year before. We used to go to many exhibitions and shows. I remember seeing a very good collection of paintings by Gauguin. And then I remember going to the Petit

Palais and to the Grand Palais. There I remember seeing some paintings by Mother and Father, hung.

Capri
[December 1923–spring 1924]
[p. 41–42, 50 (3rd series)]

Christmas was full of excitement and secresy.[12] Everyone was doing something for everyone else. Doors were locked and you had to tell your name before entering. On Christmas we had a beautiful tree, most beautifully and richly decorated. Daddy dressed as Santa Claus. We all had beautiful presents. I had several very lovely silks which Aunt Emily[13] made into dresses for me later. It was all great fun and in the evening we all dressed up. I painted myself a reddish brown, wore some little bathing suit, did my hair in two long braids with ribbons in them and a crown of feathers around my head all painted different colours. I wore many necklaces and carried a real and very large bow and arrows that Antonino[14] had procured for me. This was quite a good costume but slightly cool for a winter day. Mother was marvelous. She dressed up like an old negress with various coloured handkerchiefs tied around her. Daddy was an Arab. They both darkened their faces. . . .

On New Year's morning, I woke up and found a marvelous box full of sweets outside my door. . . .

The girls came back from England[15] and were so glad to get some bathing in. We decided to have a little paper that would come out every week. One afternoon, we sat out on the terrace off Mother and Father's room and discussed what the paper should be called, how it should be brought out and what sort of things we should write for it. . . . We finally decided to call it "Genius Burning" but we didn't know how to spell it and so called down stairs to where Mother was having a party and asked how it was spelled. From then on, we brought out G. B., as we called it for short.[16]

8

Selections from "To Frances and Claire Some Memories of Your Grandparents Earl Henry Brewster and Achsah Barlow Brewster by Your Mother Harwood Barlow Brewster Picard"

INTRODUCTION

Harwood Brewster Picard composed her second memoir at Masera, Italy, in 1977. Perhaps returning to the country of her youth provided the impetus, five decades after her first attempt, to document once again the Brewsters' lives. She was sixty-five at the time, about Achsah's age when "The Child" was written, and her mother's memoir was clearly the inspiration for her own, down to the dedicatory title. She must have consulted both "The Child" and "Fourteen Years of My Adventures" to refresh her memory (she mentions neither),[1] though readily admits that, given the many years of accumulated family lore, it was difficult to distinguish her own recollections from "a memory of someone else's memory" (1).

Just as Achsah had presented to Claire and Frances an account of their mother's childhood, Harwood in turn relates her parents' history to her daughters. Claire, now forty-two years old, and Frances, thirty-nine, knew their grandparents solely through letters, books, and paintings. Harwood's memoir fills in the periods that Achsah had only alluded to in "The Child," including particulars of Earl and Achsah's youth, education, and marriage, and their years in France. Except for a brief summary of post-1935 events, she closes with the last embrace and wave that the three exchanged, none of them imagining the finality of it.

The many small-scale but sharp details that embellish her narrative lend charm and immediacy: Earl's summer job feeding goldfish, the recurrent pawning of his gold watch, and his presence at the eruption of Mt. Etna (1–2, 4); Achsah's painting schedule and mishap with a palette (16); the demands of housekeeping in the absence of plumbing and electricity (58). (We hear, too, of Edith Lewis's belief that artists who love their work should not expect to make money from it [35]). Whereas Achsah's personality and prejudices suffuse each page of "The Child," her daughter's adult memoir is a model of self-effacement and reticence, considering that she was present at nearly every event related. Harwood writes mostly in the third person, referring to herself throughout as "the baby," "the child" (as did her parents), or "Harwood," slipping into the first person only near the end, when she observes, almost with dismay, "It seems as though my name fills these pages" (57). Eschewing any reference to her own rapport with friends such as Willa Cather and D. H. Lawrence, she prefers instead the self-deprecating story: how the priest who taught her Latin and Greek "impressed on Harwood, that one sometimes learned more from one's mistakes than from a chance correct answer!" (29); how her early violin lessons made her realize that "the violin needs real talent and perseverance. The talent, at least, was missing!" (34). She also expresses a more measured view of events that left the fourteen-year-old Harwood indignant. Her younger self had appraised the missionary school in Kandy with a vehement, "How I hated [it]!" (Picard 1926, 105 [1st series]); now she remarks only that it provided her "first real taste of formal schooling" (23).

Harwood's love for her parents and the life they shared is apparent on each page. Even at a remove of many decades, she vividly evokes the exoticism of Ceylon and India, the beauties of Capri, the daily atmosphere of intellectual engagement and creative possibility, and the circle of loyal, sometimes eccentric, friends who functioned as her extended family when her own relatives were distant. Clear-sighted about her parents' shortcomings, she is also nonjudgmental, and speaks movingly of the relationship they shared once she had left behind home and childhood, when the three became more like equals. Part of Harwood's legacy to her daughters is this clear vision of the Brewsters, presented with humor, sympathy, and understanding.

[p. 3]

My mother had a very fair skin, gray eyes and golden hair and a Mona Lisa smile![2] She had a long neck—long waist and slender build. She was the youngest and must have been doted on by all around her. My father had dark hair, hazel eyes, and an olive complexion. He could have been taken for an Italian. During his twenties and thirties he wore a mustache. My father was about one inch taller than my mother—but when sitting she would appear taller.

[1929–57]
[p. 54–59]

The Brewsters were very happy [at Château Brun]. There was no electricity, no running water, and no plumbing—but the view of La Cadière and Castelet and the pine covered hills was so peaceful. The air was good. There was a great pine tree with a bench around its trunk—a little in front of the house. There was a paved terrace at the front with a stone table where meals were eaten. Achsah had a number of benches made here and there in the garden—wherever there was a nice view. . . .

During the previous vacation [12/29], Harwood had typed Lawrence's *Apocalypse* for him. She had seen him for the last time, when back for Christmas vacation. The Lawrences were still at the "Villa Soleil." They had an orange and white tiger striped cat—called Miki Mussolini. When the Lawrences left—Miki came to Château Brun.

There were many friends who came to see the Brewsters—the Reynolds[3] came at different times. Louie Fortescue[4] stayed with Achsah while Earl was on the trip with Mukerji to India. Edith Lewis and Willa Cather stayed at a hotel nearby at Les Lecques. The Di Chiaras[5] were living in a house not very far away and many pleasant times were exchanged—either going to their place or their coming to Château Brun.

The Brewsters made friends with an American artist, Alexander Robinson,[6] who lived in Cassis (on the way to Marseilles). He was particularly fond of painting fish. He was also very fond of good wine! Near him at Cassis lived Colonel Teed and Jean Campbell in Château Fontcreuse where they grew grapes from which a good Cassis wine was made. In their garden Virginia Woolf had built a small cottage which she would be able to use—but eventually it would belong to the Colonel. Since she did not come very often, the Colonel invited the Brewsters to stay there.[7] There was a great deal of wining and feasting and picture exhibits. But it was good for Earl and Achsah to get away now and then for a few days. One time Pamela went with them to Cassis. It was on the occasion of Harwood's 21st birthday and a 1912 bottle of champagne was opened for the occasion! . . .

For me the years at St. Cyr were especially precious. I was leaving my childhood behind and finding myself as an adult. It was most wonderful to be able to talk with my mother and father on any—and all subjects. They shared with me the thoughts that concerned them. We were a family united together—and also I would visit with each one separately. Evenings—as always in the past—were spent reading.

I remember discovering that my father had grown spiritually since I had known him. From the time we went to India in 1926, he had turned to the Vedanta teachings—not that he had turned away from Buddhism—but he had widened his interest and his studies. These made him a more complete person. Achsah was able to take his interests very much to heart and she too had a very strong faith and a great deal of courage. It was not always easy to drag food home—cook on an alcohol burner—clean the house—draw water from the well, empty slops, clean lamps, etc. Both Earl and Achsah worked very hard on the house as well as on their special interests. The house was always spotless. While at Château Brun, Achsah did not paint very much. Perhaps she did not feel strong enough. But she continued to have a need to express herself, and she wrote many sketches of people she had known and experiences she remembered. People always thought my mother saw only the good in people—but she could be very caustic in her observations. She was aware both of the good and the bad, but by nature she was an optimist. Earl and Achsah had their ups and downs. They were not perfect angels—and never had been. They were both quick tempered. Earl suffered from headaches from time to time; Achsah would need a lot of rest.

The last time I saw my mother was on the terrace in front of Château Brun; I had returned having forgotten something. I kissed and hugged her—and she seemed so small and frail to me—she in whose arms I used to love to snuggle as a child.

My father came to the station and I saw him waving to me— his beautiful thick white hair shining in the sun.

This was the autumn of 1935. I had promised my parents to go back to London for at least one more term. In December they sailed for India—so I felt free to join Georges and Claire in Paris. I believe my parents thought I would follow them to India![8] They traveled in the south before finally settling in Almora. Georges and I were married on May 7, 1936.[9]

Once I was married my mother accepted the situation and wrote me her beautiful letters full of love and encouragement. My father wrote less often—always with so much understanding and sharing his thoughts. When my mother died February 16, 1945—it was very hard for my father. He missed her terribly. He had nursed her during the last five years when she had been so ill with pernicious anemia.

My father was not well the last years of his life. Fortunately he had good friends: Boshi and Gertrude Sen (Gertrude Emerson Sen, a relative of Ralph Waldo Emerson); also Dr. Premananda,[10] an English doctor, who took care of him during the last years. My father died two days before his 79th birthday on September 19, 1957.

9

Selected Letters of Earl
and Achsah Barlow Brewster

INTRODUCTION

THE LETTERS OF EARL AND ACHSAH BREWSTER AT DREW UNIVERSITY span nearly fifty years, from the Brewsters' courtship and marriage in 1910 and the birth of their daughter, Harwood, in 1912, through the death of Achsah in 1945 and Earl in 1957. Exuberant, solicitous, often poignant, and always engaging, their letters document everyday events in the life of a family for whom the "everyday" included friendships with prominent literary and political figures, nonstop intellectual and artistic activity, frequent travel within Europe and to the Orient, chronic financial precariousness, and a child linked implicitly to Jesus Christ, Marcus Aurelius, and Joan of Arc.

The collection falls into three sections, according to period and correspondent: more than three hundred letters between Earl and Achsah Brewster, dating mostly from 1910 to 1929, from the early days of their courtship up to the time that Harwood left for Dartington Hall;[1] over twelve hundred letters from Earl or Achsah to Harwood, nearly all from the start of her school years until Earl's last letter to her before his death in September 1957; and over sixty letters from Earl to Lucile Beckett, whom the Brewsters had met in Ravello in 1914, written chiefly from Almora between 1951 and 1957. Numerous subsets and recurrent themes include progress made in painting and writing, the course of Harwood's studies, the beauties of nature, an abiding spirituality, analyses of Pāli words and Hindu scriptures, daily (sometimes hourly) schedules, the dialogues of Plato, the perils of field hockey, and the perpetual quest for inexpensive housing and sufficient funds.

Their separate voices are unmistakable. Achsah sets the scene by describing the sunrise, flowers in the garden, the clothes they

181

are wearing, the music they are listening to. Her tone ranges from dry wit to bracing high spirits to rhapsodic effusions, and her letters sparkle with her delight simply in *being:* "It is such a radiant day for you and Antonino to behold new wonders outspread. You cannot fail to enjoy just being alive on such a day" (ABB to EHB 9/25/24). Confident of leading a charmed existence, Achsah is forever "inheriting the earth"[2] and "inviting her soul."[3] Aphorisms abound: "The modern ecclesiastic seems immune to all art, see any new church if you disagree" (ABB to HBP 7/4/33); "The postal service and growing a garden should teach us patience to face life" (10/5/30). Aside from the day-to-day details of their outward lives—friends seen, paintings begun, books read, or stories written—she rarely talks about herself in a more intimate way, though she could hold forth unequivocally on such subjects as careers for women[4] and the need for contemplative leisure.

In contrast, Earl is all self-reflection and nerve endings—cautious optimism when his art inches closer to his vision, despair at his truncated education and perceived ignorance, sincere pleasure in the success of others, depression over their chronic financial straits and dependence on hand-outs. His highs are rarely as high as Achsah's, his lows far lower. "Doing one's best" is a constant theme.[5] He is ever eager to engage Harwood at length on both intellectual and personal topics, from the concepts of "soul" in the English language and "unity" in Eastern philosophy, to fatherly advice about dealing with men, his bouts of depression, and his intense love of painting.[6] He encourages her to share with him, as his "greatest privilege and joy" (11/9/30), her own cares and concerns.

Of the sixty-three letters from Earl to Lucile Beckett, all but three were written between the time of Lucile's visit to India in 1951 and Earl's death in 1957. From the moment of Earl's epiphany on the Fiesole tram,[7] he had viewed Lucile as the soul mate "with whom the heavenly pilgrimage was begun" (9/17/42), his "co-disciple in past lives" (8/10/52). Despite her sometimes difficult manner, he remained convinced that "psychically in some special way you and I are related" (6/15/51). His long, affectionate letters discuss their respective spiritual beliefs and readings, his efforts at abstract painting, and the rhythm of his days.

The following letters were written over a period of five decades, from four countries, three continents, and two ships. Although but a small selection, they nonetheless convey a sense of the world in which the Brewsters moved—their family life, their circle of friends, their personalities, joys, and troubles, and their intellectual and artistic endeavors.

※※

Earl Brewster and Achsah Barlow exchanged seventy-five letters between February 23, 1910, when Earl first invited Achsah to view his paintings, and November 29, two days before their wedding. The pleasure each felt in their immediate intellectual engagement and understanding is everywhere apparent here, just the fifth letter of their courtship.

Earl Brewster to Achsah Barlow

42 Washington Square N.Y.C.
Sunday Evening April 3 1910

My dear Miss Barlow,—
Your very welcome letter and the package of books came to me last Monday. I am looking forward with much pleasure to reading "Pipa Passes,"[8] and I shall prize the book not only for its own sake but because it has come as a present from you. Thank you very much for it. The prints by Hiroshige are exquisite. In looking at them I get a sence of tranquility, and of space, such as nature gives me when I veiw there the same effects Hiroshige has rendered. And they are effects of which I am very fond.

I shall follow your suggestion and keep the book some time,— longer than did you "The Centaur"![9] How perfectly Hiroshige's technique is adapted to those sentiments one admires in his work.

I am so glad that you enjoyed "The Centaur." Yes the passages you quote from it are very beautiful. How each sentence seems to have the character which the writing as a whole possesses. It is so pleasant to lend you books and share in your appreciation of them that I am tempted to send you some others. May I do so? But perhaps that is foolish of me, for your time for reading may be so filled with that which you particularly desire that other matter would be a bit of a nuisance.

I had thought that when I returned to you the Hiroshige book I should yeild to the temptation of sending you one or two of the oriental books with which you told me you were not familiar. (I have pocket editions easily mailable!) Are you familiar with Lao-Tze's "Tao Teh King"?[10] I have just been reading it since you were here— having known only a few passages from it formerly. I like to read it. In places it is as intimate as the psalms or Walt Whitman, and sometimes will have an idea that reminds me of Ibsen. There is deep mysticisim, and someway one feels that the author had a fine sence of humor. Do you think all that a rather impossible combination?

How difficult humor is to analyze. I believe there is a certain kind of humor that resides very close to our finest qualities. I can't believe whoever it was that said there is no humor in Heaven. How close that quality is to true charity and how it develops the more we know of the illusions of the external world. Perhaps I should send you that book and the Bhagavad Gita, and another book upon which I should greatly like your impression. And how many others I should be tempted to send!

You invite long letters Miss Barlow and your sympathetic understanding calls forth many confidences. I respect so highly your judgement that it is a constant temptation to bring before it all my latest ideas and fancies.

This winter as I think I told you I have been studying Buddhism and I have come to see the logic of its teaching, (as interpreted by one school,) of the non reality, or perhaps more exactly, of the non permanency, of the <u>individual</u> Self. How often I have thought the matter out with just the opposite conclusion! But just at present, this veiw of the <u>individual</u> soul as of only a transitory nature seems more logical to me and the significance of the teaching more beautiful and more truly spiritual. It seems to illuminate many things with a new beauty.

Among some of the books I have read is a breif story beautifully and simply told and exquisitely illustrated—it surely will please you—and if you are interested illustrate to some degree the teachings to which I here refered. You will enjoy it best if you read the chapters in their regular order. For I am sending you my copy. . . .

Indeed I do <u>not</u> beleive that you were stupid at our dinner—but I have regreted my lack of judgement in selecting that particular restaurant and I have feared that you were too tired to have taken so long a walk and such a windy ride. I do hope no evil results followed. Were you none the worse for the experience?

    With kindest regards
      Your friend
      Earl H. Brewster

⁂

The Brewsters spent the first three years of their marriage in Taormina, Paris, Portofino, and Anticoli Corrado, where Flora Brewster visited them in mid-1913. At the close of her stay, Earl accompanied her to Naples for her ship home, and continued south for a week of sight-seeing and sketching in Sicily, while Achsah and Harwood remained at Anticoli.

Earl Brewster to Achsah Brewster

Palermo—Hotel Savoy
Sept 11—1913

My dearest one,—
... [W]e did not sight land until towards nine o'clock. Sicily looked like a golden vaporous cloud. And when I arrived I found it so to be. Never do I think I have seen such a day—It is scirrocco[11] I am told and about as hot as I ever have experienced with the wind blowing furiously, and fine golden dust every where. I could imagine easily that it came from the hot desert and brought much of the sand with it, and that the desert were not far away either. ...

Oh yes I must tell you of my new shirt!—Mother insisted on paying the hotel bill in Naples—and—you don't see the connection?—well it's so very hot and the flannel shirt would be so warm I bought me another kind—you've guessed the style I think!—yes one of those with open throat and collar outside of coat collar—they are comfortable and becoming I think. In Naples and Rome I saw enough to over come my timidity—but here have seen none and people look with interest at it. It's so sensible on a day like this I don't believe they can resent it.[12]

Regarding what you write of Eucken's philosophy of activism[13] I am reminded of quotations from the Bhagavad Gita. Surely both contemplation and action are necessary—but I think here in the West there is not too much of the former. ...

I was much interested to find Arnold Bennitt write with such a harmony to Buddhistic and Theosophic philosophy—as in the book "The Glimpse"[14] which I recently sent you. How did you like it?

Regarding contemplation and activity, surely they must go hand in hand. More and more am I impressed with the statement "As a man thinketh so is he" and I realize more what a great empire, what vast powers, lie within ourselves if we will have initiative enough to partake of our heritage. So much depends on will power and steadiness, consistent effort and calmness.

I feel that I have gained power for better activity, thro my meditations.

My dear dear dear one—I do love you so—and I am so glad you understand me so well—and I am so grateful to you for being what you are. May God bless us—all three,—and lead us into a life here together in which we shall be splendid and do splendidly.

God bless you
From one who loves you beyond all words
Your husband Earl. ...

After seven months of study and painting in Ceylon, the Brewsters returned to Europe in May 1922, settling into the Grand Hotel in Chexbres-sur-Vevey, Switzerland. Earl spent August 1922 traveling in Italy with John Derby, Achsah's nephew. In Florence he oversaw the preparation of their paintings for the 1922 Salon d'Automne and joint show at the Galerie Chéron, and then continued with John as far south as Amalfi.

Earl Brewster to Achsah Brewster

Napoli Aug 28 '22

Beloved—

. . . I sat out in that rotunda out side of Cooks and as I read was interested in watching a party of young men, whom I thought were Singhelese. And I must say I have seen people of all nations—young people too—these last few weeks—but without a single exception these young men took the prize for real gentlemanlyness. . . . They told me they were from Ceylon—but were Indian. They asked my advice about hotels—and that was about all. But it was a joy to see such beautifully mannered young people. It sprang from something spiritually superior—I have not the slightest doubt. . . .

Did you secure the book by Schopenhauer? I hope so. . . .

I am very sorry to say: About your paintings in Florence.—Both Magnelli[15] and I felt that that large picture of Harwood ought to be worked on some more as it has dried in badly—do to previous retouching—I knew that there would be no time before the Autumn Salon for repainting & drying so I am not bringing it, as you told me to use my own judgement.

Are you painting now & what? . . .

My after dinner coffee kept me awake most all last night at Amalfi. And I thought and thought! And I tried to think out where we should go this winter! And many problems. Yet, one day at a time, maybe is enough. Life is very simple—all we have to do is our best!

We walked up to Ravello yesterday. It was a very lovely day for that country, and you know what that means. I saw many people who asked after you—will tell you about them when I see you. And about many things.

Enjoyed Harwood's letters. Give her kisses from me. Will write to her later.

Well one thing I thought about last night was how very greatly I love you—truly more than ever

Your
Earl

This seems such a poor letter—lay it to the pen. I am sorry about the painting will explain later.

When their 1926 trip to India left them disillusioned, the Brewsters investigated the Greek island of Syra, in the Cyclades, as a possible home. In this animated letter to her sisters, written on the voyage from Bombay to Piraeus, Achsah typically says nothing of her unhappiness and ill health while away. In the event, they lasted only four days on Syra before returning to Italy.

Achsah Brewster to Alpha Barlow and Lola Derby

> S.S. Genova, Marittima Italiana
> December 12, 1926

Dearest Sisters:—

Here it is Sunday and a white gull cutting across the blue and Arabia Deserta shining against the horizon. We sailed on the seventh and touch at Aden to-morrow early, so we already have left the Indian Ocean in our wake. It is wonderful weather, and the ship is so steady and the sea so beautiful to sea-famished eyes. Earl has found several interesting pals with whom to settle the affairs of the universe. We intend to land at Port Said and after a glimpse at the Sphinx and the pyramids to embark for Greece and the "distant Cyclades."

I am greatly interested in all you say about Rachel[16] and her loveliness. Of course I wish she would fall head over heels in love with someone who is a philosopher—saint—millionaire with a keen sense of humour and an avocation as well as a vocation. I cannot quite like a "career," especially a "successful career." I do love gentleness and sweetness and womanliness and how much Rachel has all these. Really most western women seem to me of triple-plated brass,[17] shrill, hard, rushing—what would they "do" if they wedged their way in where they are pushing so hard? Of course, I also believe that every woman, married or unmarried, should also have her creative expression.

The October number of "Arts & Decoration"[18] had two good reproductions of my Singhalese paintings.

Have I told you of our thrilling visit with the Mahant of Buddh' Gaya[19] in a wonderful guest-house, eight hundred years old? The visit to the bo-tree[20] was deeply moving. Good thoughts do come to one under the trees when holy men have sat there. I will send you one of the bo-leaves. Harwood even had a chance to ride on an elephant, along the dry river bed and through the groves. It was very like an ocean voyage once you had scaled the little iron ladder, and a rather choppy sea at that. Our official reception by the Mahant was charming, perfumes and then cardamom seeds. (The Nehrus[21] sent

us golden necklaces and a silver fish perfume flask as a parting ceremony.) . . .

Harwood is enjoying swimming and deck-sports. She also is writing her memoirs. "Fourteen Years of My Adventures." They are very
thrilling. You must not mention this for she wants it to be a dead
secret. I hope she will do it up to the end of her Indian experiences
at least.

There are cinemas every evening much to daughter's delight.

The best thing at Bombay was a budget of three such good letters
from you, with such happy chronicles. What fun to see dear Edith! I
don't see why anyone wants to live at that northern corner of the
world.[22] Give me the south and a blue, shining sea.

With more love than ever for you all, beloveds, from

> Your devoted,
> Achsah

※

Shortly after Harwood began school at Dartington Hall in England in September 1929, Earl and Achsah moved from Capri to
St. Cyr-sur-Mer, near the Côte d'Azur, to be closer both to her
and to D. H. Lawrence, who was living at Bandol. In late February 1930 Earl left with Dhan Gopal Mukerji on a two-month trip
to India.[23] When their ship docked at Port Said, en route to Bombay, he found Achsah's telegram with the news that Lawrence
had died at Vence nearly two weeks before, on March 2. The
postscript to Earl's reply makes clear that the idea to publish
Lawrence's letters came to him almost immediately.

Earl Brewster to Achsah Brewster

> S.S. Cracovia
> The Red Sea March 15 1930

Most dearly Beloved:

Yesterday just as I was about to leave the steamer for a few hours
at Port Said I was handed your telegram of March 11th. I am very
grateful to you for telegraphing me and I feel releived in thought to
have your words concerning yourself;—the news of David's death
came as a great shock to me and I have felt dazed and sorrowed ever
since. I had believed that he would live at least a few years more. He
had been frequently in my thought and in our conversation, but that
is as it usually is,—and no intuition that he had passed on had come
to me. Indeed I wrote to him from Venice about March 7th.

We shall miss him greatly—more even than we now realize. But
we shall honour him most, and keep his presence and friendship
best, by trying to live in the realizations of those truths he had real-

ized. His personality was so vital and so tremendous that it seems impossible that already he should not have awakened and begun to manifest himself somewhere. You will write me some details of his last days. Was his death sudden? Of course you went over to Vence? Was the body cremated? And where is Frieda staying now? I will enclose a letter to her for you to please forward. I cannot but feel that David has found the peace and rest, which he desired, from which his soul will come forth again to an even fuller, happier expression.[24]

Although we are now on the Red Sea it is still gray and cold on one side of the sky! I am dressed as warmly as ever—yellow sweater and all! I felt keenly the entrance into another world yesterday as we neared Port Said. . . . I must confess this part of the world stirs something within me and thrills me, moves me, satisfies me as much—nay more—than ever. It is as though—for me—in being nearer the sun I had come nearer to Life and God. . . .

I pray that you may be very well, serene and happy. I give you all the blessings it is in my power to bestow—and I know that you have the blessings from far greater ones than me. I put my arms about you and love you more than ever

Your
Earl

Later—March 19th—9 o'clock a.m.

Most dearly Beloved:

We are due at Aden at noon. . . . Dhan and I spend much time in meditation—four or five times a day we have periods of meditation. This morning we have been reading from Wm James "Varieties of Religious Experiences": it seemed a better book than I remembered it. Also these days we have been making our own translation of the Kena Upanishad—I think that I have truly done some good work at it. . . .

Well, my own dearest one, I am sure the happiest moment of my journey will be when I return to France and find you well.

Always always I am thinking of you and loving you more than ever

Your—Earl

Don't let anyone have access to my letters from David, until I return.[25]

***

Harwood thoroughly enjoyed the classes, extracurricular activities, and camaraderie at Dartington Hall. Achsah's letter below was the Brewsters' sixth and final attempt to dissuade their eighteen-year-old daughter from the dangers of playing field hockey. ("Surely tennis is a splendid game" [EHB to HBP 10/30].) Harwood stood her ground.

Achsah Brewster to Harwood Brewster

Château Brun
St. Cyr-sur-Mer,Var, France,
October 8, 1930

Dearest Harwood:—

Your dear letters of the 1st and 3rd and Aunt Alpha's enclosed are most precious.

Your letter distresses me very much, for you know that I feel you are of an age to decide things for yourself and that one human being has no right to enforce his will upon another. You must decide the hockey for yourself. For my part, I think it unwise, unless you wear a face-mask. Everyone I consult feels this way. Mr. Fitzpatrick who was here last week, had a crooked broken nose—broken three different times in hockey. Jim nearly lost an eye and you lost a tooth in a few games. I know the "esprit de corps" and all that and I remember that my room-mate Persis Paulsen played basket-ball with a broken rib and at times she should not have done so. She hurt herself so that she has not been able to have children and has adopted two. It is not even as if you were staying on at Dartington with an established group, and you surely cannot be the whole hockey team! No one is that important.

I do not like to write this and I wish you might feel as I do about the matter. I am most miserable at the thought of your playing hockey.—Basta!

We have had a lovely drive in Victor's[26] bran[d] new car that ran as if on wings, and looked a gleaming dark blue elegance. It seemed sacriledge to bring back groceries and plants in it, but we did—roses to climb over the walls and oleanders. Father and Emil[27] and I have been planting them all the afternoon and I hope they will be in full flower when you and Pop[28] are here at Christmas. . . .

I have begun a lunette of angels for the top of the mural I have been working on. Pray that they are really beautiful.

Father is writing such interesting memoirs of Uncle David.[29] We both are most busy and the days slip fast. . . .

All love and blessings, darling daughter
  from your devoted mother,
    Achsah

✹❂✹

During their years in France, the Brewsters turned increasingly to writing as a means to earn money; in addition to their book on Lawrence, they sent a steady stream of stories, novels, and essays to various popular and scholarly publications. The following five letters refer to several such projects, to their extensive reading, and to Harwood's study at the London Royal Free Hospital School of Medicine for Women. In two letters written on October 22, 1932, Earl and Achsah each express satisfaction at the upcoming marriage of Boshi Sen to Gertrude Emerson, the editor of *Asia* magazine. Achsah's pleasure at Gertrude leaving her salaried position at *Asia* is in striking juxtaposition to Earl's request to Harwood for a loan of 250 francs. Harwood's schooling in England was in turn being funded by Alpha.

Achsah Brewster to Harwood Brewster

> Château Brun,
> St. Cyr-sur-Mer,
> Var, France,
> October 22, 1932.

Dearest Harwood:—

. . . We both are busy writing trying to lick into shape some magazine things. I sent off what is called a "short short," under one-thousand words about the death of Rose's mother,[30] posted it to "Liberty," hoping for one-hundred dollars from them. Now I am doing a Ceylon article and shall send some reproductions of my paintings with it to "Asia" by Gertrude's suggestion. It is coming along quite well. . . . [31]

Perhaps you are all singing together. I hope so. Last night father was reading me a long argument in favour of music, and praising its therapeutic powers in treating insanity and many sicknesses.

We shall be hearing from Gertrude this week, I should think from Port Said. She was a dear and how she adores Boshi. I am sure she is glad to leave the grind of the business world and being efficient and will be content to rest and invite her soul after the Hindu manner.

Bless you, darling. More love than ever from—Mother—Achsah.

⚬⚬

Earl Brewster to Harwood Brewster

> Château Brun
> St. Cyr-sur-mer Var France
> 22 October 1932

Beloved Harwood:

It is a rather nice morning of fleeting sunshine and flying clouds, warm enough to sit in my third floor room with the window open. My watch says nine o'clock—bath, pranayama,[32] chanting, meditation, breakfast, dishes, sweeping and all the house work is finished and the post has not yet arrived. Mother frequently remarks "Well, we may have a letter from Harwood to-day—we might." I say "Of course why not?"

Now the post has come—it brought the Prabuddha Bharata and the Mahabodhi[33] magazines and a receipt from the New Statesman & Nation. Thank you so much for subscribing for that for us. . . .

I long to know more about your life. How much of your time is occupied in the care of your room and preparing your food? Do you have all your food in your rooms? Did you have to buy much for your room—bedding, dishes or furniture? Can you really make it warm? How much time do your lessons require in their preparation? . . . Tell us what you have to eat. I would so much like the schedule of your usual day. . . .

We enjoyed Gertrude's visit, as mother has doubtlessly written you. I think the chances are good that she and Boshi will have a happy life together. I sent two paintings to Boshi—one of Swamiji and Kailash[34] and a sketch of the Himalayas. Mother gave Gertrude various things. Gertrude liked very much "My Lady Poverty"[35] and persuaded me to send it to The Yale Review—so I must write Vijoy[36] to release me from my promise to send it to the Prabuddha Bharata. . . .

My dear daughter, there is one thing I do especially feel somewhat worried about—and that is the lack of a chaperon for you! It seems to me that your room must be ideal in many many ways—and you are over twenty years old—but one is not so awfully wise even at twenty! I beg you to be very careful what gentlemen—young or old—that you invite to your room—in fact I wouldn't invite any alone, without another woman present with you. This is just sound and important advice Harwood dear. Boys and men are just devils—and surely I ought to know belonging to that devision of the race.

We are hard up, financially. If it will not embarress you too much, would you please send us 250 francs in a registered letter—(that is $10—you can get the $10 exchanged into French money easily, $10 = 250 francs +). Maybe I can even return the sum to you some day. But you know I am not good at that. If not too inconvenient please do this for us as soon as you can without interfering with your school and other engagements.

Bless you my dear dear daughter. May you grow in strength of body, mind and spirit. May your life be rich in all good things. Your letters are a joy and a blessing.

With more love than ever
    Your devoted
    Father

Achsah Brewster to Harwood Brewster

Château Brun
St. Cyr-sur-Mer,
Var, France,
January 16, 1933.

Darling:—

The post man has just come bringing bread and a letter from Aunt Berta, a "Times" from Mr. Billson[37] and your blessed telegram, so we are full of peace on this sunny morning, picturing you off to register for the new term and possibly dissecting dog fish this very minute. I refuse to believe my nervous system is fully explained by the dog fish! Father read me a long article from the "New Statesman" yesterday establishing the Mendelian law of heredity by means of little flies bred in bananas! One must keep abreast with one's daughter, you see!! . . .

Father read the twelfth book of Plato's "Laws" and a good deal of Jowett's introduction to the "Laws," a very interesting treatise. It seemed good to be reading something with such enduring values, an[d] a true relationship to all times and all people. If you build on the heart of man, it is a firm foundation. Yet the "Laws" were written by Plato in his old age, seventy-four, and lack the joyous spontaneity of youth and the dramatic beauty and clear romance of his earlier work, but by way of compensation there is a view of religious conviction and a breadth of vision. . . .

It is early, not yet nine of the clock, and yet we are in full blast, even the datura with its head uncovered to the sun and the floors gleaming like the crystal palace.

All love for you, darling, and every blessing from Father and me.

Your devoted mother,
Achsah

※

Achsah Brewster to Harwood Brewster

Château Brun
St. Cyr-sur-Mer
Var, France,
January 24, 1933.

Beloved Harwood:—

. . . Father has nearly finished Pearl Buck's "Good Earth". It is written in solid Biblical phrases and is quite wonderful, but oh so depressing and I cannot but believe false. There is not one really lovable person in the book, except Olan the wife who is scarcely more than a beast of the field. Yet the enduring earth and its healing power one feels wonderfully and the recurring rhythms of despair in life when one has to wait for nature to heal one. Don't read it. I go to bed weeping from it, each time and I know it is false. There may be sorrow, but there is much joy, and one can reach tranquility and balance. . . .[38]

All the time you were home I marvelled at the contentedness and good cheer you kept unbroken, under the most trying circumstances. I appreciated it more than you may know. It seems to me just to be cheery is the best thing almost in the world. To really have a zest and enjoyment in this game of life.

My dialogue with Jeremiah keeps on apace.[39] To-day I have cut out of the New York Herald a notice of another prize, only 10,000 lire this time, offered for the best book about Italy which would cause people to travel there immediately! . . .

I wonder where Frieda is and when we shall hear. She may be in California by now.

More love than ever for you, our treasure, and all blessings.
Devotedly—
Mother.

Earl Brewster to Harwood Brewster

Château Brun
St. Cyr-sur-Mer
Var France
April 30 1933.

Most dearly Beloved Harwood:
Sunday afternoon. Four o'clock. Tea just over, consisting of fresh bread and butter and hot raisin-buns buttered & honeyed. Mother now at the piano. Out of doors gray, and a hottish wind blowing—inside cool enough for a fire. It has been a quiet day—Mother prepared coffee,—then Plotinus—a wonderful part—The Fifth Ennead, I The Three Initial Hypostases—division 14 and 15.

When the post-boy came fortunately—very fortunately—there was a letter from you to help break the effect of the shock which dear Mother had on the same mail in hearing from The Atlantic Monthly that she had not won the $5000. prize.[40] But even your precious precious letter didn't entirely drive away the shock. I suspect she had spent the money,—well at least there may have been a little satisfaction in that! Alas! Alas! Alas!

Then we read, after the house-work was finished, The Lesser Hippias by the divine Plato. I bow more reverently than ever to his divinity, and thank the Great Fate, for the fact that Plato is. The Lesser Hippias I find amusing,—good and very significant. Its problem is whether it is better to lie voluntarily or involuntarily. Socrates argues very well indeed that it is better to lie voluntarily, then at the end of the dialogue he confesses that he does not really know which is the better. I remember when we were visiting Edith Lewis in New York we discussed with her whether it was better to sin in ignorance or sin with the knowledge one was sinning—If I remember rightly we all finally came to the conclusion for which Socrates argued. But Physics and Biology and Chemistry are far removed from all sophistries of that kind I suppose.

This afternoon we have read the New Statesman and Nation. So the day has gone. Tomorrow I hope to be painting. I think you would like my Buddha and the Elephant which I have recently practically finished, I think. . . .

To return to the subject of painting—I have also been working on some "abstracts" which interest me very much. But tomorrow I expect to begin a large canvas. . . .

I borrowed from Ferdinando[41] "The Nigger of the Narcissus" by Conrad. I have never read it. It is so well written—a great book. Huxley's "Brave New World" is a purgative—but I don't believe that I needed it: Mother couldn't read it.

Do give me a few items concerning your visit to Mrs. Rhys Davids. . . .

Mother can now type like a regular professional!

May the Lord protect you from all harm, while you grow in goodness beauty and truth.

More love than ever

Father

⚜

In December 1935 the Brewsters left France for India. They never returned to Europe, and never again saw Harwood. The years in Almora were extremely prolific for both their painting and writing; Earl's work in particular was much sought after, though he earned as little as ever from it. In May 1936 Harwood married Georges Picard; their daughter, Frances Diana, was born in October 1938.

When Achsah's illness during the late 1930s left her too weak to write, she dictated her correspondence to Earl, which he noted at the head.

Achsah Brewster to Harwood Brewster Picard
(Dictated by Mother)

> Bhawani House, Snow View Estate,
> Almora, U.P. India
> 19 Dec 1938

Beloved:

It is a bright shining day, and I hope that you are all out for a drive in the happiest of spirits and abounding health. Here it is the

19th—so Frances must be two months and nineteen days old, quite venerable. We have nearly worn out the one picture we have, and are looking forward to some of Georges' art products before long. . . .

Next to us are staying Jawaharlal's daughter Indira—a charming girl of about eighteen, who has been studying at Oxford: her particular interest has been political philosophy.[42] She is very beautiful, with a delicate pale flower beauty, blue black hair, black arched brows and eyes that you must describe as lotus eyes. Her features are beautifully chiselled, and her hands so delicate that they seem like transparent flower buds. In great contrast to her aunt Krishna Hathee Sing Devi,[43] the youngest sister of Jawaharlal's, and her two little boys of three and four years of age. She is wonderfully vivid; curls swept back from her shining face with its great dark eyes. She must be a good deal of an artist judging by the way she carries herself, and the interesting clothes she wears. I found it perfectly delightful even to the beautiful ring on her left hand of emeralds and a huge diamond. I am hoping to see more of them when they are rested from their journey but we had a most lovely visit. . . .

Such a dear letter came today from Aunt Edith. She says that dear Isabel Hambourg died early in October at the Cocumella in Sorrento. Poor Willa has lost her farvourite brother and Isabel both within a few months,[44] and the shape of earthly life is much changed for her. She is writing at the Shattuck Inn at Jaffrey—New Hampshire.

Father has just finished a very fine review of Russell's Power[45]— which we consider an excellent book.

On this last post a great big volume of Uncle David's posthumus stories Phoenix arrived as a Xmas gift from Maj. Alexander.[46]

The narcissus are still blossoming in our garden and in the rocks.

Everyday father reads some hymns from the Ṛg Veda to me—or I to him. They are full of the life of nature and the little green leaves and the breezes seem so much more significant because of them, just as they do for reading David's psalms.

Father and I are with you dear children—during these holidays and all days—I am so glad that Francis is a good baby. You never cried either—and if you did the first movement of The Moonlight Sonata was balm to your spirit.[47]

Well my precious this brings you our deep love and admiration. . . .

More love than ever from your devoted Father and Mother

Achsah Brewster died of pernicious anemia on February 16, 1945. Writing here to his brother Ara, Earl pays tribute to her stalwart faith in him, and her gift for living each day to the fullest. Earl also described for Ara what must have seemed a particularly exotic and unlikely retirement for a man from Chagrin Falls, Ohio.

Earl Brewster to Ara Brewster

Bhawani House Snow View Estate
Almora U.P. 4 April 45

My dear Brother:

I was more glad to receive your dear letter of Feb. 24th than I can say.[48] It was the first letter to reach me from America written after Achsah's death, it comforted and helped me, and I am indeed grateful for the words you write and the love and sympathy from yourself and the others which you give me. . . .

Under present world conditions, travel being very difficult and expensive and perhaps dangerous, it seems best for me to remain just where I am. . . . I live as simply as I can, considering that I myself am suffering with aenemia and cannot walk far. . . . Medicines are very very expensive, such as are prescribed for me for aenemia. I don't really know whether the doctors think I am going to recover from aenemia or not. The money which Achsah inherited from her aunts has been largely spent during her illness, plus, of course, what we have earned as well. But I hope what is left will keep me going for a few more years, if I live. I work quite strenuously painting and have sold quite a lot here in India. Old age with out any money is not very jolly to contemplate—I don't think much about it, all I can do is to work as hard as I can and as well as I can and leave the rest to the Lord. Paint and brushes are getting scarse: I shall feel very sorry indeed if cannot always get what I need of them. Naturally I would like awfully to see you and Harwood and her children and Nora[49] and your children—but travel would so eat into what money I have that I do not know whether I should dare attempt it.

I miss Achsah terribly and sometimes I secumb to the feeling that life is too barren for me to go on living. But I think that such an attitude is rather cruel toward Achsah, who gallently put up with me for nearly 35 years, and that for her sake as well as my own and everyone connected with me, I must pull myself together and go on with my life just as well as I know how to do. I am so glad to remember that all through our life together, even during her recent years of illness, Achsah never ceased to enjoy life: she would frequently remark on what a blessed happy life we had always had and were continuing to have as long as she lived. Whether I have the strength of will to live now according to those ideals we held in common remains to be seen.

I have a boy of about 27 who has been with us several years and who looks after me quite well.[50] He is a fairly good cook, and a vegetarian like myself: he shaves me every morning after my coffee, rubs me down after my bath, keeps the house in order, warns callers not to stay too long!! accompanies me on my walks if I wish, and gives me a massage when I go to bed. I do not think he would eat anything which has been placed before me on the table, and certainly nothing which a Mohamedan had cooked, nor anything with eggs. But cigarettes he will accept gratefully. . . . Such are the customs of his caste—which is the Ksatriya[51] caste—the caste of the rulers and warriors. He is not supposed to have food from my supply, and he receives from me a salary which I have more than doubled since he entered my service, and is high for these parts, that is, thirty rupees a month, which is $9. and I give him frequent presents of clothes and extra money. All of which details I thought might interest you and amuse you.

I have many good Hindu, English and American friends here and throughout India who are very kind to me. My nearest neighbor is a fine young French student of Hindu music & philosophy, with him lives a young Swiss man who inherits the fortune of a famous choclate concern in Switzerland. They live winters in Benares coming here for the summer.[52]

Hoping to hear from you soon and with deep love—Your brother Earl. . . .

☙☙

The following letter underscores the high regard in which Earl was held by the Nehru family, and illustrates his quasi-celebrity status among Indians and expatriates alike. Often inundated with visitors, he was preternaturally courteous, even when most unwilling.

Earl Brewster to Harwood Brewster Picard

Bhawani House, Snow View Estate,
Almora U.P. India 17 June 1945.

My beloved daughter:
. . . Your cable arrived June 15th, two days en route. It was brought to me while Jawaharlal Nehru was making a call upon me. How glad I was to have you present to participate in so happy a time. For I was deeply touched and honored that he should come to see me on the first day of his release from prison. He had just been transfered to the Almora jail a day or so before his release.[53] Already he is on his way now, I am told, for the plains. He told me that his daughter Indira had telegraphed him that she would meet him there. Like me, he also has not yet seen his grand child, (Indira's son.) . . .

Now it is June 19th—for four days I had just a continuous stream of visitors, all day long, last evening at about 6 o'clock I fled to my bedroom, undressed & went to bed; having a bad cough & feeling utterly exhausted, in spite of my increased blood count. One awful, awful woman came, earlier in the day, insisting that I should explain to her my religious conceptions, but she herself occupied all the time talking about hers! My dear little phaesant[54] saw that I was becoming utterly exhausted, and he began to attack her!—but that meant that I had to stand and protect her as well as listen to her talk. All this during the middle hours of a very hot day and when I had previously had one of the Ramakrishna swamis all the morning and for lunch, who had elected to come and see me. . . . You ask how I spend my time—well the foregoing is the way it passes some times. I hope after four days like that the gods will protect me for a few days and let me return to painting & study. . . .

With much love to you, all four,
Your devoted
Father

June 20th: Yesterday, about one o'clock, I saw coming up my path another lot of American soldiers to call upon me—about 50 I should think—but I am very sorry to say I felt so exhausted and feverish at that hot hour of the day—that I went to bed with orders to Uttama to say that I was too ill to see them—which I felt was indeed the truth: but I am very sorry that I had to do that.

Oh my daughter, youth fortunately cannot know how tragic old age is for most of us.

⚶

Earl's last letters to Harwood speaks increasingly of his poor health, his deep sense of loss and regret at the time and distance between them, and concern that his affairs be put in order before his death. His pleasure in painting and reading continued unabated. Earl died at the hospital in Bareilly on September 19, 1957, less than five months after this letter was written.

Earl Brewster to Harwood Brewster Picard

Snow View Estate
Almora U.P. India
28—IV—'57

Beloved Daughter,—
. . . My illness seems to have taken on a different character. My heart is affected, which at times affects my breathing and I am much weaker. Haridas[55] on his return from a minor operation in Lucknow

has just been with me for several days. He warns and urges me to be far more careful than ever before not to do work that tires me—such as the washing (!) and carrying water etc, or he says I'll find myself confined to the bed, and that I must not climb the steep hill between this house and my neighbors, who live at a lower altitude. I always enjoy his visits very much. He sits on the floor and I on the couch while he reads for long to me. He is very fond of Willa Cather's writing. Previously he had read to me her Tom Outland's Story which we think is great writing. This time he read to me The Professor's House (of which Tom Outland's Story forms a part), and he read "My Mortal Enemy" which impressed us tremendously, as very, very great writing indeed, so sensitive and keenly seen and felt! Perhaps it is the greatest writing Willa did. The "mortal enemy" is a part of the main character in the book, she is her own mortal enemy to herself. But perhaps you have read the book. We also like very much the tender, true, shortish long story Neighbour Rosicky. . . .[56]

I am so glad that it is now generally warm enough to go without fires. I have been revelling lately in wearing one of the very fine white shirts you sent to me and that fine white blouse and socks along with a pair of white flannel trousers and a deep purple silk tie. (!) . . .

When do the vacations begin for Claire and Frances? May you all three be very well and happy. With very much love to you all three, I am as ever yours devotedly

Father

Notes

CHAPTER 1. EARL AND ACHSAH BREWSTER

1. Poems: "Elephant," "Apostrophe to a Buddhist Monk"; short stories: "Things," "Nobody Loves Me"; novella: *The Escaped Cock;* travel book: *Sketches of Etruscan Places.*

2. I am grateful to Robin Rausch, Music Division, Library of Congress, for this information.

3. "Recognition" (Cather 1923, 65, and inscription); "The Moon is a Painter" and "My Lady in Her White Silk Shawl" (Lindsay 1914b, 130–31, 139, and inscription); "Epilogue" (Lindsay 1914a, 185–86, and inscription); John Stanwell-Fletcher, *Pattern of the Tiger* (Boston: Little, Brown, 1954), 50–54; Mukerji 1930, passim; Cerio 1950, vol. 2, 507–13; Claude Washburn, *The Prince and the Princess* (New York: Albert & Charles Boni, 1925, in which the hero, Conrad Brooke, shares some biographical details and personality traits with Earl); Washburn 1968, 1–24 (Achsah mistitles this essay "On Dining Abroad" in A. Brewster 1942, 134); Francis Watson, "Portrait of a Buddhist" (typescript of BBC broadcast for the program "This Day and Age," June 11–12, 1956; EHB to HBP 11/11/52; EHB to Lucile Beckett 11/16/52, 5/22/53. In chapter 2 David Porter demonstrates the links between the Brewsters and Cather's *Death Comes for the Archbishop,* "Old Mrs. Harris," and "The Old Beauty."

4. Oberlin Academy (1833–1916), originally called the Preparatory Department of Oberlin College, focused on preparing high school students for college.

5. For the links between antimodernism, Buddhism, Theosophy, and spiritual art, I am indebted to the work of T. J. Jackson Lears, Joseph B. Tamney, and Thomas A. Tweed.

6. EHB to HBP 9/22/29, 8/22/53; EHB to Lucile Beckett 9/22/53. Other female influences on Earl's education in Eastern religious thought were Lucile Beckett, Caroline Rhys Davids, and Josephine MacLeod.

7. German-American philosopher Paul Carus (1852–1919), editor of *Open Court* magazine, was an influential voice in the public discussion of Buddhism (Tweed 1992, 65); the American Lafcadio Hearn (1850–1904), who moved to Japan, interpreted Buddhism and Japanese culture for American readers (Lears 1994, 176).

8. Elizabeth Casy, "Paintings of Merit by Three Artists," *New York Times,* April 26, 1908 (clipping from a private collection). Casy noted the artists' attention to the "artistic problems of light and air," and was particularly appreciative of Earl's work. EHB to WM 4/29/08 responded to Macbeth's interest in the exhibition. William Macbeth (1851–1917) was unusual among American art dealers of the period in showing only American artists.

9. Artist, engraver, and book designer Rudolf Ruzicka (1883–1978). As

mentioned in the introduction, we have retained the original spelling in the Brewsters' letters.

10. Obituary for ABB from a New Haven paper, February 1945 (clipping from a private collection).

11. Alpha and Lola were Smith College class of 1896 and 1899, respectively. Lola married John Derby in 1900.

12. See note 3, dedicatory inscriptions in Lindsay 1914a and 1914b.

13. John Barlow to ABB 11/26/06, 1/11/07, 5/13/07 and VL to ABB 12/22/06 make clear Achsah's high aspirations for her art work.

14. John Barlow to ABB 11/26/06; see also A. Brewster 1942, 204.

15. See also EHB to Lucile Beckett 5/16/56; Picard 1984, 209. According to Achsah's Smith College registration form, and an Oberlin Academy questionnaire to which Earl responded, at least through 1908 Achsah and Earl formally identified themselves as Baptist and Congregational, respectively (Class Records, Smith College Archives; Student File [Earl Brewster], Alumni & Development Records, Oberlin College Archives).

16. They themselves were always well aware of the contrast, e.g., ABB to HBP 7/8/31, 2/8/33.

17. See also Emerson 1983, 467, which Schreiner paraphrases.

18. Smith College Museum of Art, Northampton, Massachusetts. "Gift of Mr. and Mrs. Earl Brewster in honor of the tenth reunion of Mrs. Brewster (Achsah Barlow, class of 1902)."

19. Class Records, Smith College Archives.

20. Aristophanes's term (*The Birds*, line 817) for a fantastical city in the sky.

21. Picard 1984, 205–6. Achsah was perhaps influenced by her former teacher, Robert Henri, who counseled, "'Work with great speed. . . . Finish as quickly as you can. . . . Do it all in one sitting if you can'" (Perlman 1991, 59).

22. "Happiness is desirelessness. Desirelessness is happiness. . . . (I do not mean all volition—but grasping, asking, greed)" (EHB to CW 1/24/25).

23. Language of the earliest Buddhist scriptures.

24. Lucile Beckett Czernin Frost (1884–1979), author of several philosophical works. The "magnetic force" that drew Earl to Lucile was what he had earlier felt for Annie Besant (9/22/53).

25. They were apparently unaware that Pablo Picasso had lived at 53b earlier in the year—cf. *Picasso a Roma, 1917: "Mon atelier de Via Margutta 53/b,"* an exhibition held at Galleria Valentina Moncada, Rome, February 27–March 30, 2007.

26. EHB to CRD 12/3/18; A. Brewster 1942, 101, 118; he knew also the work of William James (EHB to RR 7/4/16 and to ABB 3/15/30) and Rudolf Euckon (EHB to ABB 9/11/13).

27. Picard 1984, 204. Numerous letters refer to Christmas and birthday checks sent by Alpha, Lola, Flora, and Ara.

28. See Sulloway 1997, 117, for the inclination to travel, rooted in "childhood daydreams," as a way for younger siblings to find their niche; Lears 1994, 228, notes that "protracted, restless travel" is a form of "withdrawal from active engagement with the world."

29. Ernst Lothar Hoffmann (1898–1985), later called Lama Anagarika Govinda.

30. Class Records, Smith College Archives.

31. Gauguin, too, was influenced by Puvis de Chavannes (Nonne 2002, 78–82).

32. For the Brewsters' and Lawrence's attitude toward machinery, see also Brewster 1934, 172; EHB to ABB 7/31/29; A. Brewster 1942, 20, 269; *LL* 7 #5307.

33. Busich 1981, 9–14, http://bibliotecaviterbo.it/Rivista/1981_4/Busich.pdf.

34. In none of their surviving letters do the Brewsters mention Ernest Hemingway, Ezra Pound, or Gertrude Stein, who were also in Paris at this time. In *A Moveable Feast* (New York: Bantam Books, 1968), Hemingway notes that the Hôtel Voltaire attracted an affluent clientele (42).

35. Some critics were confused by the mingling of Eastern and Western images. The *New York Herald,* Paris, 1923, noted the influence of the "pre-classical Italians, in their case particularly Giotto, but they have added Oriental elements which somewhat confuse the issue"; for another reviewer, however, the Brewsters "accomplished an unconscious synthesis of influences historically and geographically remote from one another, but intrinsically of the same web and woof" (clippings from a private collection).

36. Archivio della scuola romana, http://www.scuolaromana.it/artisti/brogli om.htm. For a fuller discussion of the book, see chapter 2.

37. *American Art News* of 1/6/23 described their work as "a vehicle for the expression of poetic ideas," and the "union of art and idealism" (clipping from a private collection). Years later, Syracuse professor Raymond Frank Piper, who hoped to include examples of the Brewsters' work in his book about cosmic art, *The Hungry Eye,* explained, "Since [cosmic art] deals with ideas, it must be expressive and more or less abstract" (Piper 1956, preface).

38. The Brewsters' essays seemed to reflect their familiarity with the Theosophical system that attached spiritual and emotional significance to specific colors: e.g., just as color and form combined to create emotion, the artist's own "psychic conditions" invariably led him to choose certain colors and forms to express these conditions (Brewster 1923, 10, 15–16). See EHB to Lucile Beckett 3/27/56 for a description of this process in regard to an abstract painting that Earl had sent her. The notion was conceived and diagrammed by Theosophists Annie Besant and Charles W. Leadbetter in a chart, "Key to the Meaning of Colors," which appeared in their book *Thought-Forms* (Ringbom 1986, 135–37). See also Tamney 1992, 24, for the influence of these texts on abstract artists.

39. From a private collection.

40. Achsah had originally offered the triptych to Smith College in late 1921 as a twentieth reunion gift. It was shipped from Capri to Massachusetts, but the college could find no suitable place to accommodate the thirty-foot painting, and sent it back to her (Office of the President, William Allan Neilson Files, Box 4, Smith College Archives). The painting is still in the church of St. Georges at Crécy, though misattributed to another artist. I am grateful to Yvette Kirby for her invaluable assistance in helping me locate it and attempt to have the error rectified.

41. EHB to CRD 3/8/24, 3/18/24, 3/31/24, 4/27/24.

42. Earl also questioned both Washburn (3/18/24) and Ruzicka (7/5/24) as to the potential financial success of a proposed book about pilgrimages to Buddhist monasteries in India, Ceylon, and Burma, but neither was encouraging.

43. Dhan Gopal Mukerji (1890–1936), who lived in the United States, wrote children's books and other works that helped to familiarize western readers with Indian culture and religion.

44. Chief disciple of Ramakrishna and founder of the Belur Math mission,

Calcutta. He had addressed the World Parliament of Religions at the 1893 Columbian Exposition to great success and celebrity.

45. According to David Edward Shaner, Earl's *Life of Gotama the Buddha* (one of ten biographies of the Buddha published between 1925 and 1929), relies exclusively on Mrs. Rhys Davids's translation of the Pāli Canon. "In its time, and to a limited extent now, [Earl's] work occupied a[n] important niche as a primary companion to narrative biographies written for nonspecialists" (Shaner 1987, 314–15). It is clear from Earl's correspondence with Mrs. Rhys Davids that he consulted a number of other biographies and translations, as well as some of the original texts, and made his own lists of the selections he wished to include (EHB to CRD 3/8/24, 3/18/24, 3/31/24).

46. Earl also now gave Claude Washburn's sister a roll of paintings to take to Edith Lewis in New York, presumably for placement in a gallery (EHB to CW 3/16/26).

47. From a private collection.

48. See also Lears 1994, 143, for the antimodernist trait of elevating "becoming over being, the *process* of experience over its goal or result."

49. See A. Brewster 1942, 339, and Picard 1977, 33, for the contrast between the two brothers.

50. In "Nobody Loves Me," Lawrence describes his New England friend as girlishly naive in her sense of living in real peace with her fellow man (Lawrence 1961, 205); he acknowledged to the Brewsters that *Lady Chatterley's Lover* "isn't in your line, either of you—neither Buddha nor Mary" (*LL* 7 #4795), and teasingly suggested that Achsah send "her most spiritual and purely pure friends," including Mrs. Rhys Davids, an order form for the book (*LL* 6 #4356). Aldous Huxley joked with Lawrence about the lesbian bar he had visited in France: "It was just the place for the Brewsters!" (Huxley 1969, 305). Yet the Brewsters were by no means prudish. Earl wrote appreciatively to Claude Washburn about *Sons and Lovers* and *Women in Love,* defending the "degree or detail" of Lawrence's treatment of sex, "an engrossing subject" (EHB to CW 7/17/21). Achsah thought *Lady Chatterley's Lover* "tender and beautiful and with some of his best writing," though "not true psychologically" (ABB to HBP 3/10/33).

51. See dedicatory inscription, December 6, 1914, in Lindsay 1914b.

52. "As you probably know by intuition, your Father and I have led an absolutely brahmacharin life since months before your birth and our strength and vitality have not been frittered away. I am thankful that our life together has been of the spirit rather than of the flesh" (ABB to HBP 10/12/36). The Hindu concept of "brahmacharya" refers to the vow of celibacy taken by those who renounce material and sensual pleasures for a higher spirituality. It is interesting to note that the change in their relationship may have occurred at about the time of John Barlow's death in March 1912. Achsah knew that Harwood was herself pregnant at the time she wrote this letter.

53. Writing to Claude Washburn on 2/9/24, Earl questioned "whether it is better to renounce the joys that come from outside—from contact with people and things—finding ones joy only in ones work and ones thought—or whether one needs the other kind of thing to keep one from drying up. The usual answer is, I know, that one needs both work & play—solitude and contact. I am beginning to doubt it."

54. *LL* 6 #4534; ABB to HBP 12/26/38.

55. Undated letter, written between 1919 and 1923.

56. Edith Lewis to HBP 7/7/[47], [5/51], 6/15/51, 7/12/63; A. Brewster 1942, 213, 250; ABB to HBP 9/21/31, 5/6/33.

57. Five years earlier Claude Washburn had taken the collective measure of the Brewsters' various homes as a "Tour of Discomfort" (Washburn 1968, 21).

58. EHB to ABB 3/15/30; he wrote similarly to Harwood on 3/17/30, "Save very carefully any bit of writing you may have from Uncle David." For Earl's role in later arrangements to have Lawrence's remains disinterred and cremated, see EHB to Frieda Lawrence 10/14/34, 12/14/34; EHB to Angelo Ravagli 1/1/34 [i.e., 1935], 1/12/35.

59. For Mukerji's characterization of his companion, "Mr. John Earl," see Mukerji 1930, 15–16; ABB to HBP 10/15/30.

60. EHB to HBP 4/3/33 and 4/9/33, and frequent mention of this project in the preceding months.

61. Earl was concerned as well about meeting the tuition, which Alpha consented to pay.

62. ABB to HBP 10/28/31, 11/2/31, 11/15/31; EHB to HBP 10/4/31, 11/11/31.

63. She did not win either contest.

64. Never published. See also EHB to HBP 10/22/32 for his other attempts to publish the essay.

65. Bimala Churn Law, ed. *Buddhistic Studies* (Delhi: Gajendra Singh, 1931), [284]–328; EHB to HBP 10/17/31.

66. Edith Lewis (to ABB and EHB [spring 1934]) and Willa Cather (to ABB and EHB 7/1/34) were particularly enthusiastic.

67. Sponsored by the Mount Holyoke Friends of Art (Class Records, Smith College Archives).

68. It seems unlikely that they could have paid for this trip themselves.

69. He was the nephew of author Ernest de Sélincourt.

70. Class Records, Smith College Archives.

71. ABB to HBP 2/26/36; EHB to HBP 3/31/36.

72. ABB to HBP 7/12/36, 8/2/36, 8/15/36.

73. Never published.

74. Class Records, Smith College Archives.

75. The Brewsters' spartan vegetarian diet may have aggravated the disease.

76. ABB to HBP 6/7/36, 11/15/36, 9/26/38, 8/1/39, 9/15/40.

77. For a fuller discussion of "The Child," see chapter 6.

78. "I don't care a damn for public exhibitions, societies etc. in my present life" (9/29/45).

79. EHB to HBP 2/21/45; EHB to Frieda Lawrence 10/6/46.

80. From a private collection.

81. Class records, Smith College Archives.

82. EHB to Lucile Beckett 2/28/52, 11/16/52; EHB to HBP 5/27/50, 8/1/50, 5/23/55, 4/4/56.

83. Published in two installments in December 1952 and January 1953.

84. Most of Earl's letters to Harwood between May 1954 and April 1956 discuss the disposal of Lawrence's letters; see also EHB to Frieda Lawrence 8/4/54, 9/1/54.

85. EHB to HBP 11/11/52; EHB to Lucile Beckett 11/16/52, 5/22/53. The article apparently never ran. See: http://images.google.com/hosted/life

86. "Not a good title, for I have not considered myself a Buddhist for some 25 years" (EHB to Carl Brewster 9/19/56; from a private collection).

Chapter 2. "Happy Working Days"

This chapter draws on and expands my earlier essay, "'Life is very simple—all we have to do is our best!': Willa Cather and the Brewsters" (Porter 2008a).

1. According to Lewis, Cather visited her at 60 S. Washington Square in 1904 and 1905, took her own studio there in 1906, and began sharing an apartment with Lewis on Washington Place around 1909 (Lewis 1953, xiii–xviii). In an 11/16/10 letter to Earl, Achsah mentions that she will stay with Edith when she visits him the following weekend. In a 1/1/44 letter to Harwood she recalls that she and Lewis "used to go to some [restaurants] on 8th Street, not sumptuous but thrilling to us."

2. Achsah dates this first meeting with Cather to 1903, a date that seems too early (cf. evidence cited in note 1 above). Merrill Skaggs has argued, however, that Cather may have been in the East, and in contact with artists at Cos Cob, "between October of 1902 and late April of 1903" (Skaggs 2000, 51). Could Achsah and/or Earl, who were in New York by 1902 and had ties to the Cos Cob group, have been part of these same conversations? Harwood mentions that on the Brewsters' 1923 return to the States she found in New Haven "a roll of documents showing that Mother was the Duchess of Cob for she had been away one summer with some friends who called her that" (Picard 1926, 18–19 [third series]).

3. See Porter 2008b, 154–59.

4. Achsah and Earl discuss asking Edith to dinner during Achsah's November visit to New York but do not mention Cather (EHB to ABB 11/16/10; ABB to EHB 11/18/10).

5. On the trip, see Lewis 1953, 158–60; Brown 1953, 278–79; Woodress 1987, 420–22. Cather sailed in mid-May and returned in late September (cf. note 76 below). We don't know the dates of Cather's visit with the Brewsters, but she probably arrived in late July. She was in Aix by August 21, as we can see from a letter to Louise Burroughs that she wrote from there on that date (Burroughs Archive, Drew University). In "A Chance Meeting" Cather puts her encounter with Madame Grout in "the latter part of August 1930" (Cather 1936, 5), and a note in my possession (consisting solely of Cather's signature) was mailed by Cather from Aix-les-Bains to a U.S. correspondent on August 31, 1930. See also Cather 2002, #1015 and 1016.

6. In his 1949 memoir Earl writes that Cather visited them in 1935 (2), but he does not mention her 1930 visit, and it seems likely that he has confused the two dates, esp. since in an 8/24/35 letter to Harwood he cites a letter from Lewis saying "that Willa will probably go to Paris and that she will come here by herself." This is apparently what happened.

7. For detailed information on the copies of Cather books owned by the Brewsters, see chapter 4.

8. Although Achsah here misquotes the title of *The Country of the Pointed Firs,* she evidently had long known Jewett's writing. So had Earl, who comments in his 1949 essay on Cather that he had grown up reading Jewett (see chapter 5). Cather had in 1925 edited a selection of Jewett's stories, and conversations about Jewett during her 1930 visit with the Brewsters may have prompted Achsah to return to Jewett's writings in the months preceding her October 1931 letter to Harwood.

9. ABB to HBP 1/12/41, 3/17/41, 3/23/41; EHB to HBP 3/28/41.

10. 1/17, 1/25, 1/30, 2/8, 2/12 letters (all 1944) from Achsah and Earl to Harwood.

11. EHB to HBP 4/28/57 and 5/15/57, the first of which will be found in chapter 9; for more on Haridas, see chapter 8, note 10.

12. See, e.g., ABB to HBP 12/13/37: Achsah has just received a photograph of Harwood with Edith Lewis; ABB to HBP 12/14/42: Harwood has reported on Willa's illness and operation; ABB to HBP 1/29/43: Harwood has moved and has just received a plant from Aunt Edith; ABB to HBP 4/23/44: Edith has been "singing [Harwood's] praises."

13. In the summer of 1910 Achsah writes frequently from Mountain View Farm, East Jaffrey, to Earl in New York. In a 9/12 letter she notes her delight in Mt. Monadnock, where Cather would so enjoy walking in later years. It was apparently Isabelle and Jan Hambourg, not Achsah, who introduced Cather to Jaffrey, but one is nonetheless struck by the coincidence, especially given Lewis's early friendship with Achsah.

14. In September 1912, just months after Harwood's birth, Earl wrote Macbeth that this painting, "one of my most recent and beautiful canvases," had been accepted by the Autumn Salon in Paris, and in December he mentions having sent this and three other paintings to Macbeth (letters of 9/25/12 and 12/22/12 from EHB to WM); a letter of 11/27/16 gives Macbeth his instructions concerning Lewis and these paintings. For more on this episode, see chapter 1.

15. On Cather's fondness for this passage, see Slote 1966, 83–84, 249.

16. See Picard 1977, 17: "One long walk the family especially enjoyed led to the three scalops. This was at the end of the peninsula and already facing the bay of Salerno with a view of the nearby Islands of the Sirens. These three rocky scalops were very bare—all the surrounding mountains and rocks would be bare in summer." Achsah in "The Child" mentions picnicking by the "Three Scallops" with Edith Lewis during her 1920 visit (165), and both she and Harwood comment that Earl made sketches of them.

17. It may well be, however, that this particular purchase was of *Le Négre bleu* and was for the Hambourgs, not the Cather-Lewis home: see chapter 5, note 5.

18. E.g., ABB to EHB 9/25/24, ABB to HBP 9/13/31.

19. *Sic*—but this is a letter written by Earl from Achsah's dictation, at a time when she was virtually unable to write. Achsah regularly spells Isabelle's name correctly.

20. See, for example, her comments to Dorothy Canfield Fisher (Cather 2002, #635 and 849) and to Zoë Akins (#1474), and compare Lee 1989, 187. In his 1949 essay on Cather, Earl Brewster writes that he "was touched and somewhat surprised" that a writer of Cather's stature would comment so warmly on their book (E. Brewster [1949], 3).

21. Cf. her comment in *The Song of the Lark:* "Artistic growth is, more than it is anything else, a refining of the sense of truthfulness. The stupid believe that to be truthful is easy; only the artist, the great artist, knows how difficult it is" (Cather 1915, 477).

22. Lewis 1953, 119; Woodress 1987, 310; Cather 2002, #505.

23. Lewis 1953, 121; Cather 2002, #509.

24. Woodress 1987, 311; Cather 2002, #510 and 511.

25. Cather 2002, #512 and 513; Woodress 1987, 311.

26. See Lewis 1953, 121; Cather 2002, #513; Woodress 1987, 311.

27. On Cather's 1923 trip, see Brown 1953, 226–27; Lewis 1953, 131–33;

Woodress 1987, 338–40. Woodress (339) dates Cather's sailing to October 23, but on 11/9 she writes Duncan Vinsonhaler from France that she will sail on November 17 (Cather 2002, #704), and on 11/29 she writes both Dorothy Canfield Fisher (#706) and Achsah Brewster (see chapter 4) that she has just returned. Frank Swinnerton, who was on the boat with Cather, also dates the sailing to November (Swinnerton 1936, 316).

28. See, e.g., A. Brewster 1942, 266; Picard 1926, 15–16 (second series); Picard 1977, 27–28; E. Brewster [1949], 2; EHB to ABB 9/26/19. The hotel is located at 19 Quai de Voltaire, between Pont Royal and Pont du Carrousel. In her 1925 story, "Uncle Valentine," Cather's title character dies close to this location, "struck by a motor truck one night at the Pont Royal, just as he was leaving Louise Ireland's apartment on the quai" (Cather 1973, 38).

29. Though she does not mention Cather, Harwood recalls going in "October or so" to Naples to meet Aunt Edith and to see her off on the White Star Line (Picard, 1926, 59 [first series]).

30. Cather was not alone in having trouble with Achsah's name. A 1921 letter from D. H. Lawrence begins, "Dear Achsah Brewster Ach! ach Gott!—tiresome name to spell you've got" (*LL* 4 #2355). Some of Earl's letters have "Achsa" on the envelopes, and even Achsah's Smith College transcript and yearbook make the same mistake.

31. See Lewis 1953, 119.

32. "Katherine Mansfield" was first published in 1925. The sentence quoted is from a new opening section that Cather added when she revised the essay for inclusion in *Not Under Forty* in 1936. Clearly her 1920 visit with the Brewsters was still in her mind.

33. ABB to HBP 2/14/42; E. Brewster [1949], 1.

34. For the trip, see Picard 1926, 9–11 (third series); her account (13) suggests that they had arrived shortly before Decoration Day, while Achsah puts their arrival on that day itself (A. Brewster 1942, 316). Harwood's recollection seems more likely to be correct: her memoir dates from just three years after the trip, whereas "The Child" was written almost twenty years later—and is frequently fuzzy in its chronology.

35. Cather 2002, #706 (but with the mention of Swinnerton omitted from the paraphrase; the paraphrase should also read "from France" rather than "for France"). See also #703, dated November 6, 1923, in which Cather writes Mrs. George Whicher from Ville d'Avray hoping that she and her husband can come to an art opening the next day and meet the artists: the opening must have been that of the Brewsters' Paris show.

36. In her helpful comments on an earlier version of this chapter, Merrill Skaggs commented on the hyperbolic ebullience of Achsah's language here (as elsewhere)—and on the way it mirrors Canfield's own tendency in the same direction (see, e.g., Canfield's letter of 12/8/23 to ABB, quoted in chapter 6, note 44). Noting that the writing of yet another of Cather's close friends, Viola Roseboro', errs in the same direction, Skaggs commented that perhaps Cather enjoyed the florid styles of such friends precisely because they gave her added incentive to try to say things simply and directly.

37. In both of her memoirs Harwood describes Edith Lewis seeing the Brewster family—i.e., all of them—off when they left New York (Picard 1926, 36 [third series]; 1977, 35).

38. Editorial changes Edith Lewis made in the typescript of Earl Brewster's 1949 essay offer dramatic evidence of her determination to minimize her role: see chapter 5.

39. E.g., Lee 1989, 71: "Cather wrote feelingly about Isabelle to friends like Dorothy Canfield or Elsie Sergeant, but she hardly ever mentioned Edith, except to say that she'd been seasick again on a transatlantic journey, or that Cather needed to have her on a trip to help her, because she had a hand injury and couldn't manage packing or dressing alone."

40. When the Brewsters' friendship with the Hambourgs began is not clear, but it must have been through the Cather-Lewis connection. In "The Child" Achsah writes that visits to Ville d'Avray were "frequent and delightful" (271), and Harwood mentions the Hambourgs visiting the Brewsters in Capri, noting that "there was a lot of music" (Picard 1977, 29, who seems to place the visit in 1924, though a 6/7/25 letter from EHB to CW suggests that it probably occurred in the first half of 1925). By the time Cather writes Achsah in February 1923, the Hambourgs had acquired Earl's *Le Négre bleu.*

41. Compare Achsah's description of Harwood in "The Child": "Sincerity and simplicity and a recognition of truth were distinguishing traits already in our six-year-old. It gave her an integrity of character that sat well with her square shoulders and firmly planted feet" (146). Honesty is central also to the Brewster family motto, which Achsah cites on the cover of "The Child": "VERITE SOYET MA GARDE" (may truth be my guardian).

42. Cf. Achsah's comment in an early letter to Earl: "I believe with Tolstoi that the only happiness of life lies in its simplicity and genuineness," language which Earl quotes in a letter to her two weeks later (ABB to EHB 9/12/10; EHB to ABB 9/25/10).

43. On Cather's relationship with Menuhin, see Lewis 1953, 168–72; Sergeant 1953, 253; Woodress 1987, 502; Lee 1989, 334–35; and esp. Steven B. Shively, "Reading the Menuhin Chapter," in *Willa Cather: New Facts, New Glimpses, Revisions,* ed. John J. Murphy and Merrill Maguire Skaggs (Madison, N.J.: Fairleigh Dickinson University Press, 2008), 19–31. Cather wrote Stephen Tennant that Menuhin was one of the most truthful people she knew (Hoare 1990, 339). Frank Swinnerton, whose honesty Cather came to admire on their 1923 voyage home, found in Cather qualities similar to those which drew her to the Brewsters and to Menuhin: "complete freedom from egotism, intense interest in life and living. . . . She talked excellently, without show of wit but with beautiful candour. . . . [S]he is full of wisdom" (Swinnerton 1936, 318).

44. See, e.g., *LL* 5 #3802, 6 #4053, and Earl's comments in Brewster 1934, 225–26, 245. Cushman 1992, 44, notes that Lawrence's story, "Things," made gentle fun of the Brewsters, Harwood that Lawrence used to tease her father (Picard 1984, 214).

45. *LL* 5 #3693. Harwood writes that despite the constant teasing, "I think [Lawrence] really admired my father" (Picard 1984, 214); cf. Cushman 1992, 47: "[The Brewsters'] way was not Lawrence's way, but he respected them, especially since they attempted with such integrity to live up to their ideals."

46. Both Achsah's language here and Earl's belief in the power of art, of forms and colors, to communicate "character" are reminiscent of what Maurice Denis wrote in a famous 1890 manifesto, "Definition du Neo-Traditionnisme," which the Brewsters must have known: "The depth of emotion is due to the ability of these lines and colors to speak for themselves, as only the divinely beautiful can" (Petrie 1997, 124). Achsah was in fact invited to join Denis' group of artists: see chapter 1.

47. It is hard to believe she would not have seen it when she returned to

Paris in 1923, just months after its appearance. The Brewsters sent D. H. Lawrence a copy when it came out (see *LL* 4 #2852, dated June 29, 1923), and the Brewsters had a copy with them by the later stages of their 1923 trip to the United States (Picard 1926, 27 [third series]). In his 1949 essay, Earl Brewster comments that Cather did not "limit her encouragement" for their writing to their D. H. Lawrence book, a suggestion at least that she'd commented favorably on the 1923 book as well (E. Brewster [1949], 3).

48. On Cather's struggle to fend off intrusions on her work, see Porter 2008b, 202–3.

49. Rose 1983, 133, in connection with the plow seen against the sun in *My Ántonia*. Rose shows that though Cather does not give full expression to these themes until 1922, they are already shaping her art in the decade that precedes (see esp. 125–35).

50. Rose 1983, 132. Rose focuses on ways in which Cather's art aligns her with "modernist," abstract painters. She does not discuss the Brewsters, but they too sought "simplification of form" (Rose 1983, 140) and repeatedly turned to primitive art, and to art not rooted in the European tradition, for their inspiration (142–43). Both Earl's own comments (Brewster 1923, 12–13) and those of Cushman 1992, 41–42, and Randhawa 1944, 29–37, suggest his close affinity with the abstract artists of his time.

51. Rose 1983, 132, who also speaks of Cather's interest in psychological archetypes, a theme close to what Earl expresses through his interest in "character."

52. Cushman 1992, 48, notes both the "presence of Puvis behind the Brewsters" and the ways in which D. H. Lawrence picked up this influence from them. Puvis finds his way also into the 1890 Maurice Denis essay cited in note 46: see Shaw 2002, 3–4, 8–9.

53. Cited in Alexandre 1905, xviii. Rose 1983, 143, sees in Puvis the same inclination toward simplification and "abstraction" that drew Cather to the Anasazi—and that also characterized both Cather's writing and the art of her own time.

54. Cf. Edel 1959, 7, quoting Howard Mumford Jones: "The tension in Miss Cather's tales . . . arises from the 'conflict between the desire of the artist to pursue beauty and the necessity of the craftsman, if he is to live, to make some practical adjustment to the workaday world.'"

55. Cf. Jim Laird's description of the banker: "Phelps, here, is fond of saying that he could buy and sell us all out any time he's a mind to" (Cather 1920, 269).

56. During this same period Cather voiced her distaste for Defoe's *The Fortunate Mistress*, about a woman who turns to prostitution. While her strictures are directed mainly at the book, Cather also suggests an affinity between the author and his subject: "Defoe seems to have had only one deep interest, and that was in making a living" (Cather 1949, 85).

57. See Harris in Cather 2006, 614, on the impact of winning the Pulitzer: "[Cather] would later confide to . . . Dorothy Canfield Fisher that success did exact a toll . . . ; before the recognition, she had been able to write as she pleased and to enjoy writing, but now she felt pressured by demands and expectations. Like an old wild turkey, she wanted to fly away." Cf. Edel 1959, 12: "I suspect that the more Miss Cather succeeded in her career, the more despair she experienced without quite understanding why"; also Lee 1989, 183–85.

58. Cf. Cushman 1992, 47: the Brewsters were "quietistic seekers after

truth" who "lived in Capri and later in India in order to remove themselves from the fray." The Brewsters' sidestepping of "the fray" may also have appealed to Cather, who in the eyes of at least some held herself inappropriately aloof and uninvolved during the period of WWI and after: see, e.g., Sergeant 1953, 127–28, 153–58, 163–66. Cather confronted that war head-on, of course, in *One of Ours*—more so than Sergeant recognizes—and in her essay "Escapism" argued that an artist's mission is to deal not with the particular issues of the day but with the eternal issues of the human condition (Cather 1949, 18–29).

59. Chapter 1, p. 59.

60. *On the Divide: The Many Lives of Willa Cather* (Lincoln: University of Nebraska Press, 2008). On the conflict described here, see also Porter 2002, 2003, and 2005.

61. On Cather and Eddy, see Porter 2007, esp. 298–304.

62. Cf. EHB to HBP 6/1/45: "I am grateful for individual appreciation of my work, but I hate publicity . . . [B]y 'publicity' I mean the write-ups and critics cackle." And Lucy Marks quotes Earl commenting in a 1932 letter to Ralph Ruzicka that "the world seems as little aware of us as always—which I do not mind" (chapter 1, p. 66).

63. By the time Cather visited the Brewsters in 1930, this divide had become yet more apparent. Since the last time Cather had seen the Brewsters, she had published *The Professor's House, My Mortal Enemy,* and *Death Comes for the Archbishop,* and *Shadows on the Rock* was nearing completion. In contrast, by 1930 it was becoming clear that the Brewsters' work would never gain a significant following, and that in the future they would be largely dependent on others for their living.

64. Though Cather traces her interest in Puvis to her 1902 visit to Paris, she knew of him before that trip: Giorcelli 2003, 71, note 1; see also the summary under Puvis in Polly Duryea, "Paintings and Drawings in Willa Cather's Prose: A Catalogue Raisonné" (dissertation, University of Nebraska, 1993).

65. The right-hand panel of Achsah's *Sermon on the Mount,* which she displayed in the 1923 show, has close similarities to Puvis' Pantheon panel of *St. Geneviève at Prayer.*

66. See John Murphy's "Historical Essay" on *Archbishop* in Cather 1999, 332–38. Note, for instance, how Bishop Latour specifically links the golden stone of his new cathedral in Santa Fé with the rock of the Palace of the Popes at Avignon: Cather 1927, 242.

67. If the description of Latour in this passage near the start of "The Vicar Apostolic" suggests the state of mind sought in Buddhist meditation, the words he speaks at the very end of this same first book suggest Buddhist "mindfulness," one's close attention to one's own body, feelings, state of mind, and experience: "The miracles of the Church seem to me to rest not so much upon faces or voices or healing power coming suddenly near to us from afar off, but upon our perceptions being made finer, so that for a moment our eyes can see and our ears can hear what is there about us always" (Cather 1927, 50–51).

68. On these and other materials in this section, see Murphy's excellent discussion in Cather 1999, 326–39, a section on which I have drawn heavily.

69. A. Brewster 1942, 91; for the full passage, see chapter 6. Cf. Achsah's description of her father in "The Child": "Belonging to no church, he gave to all creeds and denominations. His imagination entered into whatever others were doing" (204); Achsah herself was never baptized. Compare Lucy Marks's com-

ments on the "deeply spiritual and strikingly cross-cultural sensibility" which characterizes Earl and Achsah's exchange of letters during their courtship (chapter 1). Among the topics they discuss are Buddhism, Lao-Tze, the "psalms or Walt Whitman," 1 Corinthians 13, the *Bhagavad Gita,* and the Golden Rule. On the eclecticism of the Brewsters' religious leanings, see chapter 1, above. As Lucy Marks shows, even their fierce resistance to Harwood marrying the Catholic Georges Picard was motivated by a sense that Catholicism was narrow and closed minded.

70. On the Middle Path, see Earl's translation of the Buddha's First Sermon in E. Brewster 1926, 61, a passage that explicitly urges monks to avoid the extremes of "[a] life given to pleasures" and "a life given to mortifications"—the extremes that in many ways define book 5 of *Archbishop,* "Padre Martinez." On the novel's religious openness, E. and L. Bloom 1964, 213, note how Cather in *Archbishop* "fuse[s] a relatively sophisticated Catholicism with the ancient paganism of Indian rites on the one hand, and with primitive Mexican devotion to Catholicism on the other."

71. On the differences between Latour and Vaillant and the ways they nonetheless complement each other, see esp. Lindemann 1999, 116–26. Harwood comments frequently on the differences between her parents, and how these differences coexisted and complemented each other in their marriage: see, e.g., Picard 1984, 205–6.

72. One wonders if it was this perceived closeness that led Achsah in "The Child" to describe Harwood's eyes in terms very like those she uses for Willa's: cf. 19 and 318.

73. Cf. Achsah's comment on the "noble quality" of *Shadows* and its relationship to the sincerity and beauty Achsah associates with Sarah Orne Jewett (ABB to HBP 10/1/31).

74. Cf. Richard C. Harris, "Cather's *A Lost Lady* and Schubert's *Die schöne Müllerin,*" *Willa Cather Newsletter and Review* 51 (2007): 39. "In an April 1945 letter to Carrie Miner Sherwood, Willa Cather remarked that she had not so much invented her fictions but rather had remembered and arranged people, places, and situations from her past, had ordered various elements that coalesced as they came to mind."

75. A. Brewster 1942, 55, 271–72 (both included in chapter 6). For Cécile and stories, see, e.g., Cather 2005, 45–46, 100–102, 128–29, etc.; for the clothes she receives from France, without initially understanding that they herald her coming of age, see 245.

76. Cather and Lewis sailed from Paris to Quebec on September 27: see ABB to HBP 9/27/30; Cather 2002, #1017. On the composition of *Shadows,* see Cather 2005, 555–56.

77. See Achsah's 10/8/30 letter to Harwood in chapter 9. On the fierce debate with her parents as to what she should study at university, see chapter 1.

78. Cf. Achsah in "The Child": "Lawrence kept on reiterating that Harwood must go to school" (409).

79. Chapter 1, p. 60. Ms. Marks notes also that "Earl himself recalled his boyhood sadness when he grew too old to wear white" (Brewster 1923, 6).

80. See, e.g., A. Brewster 1942, 19 (Harwood's "self-sufficiency was fostered in every way") and 146 ("One never felt like talking down to Harwood").

81. As Lucy Marks shows, "child" itself was a loaded word for Achsah: see her discussion in chapter 1.

82. Lucy Marks points out that Mrs. Templeton's comments on Vickie's ten-

dency to "overdo it" recall the sorts of remarks Achsah kept making as Harwood pressed forward toward a career in medicine, remarks that undermined Harwood's goals and chosen career: "touch the harp lightly"; nothing matters except goodness, truth, etc.; Harwood shouldn't grasp "to learn too much"; there were "too many specialists"; women's sphere was in the home, nursery, and garden; something seems to dry up within professional women, etc. Harwood's interest in pursuing a medical career had been a bone of contention even before she headed for Dartington (see, e.g., *LL* 7 #5122, 5214, 5305), and Cather may well have picked up intimations of this tension during her 1930 visit and subsequently written them into the relationship between Vickie and her mother.

83. Woodress 1987, 438.

84. On Cather and her mother during Willa's teenage years, see O'Brien 1987, 101–5.

85. Earl's keen interest in Harwood's daily schedule found a counterpart in the care with which he watched and recorded his own; his inclinations in this regard may well show the influence of the Buddhist concern with establishing and following a controlled regimen.

86. For Earl's 10/22/32 letter (along with one Achsah wrote Harwood the same day), see chapter 9.

87. On the meeting with Grout and "The Old Beauty," see Lee 1989, 354; Stout 2000, 261.

88. My language draws on that of the Richard Harris article cited in note 74.

89. Earl specifically links the poem with the 1920 meeting in Naples: "The scene of departure from that Italian coast was in Willa's thought when she wrote her poem 'Recognition'" (E. Brewster [1949], 1).

90. Earl and Achsah's discovery in the summer and fall of 1910 that they both loved Italy influenced their decision to marry as soon as possible—and to leave immediately for Italy (see, e.g., EHB to ABB 8/14 and 9/25/10; ABB to EHB 9/12 and 10/2/10).

91. The poem recalls a passage in "The Sculptor's Funeral," one of the stories in the book Cather gave the Brewsters when she met them in 1920: "the yearning of a boy, cast ashore upon a desert of newness and ugliness and sordidness, for all that is chastened and old, and noble with traditions" (Cather 1920, 262).

Chapter 4. The Brewster Archive

1. Identifications of edition and issue follow Crane 1982. For full bibliographic details, see the checklist contained in chapter 3.

2. The "rather inscribed" is added above the line in Achsah's letter.

3. The three posthumous volumes that Edith Lewis sent the Brewsters in India are the only copies in the archive that retain their dust jackets.

4. There is solid evidence that Cather and Lewis had a small stock of these two early books and used them in later years as gifts: among my own books are copies of *April Twilights* and *The Troll Garden* which Cather inscribed for friends in 1912 and 1925, respectively, and in the Burroughs collection at Drew there is a copy of *April Twilights* inscribed by Cather in 1940.

5. On this painting, and the way Lewis and Cather acquired it, see chapter 2, note 14.

6. On Cather's delight in the letters she received from servicemen about *One of Ours*, see Lewis 1953, 122–23.

7. On this painting, see chapter 2.

8. On *The Three Scalops*, see chapter 2.

9. For Swinnerton's account of meeting Cather on the crossing, see Swinnerton 1936, 316.

10. Dorothy Brett, *Lawrence and Brett. A Friendship* (Philadelphia: J. B. Lippincott, 1933).

11. The book referred to is *Lucy Gayheart*. For the circumstances of its completion, see Woodress 1987, 455–56. Woodress comments, however, that "the delay forced [Cather] to stay in town well into July to finish the revisions of her novel," whereas this letter to the Brewsters suggests that she was done by July 1.

CHAPTER 5. "WILLA CATHER-LIVING"

1. "Paul's Case" appeared in *McClure's* in May 1905. Cather's first story in *McClure's* was "The Sculptor's Funeral," which had appeared there the previous January.

2. Compare Achsah's comments on Jewett and Cather in chapter 2.

3. Earl's memory is at fault here: Willa Cather received her honorary degree from Yale not in 1923, when the Brewsters made their only trip back to the States, but in 1929. (In June 1923 Cather was in fact in France, where she saw the Brewsters both before and after their American trip—as Earl himself mentions in this very essay.) As Harwood notes, it was John Derby, the son of Achsah's sister Lola, who received a degree at the Yale commencement the Brewsters attended in 1923 (Picard 1926, 18 [third series]). Interestingly, Achsah also mentions seeing Cather receive her honorary degree from Yale (ABB to HPB 6/1/44); she and Earl must have shared this "memory" until it became real.

4. Earl is describing their Paris reunion with Cather in the fall of 1923. The house he mentions "near St. Cloud" is that of Isabelle and Jan Hambourg in Ville d'Avray.

5. It seems likely that the painting to which Earl here refers is *Le Négre bleu*, which Achsah in chapter 131 of "The Child" recalls Cather purchasing at the Brewsters' 1922 show (see chapter 6). As we show in chapter 2, although Cather apparently arranged with the Brewsters to purchase this picture for the Hambourgs, she cannot have done so at the 1922 show.

6. Earl's chronology is off. It was in 1930 that both Cather and Lewis visited the Brewsters in St. Cyr, after which she traveled to Aix-les-Bains and met Madame Grout; in 1935 Lewis alone visited them. See chapter 2.

7. The parenthesized exclamation point is Earl's—apparently a bemused comment on his shaky memory as to Petrarch's relationship to the monastery!

8. On the clear echoes of this outing in Cather's "The Old Beauty," see chapter 2.

9. The book in question is *Not Under Forty*, which Cather retitled *Literary Encounters* when it came out in the 1938 complete edition of her works; Earl's title, "Literary Encounter," suggests that he knew this later title, though there

is no evidence that the Brewsters owned a copy of this 1938 edition. Earl's parenthetical comment that Cather's visit to Aix-les-Bains was "perhaps in a previous visit" suggests his own uncertainty as to the date of her trip to see the Brewsters in southern France (cf. note 6).

10. Earl here considerably overstates Frieda Lawrence's role in the inception of the book. Almost from the moment Earl learned of Lawrence's death, he began to consider writing a potentially lucrative book that would include the letters they had received from Lawrence along with reminiscences about him: see his letter of 3/15/30–3/19/30 to Achsah in chapter 9; he also wrote to Harwood on 3/17/30 urging her to keep any communications she had received from Lawrence (see chapter 1, note 58).

11. In locating the Brewsters' Lawrence book (published in 1934) "a few years before Willa's visit," Earl is again erroneously dating Cather's visit to St. Cyr in 1935 (in fact, work on the book began in the fall soon *after* her 1930 visit: see chapter 1). His memory of Cather's praise for this book, however, is correct: see her letter of July 1, 1934, to the Brewsters (chapter 4).

12. There is no evidence that Alpha visited the Brewsters in St. Cyr in 1930, and we have found no other specific reference to a 1930 meeting there between Cather and Mrs. Rhys Davids. That said, a 9/30/47? letter from Edith Lewis to Harwood Brewster may allude to a time when Mrs. Rhys Davids, Harwood, Lewis (and perhaps Cather?) spent time together (e.g., in 1930 at St. Cyr, which is the only time at which such a meeting could have taken place).

13. One must assume that Earl here is thinking of Cather's *Death Comes for the Archbishop* and *Shadows on the Rock,* the latter a work that Achsah especially loved, and the former the work that Earl rereads in 1955 with such pleasure (see chapter 2).

Chapter 6. "The Child"

1. Achsah may have been inspired by a letter she received from Richard Reynolds, in which he reported writing his memoirs for Hermione and Claire (ABB to HBP 5/25/41). She began her own memoir just a month later (ABB to HBP 6/29/41).

2. ABB to HBP 9/2/42.

3. Achsah had previously composed sketches of her aunts, sisters, and nephew: see ABB to HBP 5/17/37, 5/28/40, and 6/4/41; on 8/22/42 and 9/2/42 she mentions a "sketch" and "remembrance" of Rachel Derby, and on 8/22/43 tells Harwood, "I am sending off my meandering about old age which may divert you to type off at leisure for me."

4. ABB to HBP 5/25/41.

5. "It is so long since we have heard from you that the basis of life seems to have dropped out, leaving us pendulous in mid-air" (ABB to HBP 2/10/41).

6. ABB to HBP 12/14/41.

7. Achsah did not shrink from recording a number of compliments to herself, from praise for her face cream (122), to homage from a peasant woman in Florence (88), to admiring comments from Charles Loeser (59), Algar Thorold (99), D. H. Lawrence (351), and Llewelyn Powys (392).

8. Numbers in brackets at the top of each selection give page numbers in the original typescript of "The Child."

9. Harwood was born on August 22, 1912.

10. Helena Petrovna Blavatsky (1831–91) was the founder of Theosophy. Earl would retain a sense of positive connection between Harwood and Madame Blavatsky. On 9/11/30 he wrote to Harwood, "You may wonder why I was so anxious some days ago to receive your letter—why because I had a dream that worried me—I thought we were visiting at some place where Mme. Blavatsky was one of the guests! You disappeared and we could not find you but as Mme. Blavatsky had also disappeared, in the dream we felt relieved and said you had gone away somewhere with her."

11. John Barlow had in fact died five months earlier, on March 15, 1912.

12. Villa Faulkner Page, friend and patron of Fred Shaler, was active in the New Thought Movement.

13. This sentence is confused in the typescript; printed text follows Harwood's editing. For Uncle Fred [Shaler], see chapter 1.

14. Compare this description of Harwood with Achsah's description of Willa Cather in chapter 163.

15. Achsah is thinking of the *Dhamma Sangani,* the first book of the Theravada (called also Hinayana) *Abhidhamma Pitaka.* Mrs. Rhys Davids's 1900 translation of the work for the Pali Text Society was entitled *Buddhist Manual of Psychological Ethics.* See also Earl's correspondence with her on this subject, 8/14/16.

16. Lewis's visit apparently took place in June 1914: a 5/14/14 letter from Willa Cather to Ferris Greenslet, her Houghton Mifflin editor, mentions that Lewis will sail for Europe at the end of the month.

17. At the period described in this chapter, the Brewsters were living in the Villa Pestellini in Florence, where they had moved in the spring of 1917.

18. Achsah is probably thinking of Tolstoy's "The Foundling," in which Másha goes to fetch water, finds a baby outside the door, and begs her mother to allow her to keep it.

19. Achsah's description of Alberto Magnelli seems colored by her recollection of Cather's portrait of Don Hedger in "Coming, Aphrodite," a story which Acshah knew well, and to which she refers elsewhere in the "The Child" (see her description of Cather in chapter 163). Like Magnelli, Hedger is "one of the first men among the moderns. That is to say, among the very moderns," and like Magnelli, Hedger "is always coming up with something different, . . . is changing all the time" (Cather 1920, 77; see also 18, where Hedger is described as "chiefly occupied with getting rid of ideas he had once thought very fine").

20. Earl (to whom Edith Lewis had given Berenson's *Sketch for a Self-Portrait*) found Berenson very self-centered and conceited. "I don't believe that he has much if any significance to painters themselves. I have never known an artist to whom he meant anything. But to the dealers, the historians of painting, the intellectuals, he means a very great deal, and to the critics. What a contrast he is to Mrs. Berenson. I hope you remember her—a dear & charming woman. I don't wonder at Walt Whitman leaning out of the window of his house and putting his arms about her and giving her a kiss as she rode past, on horse back under his window, the first time they met!" (EHB to HBP 12/3/51).

21. See Byron, *Childe Harold's Pilgrimage,* canto 4, stanza 78. The chapter begins with Achsah's account of the Montessori school which Harwood and Manfred attended. For further details on the Brewsters' move to Rome, see chapter 1.

22. Latvian-born American painter (1877–1957).

23. Marjorie Wise was headmistress of Dartington Hall: see chapter 213.

M. S. Randhawa was deputy commissioner at Almora and a strong supporter of the arts who wrote a book on the Brewsters (see listing in References).

24. According to Achsah, Theodora Synge (1861–1941) was a cousin of the Irish playwright John Millington Synge. She is buried in the Protestant cemetery in Rome.

25. Achsah here repeats the quotation from Byron with which she began (see note 21) and pairs it with *cor cordium,* "heart of hearts," an inscription from Shelley's grave in Rome.

26. Many years later Achsah wrote to Harwood in a similar vein about an acquaintance in Almora, a Seventh Day Adventist who treated people suffering from tapeworms: "She does not seem to me to do it for love but to prove that her god is better and mightier than other gods! It helps one to comprehend the war" (ABB to HBP 9/14/42).

27. The qualities Achsah identifies in the young Harwood are those that she and Earl emphasize repeatedly, and that they also saw in Willa Cather: see chapter 2.

28. On the makeover of Hôtel Quai de Voltaire, cf. chapter 161.

29. The blooming of the horse chestnuts in Paris is a recurrent (and seasonally flexible!) motif with both Earl and Achsah. In an April 9, 1949, letter to Harwood, for instance, Earl recalls them being in bloom in May 1905, at the time when he first came to Paris.

30. The chapter's title alludes to an afternoon when Mrs. Harrison along with her son, Ian, friends of the Brewsters from Capri, tried to pick up Harwood at school—and was strongly resisted by Harwood, who feared she was being kidnapped. It is one of several stories that clearly were told and retold across the years by all three Brewsters, assuming in time the status of family legends.

31. Achsah here has "Ossip" rather than Boris as the 'cellist of the Hambourg Trio.

32. Achsah's typescript reads "Gilbert" here instead of Sibert.

33. Achsah's account is confused here. Judge McClung lived in the wealthy Squirrel Hill section of Pittsburgh; Isabelle's mother was born in the Cherry Valley section of New York, not far from Cooperstown and Lake Oswego; Cather and Isabelle rented a cottage in Cherry Valley for several months in the fall of 1911. See Woodress 1987, 139, 213–14; O'Brien 1987, 393–94.

34. Cather arrived in Paris in April 1923: see chapter 2 for her 1923 trip.

35. The show here described is that held at the Galerie Chéron in 1922. Achsah's language suggests that Cather herself was present to purchase this painting, which she cannot have been, since she did not arrive in Paris until spring 1923. For her gift to the Hambourgs of this painting (more felicitously called *Le Négre bleu* in the Brewsters' 1923 book), see chapter 2.

36. The "Little Flowers" is a collection of popular legends about St. Francis of Assisi.

37. The Hardens were a family with whom the Brewsters spent a great deal of time on their Paris stays. Pierre Caous was a painter friend who subsequently became a distinguished French judge—and who provided the French translations of Earl's and Achsah's essays for their 1923 book. Achsah describes all of these friends in chapter 131 of "The Child."

38. The blooming of the horse chestnuts this time accompanies Cather's return to Paris in the early fall of 1923; she sailed home in November.

39. Earl's reaction to the writing space provided for Cather at Ville d'Avray was far less enthusiastic than Achsah's: see chapter 5.

40. Achsah's typescript has "Red Rock, Kansas," presumably a misremembered "Red Cloud, Nebraska." The painting was in fact commissioned by the women of the Omaha Society of Fine Arts to be hung in the Omaha Public Library (Sergeant 1953, 188).

41. Theodore Leschetizky (1830–1915) was one of the great pianists and piano teachers of his era.

42. For Achsah's mural, see chapter 1, note 40.

43. Achsah's painting of Jeanne d'Arc was one of the illustrations included in the Brewsters' 1923 book.

44. Achsah's typescript reads "Caulfield" here. Achsah subsequently sent Dorothy Canfield Fisher a copy of their 1923 book. On 12/8/23 Fisher wrote to express her gratitude for the book: "[H]ow divining of you to know that ever since I saw your work I have been hungering for it. . . . [F]or what it gave me that day I saw it with you, and another dark day when I stepped in again from the dark, noisy chaos of the street, and felt myself calmed and strengthened by that calm strong beauty you two are creating, benedictions on you!" (Fisher's letter is in a private collection.)

45. Achsah's chronology here is confused, as it is elsewhere in her account of the Brewsters' 1922 and 1923 Paris visits. Their trip to the United States took place in the summer of 1923, between Cather's spring 1923 visit to Paris (chapter 130) and her return there in the early fall (chapter 161).

46. Achsah has "Edward Garnett," though the book in question was written by David Garnett.

47. Achsah's language recalls a familiar passage from *One of Ours,* the novel Cather had inscribed so warmly to the Brewsters in 1922, and which had won the Pulitzer Prize just before the Brewsters' 1923 visit to the States. Describing Claude Wheeler and his companions sailing past the Statue of Liberty to Europe and the war, Cather writes, "[T]he scene was ageless; youths were sailing away to die for an idea, a sentiment, for the mere sound of a phrase . . . and on their departure they were making vows to a bronze image in the sea" (Cather 1922, 274).

48. Typescript reads "Georges," a slip perhaps influenced by the name of Harwood's husband, Georges Picard.

49. This is one of several places where Achsah's typescript has "April Twilight"—apparently just a slip, since elsewhere she gets the title right.

50. A fall 1903 meeting with Cather in New York squares both with her 1903 publication of *April Twilights* and with her May 1, 1903, conversation with S. S. McClure, at which the possibility of his publishing a book of her stories was indeed mentioned (see Woodress 1987, 171). *Alexander's Bridge* did not appear until 1912, however, and its inclusion here, in concert with the shakiness of Achsah's chronology elsewhere in "The Child," makes one skeptical about her fall 1903 date for this first meeting between Cather and herself; see chapter 2.

51. Lewis and Cather did not begin sharing an apartment until around 1909 (Lewis 1953, xviii).

52. In what is among the more interesting of Achsah's slips, she calls this story "Coming, Aretheusa" in the typescript, substituting for the sensuous love goddess Aphrodite the name of a fountain nymph who flees the love of the river god Alpheus.

53. Achsah jumps abruptly here to the visit Cather and Lewis paid the Brewsters in southern France in 1930.

54. Achsah here miscopies the date of this inscription, May 14 instead of May 16. On the circumstances of Cather's presentation of this book to the Brewsters, see chapter 2.

55. At this point Achsah includes the full text of "Recognition," which we omit here since it has already been quoted in both chapter 2 and chapter 5.

56. "Tantine" is Josephine Macleod. For the Brewsters' long friendship with her, see chapter 1.

57. Note how Achsah here colors her account of the journey to Dartington with language drawn from the Cather poem she has just quoted—the sea, sails, arrival.

58. The poem Achsah names here, and from which she quotes, is Rilke's "The Spirit Ariel." In a letter of 2/24/39 to HBP she indicates that she has just received Marie Billson's translation of Rilke's poems, and Rilke is clearly very much on her mind as she writes these concluding pages of "The Child."

59. Although Achsah's reference to buildings at Dartington dating from the ninth century may be a bit overenthusiastic, the great hall does indeed date to the late fourteenth century, and the city of Totnes has other buildings whose origins are even earlier.

60. On Achsah and this passage from Emerson's "The Poet," see chapter 1.

Chapter 7. "Fourteen Years of My Adventures"

1. Diary entry for Dec. 8, 1926 (private collection). Dhan Gopal Mukerji (1890–1936) was an Indian writer whose work familiarized Western readers with Indian culture and religion. Harwood's original spelling and punctuation have been retained.

2. Harwood's 1977 memoir includes a lengthy, vivid, and enthusiastic account of the India trip.

3. Carosiello, on the Amalfi coast, was the Brewsters' home from March 1914–August 1916.

4. The Brewsters spent ten days in Athens in January 1920.

5. The Brewsters spent October 1921–May 1922 in Ceylon, first in Colombo, then near Kandy.

6. The Lawrences remained in Ceylon for six weeks, from March 13–April 24, 1922, staying with the Brewsters at their bungalow, Ardnaree.

7. A gift from Edith Lewis (A. Brewster 1942, 247); Lewis had earlier recounted these tales to Harwood during her 1920 visit to the Brewsters at Sorrento (Picard 1977, 15).

8. The Brewsters left Ceylon in May 1922, spent the summer in Switzerland with Alpha Barlow, and moved to Paris in the fall for the Salon d'Automne and their joint exhibition at the Galerie Chéron.

9. Willa Cather's friends, Isabelle and Jan Hambourg.

10. The Brewsters spent the first half of 1923 on Capri, and the summer in the United States, returning to Paris that fall for a second joint exhibition at the Galerie Chéron.

11. See A. Brewster 1942, 269, where Achsah interprets Harwood's fear as a "[revolt] against machinery."

12. The Brewsters returned to Villa Torre dei Quattro Venti in November 1923, remaining until March 1926. Harwood here describes Christmas 1923.

13. Emily Harden, whom the Brewsters had met in Paris.

14. One of the servants at Quattro Venti.

15. Diana, Hermione, and Pamela Reynolds returned to Capri during the summer of 1924 after visiting relatives in England.

16. The last issue was typed in early 1929.

CHAPTER 8. "MEMORIES OF YOUR GRANDPARENTS"

1. Common to all three memoirs are the sorts of often-repeated stories that become part of family lore: for example, how Earl and Achsah met, Earl's rescue of a dog from a roof, the "kidnapping" of Harwood from her Paris school, the parasol incident in Colombo, etc.

2. Achsah described John Barlow as a "living portrait of Da Vinci as a young man" (A. Brewster 1942, 204); she writes to Harwood on 1/31/44, "Curiously enough Frances has that Da Vinci look that marks our family."

3. Richard Reynolds and his daughters, Diana, Hermione ("Mynie"), and Pamela, friends from Capri.

4. Louise Fortescue, Achsah's friend from Smith College.

5. Nan and Ferdinando Di Chiara, friends from Capri, now living in France.

6. Alexander Charles Robinson, 1867–1952.

7. It was through Roger Fry's friendship with Peter Teed, a former British Indian army colonel, that Virginia and Leonard Woolf, Vanessa Bell, and Duncan Grant used the cottage, La Bergère. The Woolfs did not build the cottage.

8. Harwood's exclamation point seems to indicate that she never entertained such a notion.

9. Georges Picard, who had married Diana Reynolds in 1934. Diana died shortly after giving birth to Claire in early 1935.

10. Major Robert Alexander, an Englishman who later took the names Amana Priya and Haridas, was a medical advisor to Earl, and one of his closest friends in Almora.

CHAPTER 9. SELECTED LETTERS

1. More than two-thirds of the letters written between 1910 and 1929 are Earl's, many of them posted from his travels in Italy and France while Achsah remained at home with Harwood. There is also a small group of letters from his 1930 trip to India.

2. For example, ABB to HBP 2/6/40, 8/12/40, 2/23/41.

3. For example, ABB to HBP 5/6/33, 11/7/36; an echo of Whitman's *Leaves of Grass*.

4. For example, ABB to Alpha and Lola 12/12/26; ABB to HBP 3/25/31, 10/22/32, 2/12/33, 3/5/33, 3/29/33.

5. For example, EHB to HBP 6/7/36, 7/11/47, 5/24/51, 6/11/51; EHB to Lucile Beckett 2/3/52.

6. EHP to HBP 11/9/30, 10/22/32, 3/12/36, 11/12/47, 8/11/48.

7. See A. Brewster 1942, 83.

8. Robert Browning, *Pippa Passes*. As mentioned in the Introduction, we have retained the original spelling in all the letters.

9. Algernon Blackwood's *The Centaur,* which dealt with mythology, spirituality, and cosmic consciousness, seems the likeliest candidate, but was not published until 1911.

10. *Dao de Jing* (also *Tao Te Ching*) of Laozi.

11. Scirocco is the Mediterranean wind blowing sand from the Sahara.

12. Earl's enjoyment of clothes and fashion reflects his keen sense of color and style: see also EHB to ABB 10/1/17; EHB to HBP 1/21/33; ABB to HBP 11/23/32.

13. German philosopher Rudolf Eucken (1846–1926) won the Nobel Prize for Literature in 1908.

14. Arnold Bennett's *The Glimpse: An Adventure of the Soul,* published in 1909.

15. The Brewsters' friend, painter Alberto Magnelli.

16. Rachel Derby, Lola's daughter and Achsah's niece, was twenty-one years old at the time.

17. Achsah's "triple bronze" translates Horace's "aes triplex" (Ode I.3, 9).

18. *Art et Décoration,* published in Paris from 1897.

19. Chief monk at the temple at Bodhgaya, where the Buddha received enlightenment.

20. Gautama Siddhartha received enlightenment when resting under a bo tree.

21. Sridara Nehru, a cousin of Jawaharlal Nehru, and his wife Raj, whom the Brewsters had met in Sorrento in 1920.

22. Grand Manan, New Brunswick, Canada, where Edith Lewis and Willa Cather vacationed.

23. Indian author Dhan Gopal Mukerji (1890–1936).

24. Many years later Earl wrote to Harwood, "Lawrence's life seems to me quite a tragic one, due, I think, at least very largely, to the attitude which he held toward life—so very right in some ways, but too impatient toward what he considered wrong in human nature. In the very last years of his life I believe that Lawrence reached deeper and more spiritual realizations than he had previously had, which would have greatly changed his life for the better, had he lived longer. Should he be reborn I think that it will be with a wiser, greater nature" (8/1/50).

25. He writes similarly to Harwood on 3/17/30, "Save very carefully any bit of writing you may have from Uncle David."

26. Neighbor at St. Cyr.

27. The Brewsters' servant at Château Brun.

28. John Wales, headmaster of Dartington Hall.

29. Earl began work on the Lawrence book in the fall of 1930, and finished typing it by late January 1931 (ABB to HBP 1/28/31).

30. A neighbor in France.

31. On 1/22/33 Achsah reported having received fifty dollars from *Asia* for her article.

32. Breathing exercises.

33. Hindu publications. *Prabuddha Bharata,* to which Earl contributed, was the official journal of the Ramakrishna Order; the Maha Bodhi Society was founded in 1891.

34. Shivananda, successor to Vivekananda as head of the Ramakrishna Order at Belur Math; Mount Kailash was revered by Hindus as the home of Shiva.

35. Earl had previously submitted this essay to the *Atlantic Monthly* (ABB to HBP 1/27/32).

36. Their friend, Swami Vijayananda.

37. Achsah's aunt, Roberta Hubbard Fowler; the Brewsters had met Marie and James Billson on the ship to Ceylon in the fall of 1921.

38. "[Buck's] style is good, I suppose; it is certainly reminiscent of the Bible: but I cannot but think there is a kind of self-conscious pose in being so reminiscent as she is" (EHB to HBP 1/28/33).

39. Achsah's entry for a magazine competition for seventy-five thousand words on the theme of happiness, carrying a prize of five thousand dollars.

40. See note 39; also ABB to HBP 1/21/33, 2/27/33, 4/1/33.

41. Nan and Ferdinando Di Chiara, friends from Capri, now living in France.

42. Indira Nehru Gandhi (1917–84) was twenty-one when the Brewsters first met her.

43. Krishna Nehru Hutheesing, author of several memoirs about the Nehru family and modern Indian history.

44. Douglass Cather died in June 1938.

45. Bertrand Russell's *Power: A New Social Analysis,* first published in 1938. Earl had written to Harwood on 12/6/38, "[Russell] always seems to me to have such a blind spot in his vision for spiritual and religious truth that he is not a very sympathetic writer, for me."

46. *Phoenix: The Posthumous Papers of D.H. Lawrence,* first published in 1936. Major Robert Alexander, an Englishman who later took the names Amana Priya and Haridas, was a medical advisor to Earl, and one of his closest friends in Almora.

47. See A. Brewster 1942, 5. Earl mistakenly wrote "Francis" for "Frances," as he had above written "Isabel" for "Isabelle" Hambourg.

48. From a private collection.

49. Nora Pelton Brewster, Ara Brewster's wife.

50. Earl's servant, Uttama.

51. Second highest of the Hindu castes after the Brahmans.

52. French historian and musicologist Alain Daniélou; Swiss photographer Raymond Burnier.

53. Jawaharlal Nehru had been imprisoned since August 1942 (Moraes 1956, 309).

54. Earl's pet pheasant Molecule.

55. See note 46.

56. Two weeks later, on 5/15/57, Earl again wrote appreciatively of *My Mortal Enemy* and *Obscure Destinies:* "It seems to me that at her best Willa has gone as far, has written as well as any novelist."

References

MANUSCRIPT MATERIALS

Art Students League. Student Registration Records, Archives of the Art Students League of New York.

Barlow, Alpha Winifred. n.d. Memories. Typescript. Private collection.

Barlow, John Harwood. Letters to Achsah Barlow Brewster. Private collection.

Brewster, Achsah Barlow. Letters to Dorothy Brett. Harry Ransom Humanities Research Center, University of Texas at Austin.

———. 1942. The Child: Harwood Barlow Brewster. Typescript. Brewster 26, Drew University Special Collections, Madison, N.J.

Brewster, Achsah Barlow, and Earl Brewster. Letters between Achsah Barlow Brewster and Earl Brewster and to Harwood Brewster Picard. Brewster 24, Drew University Special Collections, Madison, N.J.

Brewster, Earl. Letters to Lucile Beckett. Brewster 24, Drew University Special Collections, Madison, N.J.

———. Letters to Ara Brewster. Private collection.

———. Letters to Frieda Lawrence and Angelo Ravigli. Harry Ransom Humanities Research Center, University of Texas at Austin.

———. Letters to William Macbeth. Macbeth Gallery records, 1838–1968 (bulk 1892–1953), Reels NMc5, NMc28, 2575, Archives of American Art, Smithsonian Institution.

———. Letters to Caroline Rhys Davids. Rhys Davids family, Archives of the Faculty of Asian & Middle Eastern Studies, Cambridge University.

———. Letters to Rudolph Ruzicka. Private collection.

———. Letters to Claude Washburn. Claude Washburn Papers, Upper Midwest Literary Archives, University of Minnesota Libraries.

———. [1949] For the book Willa Cather-living. Typescript. Robert and Doris Kurth Collection. University of Nebraska Libraries, Lincoln.

Cather, Willa. Letters to Achsah Barlow Brewster and Earl Brewster. Brewster 22, Drew University Special Collections, Madison, N.J.

Lewis, Edith. Letters to Achsah Barlow Brewster and Earl Brewster. Lewis 2, Drew University Special Collections, Madison, N.J.

———. Letters to Harwood Brewster Picard. Lewis 1, Drew University Special Collections, Madison, N.J.

Lindsay, Vachel. Letters to Achsah Barlow Brewster and Earl Brewster. Papers of Vachel Lindsay, MSS 6259, Clifton Waller Barrett Library of American Literature, Special Collections, University of Virginia Library.

Oberlin College. Student File (Earl Brewster), Alumni and Development Records, Oberlin College Archives.

Picard, Harwood Brewster. 1926. Fourteen Years of My Adventures. Typescript. Private collection.

———. 1977. To Frances and Claire Some Memories of Your Grandparents Earl Henry Brewster and Achsah Barlow Brewster. Typescript. Brewster 24, Drew University Special Collections, Madison, N.J.

Smith College. Class Records of 1902, Alumnae Biographical Files, Box 1617, Smith College Archives.

———. Office of the President, William Allan Neilson Files, Box 4, Smith College Archives.

PRINTED MATERIALS

Adler, Kathleen. 2006. "We'll Always Have Paris": Paris as Training Ground and Proving Ground. In *Americans in Paris, 1860–1900,* ed. Kathleen Adler, Erica E. Hirshler, and H. Barbara Weinberg, 11–55. London: National Gallery Company. Published in conjunction with the exhibition "Americans in Paris, 1860–1900" shown at the National Gallery, London; the Museum of Fine Arts, Boston; and the Metropolitan Museum of Art.

Alexandre, Arséne. 1905. *Puvis de Chavannes.* London: Georges Newnes.

Archivio della scuola romana: arte a Roma tra le due guerre. Entry for Mario Broglio. http://www.scuolaromana.it/artisti/brogliom.htm

Bhagavad Gita: Annotated and Explained. 2001. SkyLight Illuminations. Trans. Shri Purohit Swami. Annotation by Kendra Crossen Burroughs. Woodstock, Vt.: Skylight Paths Publishing. **(Abbreviated BG)**

Bloom, Edward A., and Lillian D. Bloom. 1964. *Willa Cather's Gift of Sympathy.* Carbondale: Southern Illinois University Press.

Bohlke, L. Brent. 1986. *Willa Cather in Person: Interviews, Speeches, and Letters.* Lincoln: University of Nebraska Press.

Brewster, Achsah Barlow, and Earl Brewster. 1923. *L'oeuvre de E. H. Brewster et Achsah Barlow Brewster: 32 reproductions en phototypie précedées d'essais autobiographiques.* Rome: Valori Plastici. Brewster 23, Drew University Special Collections, Madison, N.J.

Brewster, Earl. 1926. *The Life of Gotama the Buddha (Compiled Exclusively from the Pali Canon).* London: Kegan Paul.

Brown, E. K. 1953. *Willa Cather: A Critical Biography.* New York: Alfred A. Knopf.

Buell, Lawrence. 2003. *Emerson.* Cambridge: Belknap Press of Harvard University Press.

Busich, Renato. 1981. Una croce sulla Cassia. *Biblioteca e Società* 4:9–14. http://bibliotecaviterbo.it/Rivista/1981_4/Busich.pdf

Cather, Willa. 1903. *April Twilights: Poems.* Boston: Richard G. Badger. Brewster 15, Drew University Special Collections, Madison, N.J.

———. 1905. *The Troll Garden.* New York: McClure, Phillips. Brewster 16, Drew University Special Collections, Madison, N.J.

———. 1913. *O Pioneers!* Boston: Houghton Mifflin. Brewster 8, Drew University Special Collections, Madison, N.J.

———. 1915. *The Song of the Lark.* New York: Houghton Mifflin. Brewster 7, Drew University Special Collections, Madison, N.J.

———. 1918. *My Ántonia.* Boston: Houghton Mifflin. Brewster 9, Drew University Special Collections, Madison, N.J.

———. 1920. *Youth and the Bright Medusa.* New York: Alfred A. Knopf. Brewster 2, Drew University Special Collections, Madison, N.J.

———. 1922. *One of Ours.* New York: Alfred A. Knopf. Brewster 5, Drew University Special Collections, Madison, N.J.

———. 1923a. *April Twilights and Other Poems.* New York: Alfred A. Knopf. Brewster 1, Drew University Special Collections, Madison, N.J.

———. 1923b. *A Lost Lady.* New York: Alfred A. Knopf. Brewster 3, Drew University Special Collections, Madison, N.J.

———. 1925. *The Professor's House.* New York: Alfred A. Knopf. Brewster 10, Drew University Special Collections, Madison, N.J.

———. 1926. *My Mortal Enemy.* New York: Alfred A. Knopf. Brewster 6, Drew University Special Collections, Madison, N.J.

———. 1927. *Death Comes for the Archbishop.* New York: Alfred A. Knopf. Brewster 4, Drew University Special Collections, Madison, N.J.

———. 1931. *Shadows on the Rock.* New York: Alfred A. Knopf. Brewster 19, Drew University Special Collections, Madison, N.J.

———. 1932. *Obscure Destinies.* New York: Alfred A. Knopf. Brewster 18, Drew University Special Collections, Madison, N.J.

———. 1935. *Lucy Gayheart.* New York: Alfred A. Knopf. Brewster 17, Drew University Special Collections, Madison, N.J.

———. 1936. *Not Under Forty.* New York: Alfred A. Knopf. Brewster 11, Drew University Special Collections, Madison, N.J.

———. 1940. *Sapphira and the Slave Girl.* New York: Alfred A. Knopf. Brewster 20, Drew University Special Collections, Madison, N.J.

———. 1948. *The Old Beauty and Others.* New York: Alfred A. Knopf. Brewster 13, Drew University Special Collections, Madison, N.J.

———. 1949. *Willa Cather on Writing.* New York: Alfred A. Knopf. Brewster 14, Drew University Special Collections, Madison, N.J.

———. 1956. *Willa Cather in Europe: Her Own Story of the First Journey.* Introd. and incidental notes by George N. Kates. New York: Alfred A. Knopf. Brewster 12, Drew University Special Collections, Madison, N.J.

———. 1973. *Uncle Valentine and Other Stories. Willa Cather's Uncollected Short Fiction, 1915–1929.* Lincoln: University of Nebraska Press.

———. 1999. *Death Comes for the Archbishop.* Cather Scholarly Edition. New York: Alfred A. Knopf.

———. 2002. *A Calendar of the Letters of Willa Cather.* Ed. Janis P. Stout. Lincoln: University of Nebraska Press.

———. 2005. *Shadows on the Rock.* Cather Scholarly Edition. New York: Alfred A. Knopf.

———. 2006. *One of Ours.* Cather Scholarly Edition. New York: Alfred A. Knopf.

Cerio, Edwin. 1950. *L'ora di Capri.* Napoli: Edizione La Conchiglia.

Crane, Joan. 1982. *Willa Cather. A Bibliography.* Lincoln: University of Nebraska Press.

Cushman, Keith. 1991. The Serious Comedy of 'Things.' *Etudes Lawrenciennes* 6:83–94.

———. 1992. Lawrence and the Brewsters as Painters. *Études Lawrenciennes* 7:39–49.

Cushman, Keith, and Keith Sagar. 1991. An Achsah Brewster Painting Misattributed to Lawrence. *D. H. Lawrence Review* 23:191–95.

The Divinity That Stirs Within Us. 1992. Exhibition catalog. New York: Borghi.

Edel, Leon. 1959. *Willa Cather: The Paradox of Success.* Washington, D.C.: Library of Congress.

Ellis, David. 1998. *D. H. Lawrence: Dying Game, 1922–1930.* Cambridge: Cambridge University Press.

Emerson, Ralph Waldo. 1983. *Essays & Lectures.* New York: Library of America.

Giorcelli, Christina. 2003. Willa Cather and Pierre Puvis de Chavannes: Extending the Comparison. *Literature and Belief* 23.2:70–88.

Hoare, Philip. 1990. *Serious Pleasures: The Life of Stephen Tennant.* London: Hamish Hamilton.

Huxley, Aldous. 1969. *Letters of Aldous Huxley.* Ed. Grover Smith. New York: Harper & Row.

Keeler, Clinton. 1965. Narrative Without Accent: Willa Cather and Puvis de Chavannes. *American Quarterly* 17:117–26.

Knott, Kim. 1998. *Hinduism: A Very Short Introduction.* Oxford: Oxford University Press.

Lawrence, D. H. 1934. *D. H. Lawrence: Reminiscences and Correspondence.* [Ed.] Earl and Achsah Brewster. London: M. Secker.

———. 1961. *Phoenix: The Posthumous Papers of D. H. Lawrence.* Ed. and introd. Edward D. McDonald. London: W. Heinemann.

———. *The Letters of D. H. Lawrence.* 1984–93. Ed. James T. Boulton. Vol. 3 (1916–21), 1984; vol. 4 (1921–24), 1987; vol. 5 (1924–27), 1989; vol. 6 (1927–28), 1991; vol. 7 (1928–30), 1993. Cambridge: Cambridge University Press. **(Abbreviated LL)**

Lears, T. J. Jackson. 1994. *No Place of Grace: Antimodernism and the Transformation of American Culture, 1880–1920.* Chicago: University of Chicago Press.

Lee, Hermione. 1989. *Willa Cather: A Life Saved Up.* London: Virago Press.

Lewis, Edith. 1953. *Willa Cather Living.* New York: Alfred A. Knopf.

Lindsay, Vachel. 1914a. *Adventures While Preaching the Gospel of Beauty.* New York: Macmillan. Clifton Waller Barrett Library of American Literature, Special Collections, University of Virginia Library.

———. 1914b. *The Congo and Other Poems.* New York: Macmillan. Clifton Waller Barrett Library of American Literature, Special Collections, University of Virginia Library.

McGoldrick, Monica. 1995. *You Can Go Home Again: Reconnecting With Your Family.* New York: W. W. Norton.

Moraes, Frank. 1956. *Jawaharlal Nehru: A Biography.* New York: Macmillan.

Mukerji, Dhan Gopal. 1930. *Disillusioned India.* New York: E. P. Dutton.

Nardi, Pietro. 1947. *La vita di D. H. Lawrence.* [Milano?]: Mondadori.

Nonne, Monique. 2002. Puvis de Chavannes and the "Petit Boulevard" Painters: Emile Bernard, Paul Gauguin and Vincent van Gogh. In *Toward Modern Art: From Puvis de Chavannes to Matisse and Picasso,* ed. Sergio Lemoine, 71–87. New York: Rizzoli.

O'Brien, Sharon. 1987. *Willa Cather: The Emerging Voice.* Oxford: Oxford University Press.

Perlman, Bennard B. 1991. *Robert Henri: His Life and Art.* New York: Dover Publications.

Petrie, Brian. 1997. *Puvis de Chavannes.* Brookfield, Vt.: Ashgate.

Picard, Harwood Brewster. 1982. D. H. L. *Journal of the D. H. Lawrence Society* 3:10–15.

———. 1984. An Interview with Harwood Brewster Picard. Ed. Keith Cushman. *D. H. Lawrence Review* 17:195–217.

Piper, Raymond Frank. 1956. *The Hungry Eye: An Introduction to Cosmic Art.* Los Angeles: De Vorss.

Porter, David H. 2002. Cather on Cather: Two Early Self-Sketches. *Willa Cather Newsletter and Review* 44: 55–60.

———. 2003. Cather on Cather II: Two Recent Acquisitions at Drew University. *Willa Cather Newsletter and Review* 46:49–58.

———. 2005. Cather on Cather III: Dust-Jacket Copy on Willa Cather's Books. *Willa Cather Newsletter and Review* 48:51–60.

———. 2007. From Violence to Art: Willa Cather Caught in the Eddy. In *Violence and the Arts in Willa Cather,* ed. Merrill Maguire Skaggs and Joseph R. Urgo, 295–309. Madison, N.J.: Fairleigh Dickinson University Press.

———. 2008a. "Life is Very Simple—All We have to Do is Our Best!": Willa Cather and the Brewsters. In *Willa Cather: New Facts, New Glimpses, Revisions,* ed. John J. Murphy and Merrill Maguire Skaggs, 141–57. Madison, N.J.: Fairleigh Dickinson University Press.

———. 2008b. *On the Divide: The Many Lives of Willa Cather.* Lincoln: University of Nebraska Press.

Prugh, Linda. 1999. *Josephine MacLeod and Vivekananda's Mission.* Chennai, India: Sri Ramakrishna Math.

Randhawa, M. S. 1944. *The Art of E. H. Brewster & Achsah Brewster.* Allahabad, India: Kitabistan.

Ringbom, Sixten. 1986. Transcending the Visible: The Generation of the Abstract Pioneers. In *The Spiritual in Art: Abstract Painting, 1890–1985,* organized by Maurice Tuchman, in collaboration with Judi Freeman, [130]–53. New York: Abbeville. Published in conjunction with the exhibition "The Spiritual in Art: Abstract Painting, 1890–1985" shown at the Los Angeles County Museum of Art; Museum of Contemporary Art, Chicago; and Haags Gemeentemuseum, the Hague.

Rose, Phyllis. 1983. Modernism: The Case of Willa Cather. In *Modernism Reconsidered,* ed. Robert Kiely and John Hildebidle, 123–45. Cambridge: Harvard University Press.

Ross, Nancy Wilson. 1968. *Hinduism, Buddhism, Zen: An Introduction to Their Meaning and Their Arts*. London: Faber and Faber.

Schreiner, Olive. 1987. *An Olive Schreiner Reader: Writings on Women and South Africa*. Ed. and introd. Carol Barash. London: Pandora; New York: Routledge and K. Paul in association with Methuen.

Sergeant, Elizabeth Shepley. 1953. *Willa Cather. A Memoir*. Lincoln: University of Nebraska Press.

Shaner, David Edward. 1987. Review: Biographies of the Buddha. *Philosophy East and West* 37:306–22.

Shaw, Jennifer L. 2002. *Dream States: Puvis de Chavannes, Modernism, and the Fantasy of France*. New Haven: Yale University Press.

Shi, David E. 1985. *The Simple Life: Plain Living and High Thinking in American Culture*. New York: Oxford University Press.

Skaggs, Merrill Maguire. 1990. *After the World Broke in Two: The Later Novels of Willa Cather*. Charlottesville: University Press of Virginia.

———. 2000. Young Willa Cather and the Road to Cos Cob. In *Willa Cather's New York: New Essays on Cather in the City*, ed. Merrill Maguire Skaggs, 43–59. Madison, N.J.: Fairleigh Dickinson University Press.

Slote, Bernice. 1966. *The Kingdom of Art: Willa Cather's First Principles and Critical Statements, 1893–1896*. Lincoln: University of Nebraska Press.

Soria, Regina. 1970. *Elihu Vedder: American Visionary Artist in Rome, 1836–1923*. Rutherford, N.J.: Fairleigh Dickinson University Press.

Stout, Janis P. 2000. *Willa Cather: The Writer and Her World*. Charlottesville: University Press of Virginia.

Sulloway, Frank J. 1997. *Born to Rebel: Birth Order, Family Dynamics, and Creative Lives*. New York: Vintage Books.

Swinnerton, Frank. 1936. *An Autobiography*. New York: Doubleday & Doran.

Tamney, Joseph B. 1992. *American Society in the Buddhist Mirror*. New York: Garland.

Tweed, Thomas A. 1992. *The American Encounter with Buddhism, 1844–1912: Victorian Culture and the Limits of Dissent*. Bloomington: Indiana University Press.

Washburn, Claude. 1968. On Living Abroad. In *Opinions,* 1–24. Essay Index Reprint Series. Freeport, N.Y.: Books for Libraries Press.

Wattenmaker, Richard J. 1975. *Puvis de Chavannes and the Modern Tradition*. Exhibition catalog. Toronto: Art Gallery of Ontario.

Winkler, Ken. 1990. *A Thousand Journeys: The Biography of Lama Anagarika Govinda*. Longmead, England: Element Books.

Woodress, James. 1987. *Willa Cather: A Literary Life*. Lincoln: University of Nebraska Press.

Young, Michael. 1982. *The Elmhirsts of Dartington: The Creation of an Utopian Community*. London: Routledge & Kegan Paul.

Index